D0241796

LONDON'S COUNTRYSIDE

WINDSOR FOREST.

LONDON'S COUNTRYSIDE

BY

EDRIC HOLMES

Author of "Seaward Sussex," "Wessex,"
etc., etc.

WITH 102 ILLUSTRATIONS BY
THE AUTHOR

LONDON: ROBERT SCOTT
ROXBURGHE HOUSE
PATERNOSTER ROW, E.C.

UNITED STATES OF AMERICA:
MACRAE SMITH COMPANY
PHILADELPHIA

MADE IN ENGLAND

CONTENTS

ARCHITECTURAL TERMS

The following brief notes will assist the traveller who is not an expert in arriving at the approximate date of ecclesiastical buildings.

SAXON 600–1066. Simple and heavy structure. Very small wall openings. Narrow bands of stone in exterior walls.

NORMAN 1066–1150. Round arches. Heavy round or square pillars. Cushion capitals. Elaborate recessed doorways. Zig-zag ornament.

TRANSITION 1150–1200. Round arched windows combined with pointed structural arch. Round pillars, sometimes with slender columns attached. Foliage ornament on capitals.

EARLY ENGLISH 1200–1280 (including Geometrical). Pointed arches. Pillars with detached shafts. Moulded or carved capitals. Narrow and high pointed windows. Later period—Geometrical trefoil and circular tracery in windows.

DECORATED 1280–1380. High and graceful arches. Deep moulding to pillars. Convex moulding to capitals with natural foliage. " Ball flowers " ornament. Elaborate and flamboyant window tracery.

PERPENDICULAR 1380–1550. Arches lower and flattened. Clustered pillars. Windows and doors square-headed with perpendicular lines. Grotesque ornament. (The last fifty years of the sixteenth century were characterized by a debased Gothic style with Italian details in the churches, and a beauty and magnificence in domestic architecture which has never since been surpassed.)

JACOBEAN and GEORGIAN 1600–1800, are adaptations of the classical style. The " Gothic Revival " dates from 1835.

LIST OF ILLUSTRATIONS

vii

LIST OF ILLUSTRATIONS ix

Rura mihi et rigui placeant in vallibus amnes
Flumina amem sylvasque.—VIRGIL.

" The Country mounts up into little hills, and
the valleys are beautiful with an eternal verdure.
The grass here seemed to me to be finer and of a
better colour than in other places. . . . All the
Country is full of parks, which yield a delightful
prospect."—SORBIERE (*Approach to London*, 1664).

THE KENTISH DOWNS.

INTRODUCTION

THE extraordinary change in the aspect of the countryside within a radius of twenty-five miles from St. Paul's ; the rapid expansion of towns and the growth of residential areas beyond that circle is largely a phenomenon of the first quarter of the present century. It is said to be due mainly to the development of the cheap car ; but the housing problem in the inner urban ring of London is almost as acute as it has ever been, and the Registrar-General's returns do not warrant the assumption that increase of population is the main factor in the spoliation of the home counties. So we are almost forced to the conclusion that so prosperous is the condition of the commonalty that many thousands are not only able to keep the ubiquitous car, but also to run two homes ! However that may be, the once charming series of landscapes between the Chiltern Hills and the North Downs, and for some distance beyond these natural frontiers of the Thames Valley, is in serious danger of being utterly ruined by indiscriminate building, and the removal of those gracious and historic landmarks which make half the charm of the rural scene. Another modernity which has already greatly altered the character of London's Countryside is the succession of motor ways—arterial road and by-pass—converging upon the great city. Farther afield, as the spokes radiate from the hub, they are less obtrusive, and one may wander for miles without being troubled by the sight of their bald ugliness. The powers that rule over such matters have, in the neighbourhood of London, adopted a peculiarly aggressive type of iron railing to line the sides of these great thoroughfares. To the motorist, these fences are practically non-existent, but after a mile or so of their company the pedestrian feels singularly depressed. But it is useless to become petulant. The times must be served, and time may mellow even an arterial road ! One must not forget that these new ways were not intended for the adventurer on foot, and that they have diverted fast traffic from many narrow by-roads and lanes is a matter for congratulation.

With the object of gathering into one volume—a task hitherto unattempted—some record of the beauty and the interest still left to us in this district, the following chapters have been written. Besides being a mere record, it is hoped that these pages will serve a double purpose, and guide both pedestrian and motorist along the right way. If the boundaries are occasionally overstepped, it will be to visit localities having a relationship of sorts with London, and which may legitimately be claimed as within the influence of Cheapside and Piccadilly. Though the whole coast-line of southern England from Whitstable to Worthing is, in a sense, rapidly becoming suburban, there are certain oases, not so far from St. Paul's and almost within sight of the dome, that are still rural England.

There is no monotony in the scenery we are about to view, and, although the word " sublime " can never be used in a description of the natural beauties of the home counties, there are many truly delightful and lovely scenes both north and south of the Thames. Some, not the least in beauty, owe their merit to that stream itself. One can readily call to mind a dozen beautiful localities, well known to Londoners who use to advantage the Saturday afternoons of the summer time, which would not disgrace " Glorious Devon," but there are others not so well known that are equally fine and less sophisticated. To the former class belongs the much be-photographed " Silent Pool," not far from Guildford, which of late years has tended to disappear in dry weather. Within a few miles are several un-named, and almost unknown, lakelets of greater beauty. So also with that inland cliff beloved of the cyclist—Box Hill. For satisfying outline, view from the summit, and mere altitude alone, it must yield place to many eminences in the chain of which it forms a part. Fortunately for their charms of soli-tude, however, these have not a great high road hugging their very slopes, nor an up-to-date and famous hotel within a few minutes of their breezy heights. Very similar in character to the North Downs are the comparatively unvisited Chilterns. In this range, there are many summits beside which the hill above Burford Bridge would appear insignificant.

The North Downs suffer generally in comparison with the opposing line of hills in Sussex, though some of the rounded bosses, partly clothed in woods, which make a background to the picturesque villages of Gomshall and Shere are the principal objects in scenery of a really high order. Another fine view-point—Colley Hill above Reigate—has been spoilt by all sorts of amenities scattered about its southern face, and the very edge of the high escarpment above Woldingham is now occupied by a row of villas.

For those to whom the actual countryside—the wide airy flats of Essex and North Kent ; the mysterious dingles of the chalk hills ; the luxuriant hedgerows of Hertford and Middlesex and the glories of the Middle Thames—do not make the first appeal, there are a host of interesting and beautiful places—manor-houses, churches, old inns and the like—to be seen within the confines of the outer environs of London. It must be admitted that the advancing tide of building has destroyed comparatively little of archæological interest during the last few years, and there is a strong and fighting minority who are out to preserve everything ancient, even at the expense of public convenience. As regards the village church, it may be said that the " restorer " has had his will with most of the subjects within these pages, though a few, to be mentioned in their due order, have come out of the ordeal almost unscathed. Many very beautiful modern churches, called into existence by the increase in population, grace the countryside near London. Some are successful departures from the native Gothic, while most of the remainder have broken away from the jejune imitations of Victorian days. Every outer suburb and every village, almost without exception, has its war memorial. The sculptured monument usually follows one of the three or four regular patterns, of which an adaptation of the Celtic cross forms the great majority. In some places, however, the memorial has taken the far better form of village club or hall—usually a distinct addition to the architectural beauty of the locality and for obvious reasons not altogether liked by the landlords of the " White Hart " and the " Red Lion " !

In the two hundred miles or so which ring Windsor

and Aylesbury, St. Albans and Rochester, Maidstone and Guildford, the character of the native type varies as much as does the scenery, that is, where one can identify the "native" as such. A large alien population of the peasant status is to be found, for instance, in Surrey, where the new class of landed proprietor has brought with him his own dependants. It is startling on addressing a cottager leaning against his garden wall in a Gomshall lane to be answered in the soft West Highland English of the shores of Loch Awe, and to find Midlothian methods obtaining in the farming operations of central Essex ; though here the wage-earner is usually an East Saxon and only his employer—tenant-farmer or freeholder, as the case may be—hails from north of the Cheviots. The craving for "a bit of land" has resulted in some queer developments in south Essex, where large tracts of poor stubborn soil have been carved up into small plots by the speculator in real estate for the townsman to try his luck at the difficult feats of poultry-farming or intensive market-gardening. The pages of the press devoted to such business are crowded with advertisements of these small properties, emanating either from those who have invested their capital in like hopeless undertakings and desire to "unload," or from the professional who has bought cheaply from an unfortunate freeholder in a small way, and retails at a profit of five or six hundred per cent.

The oldest race of men within our district is to be found in the narrow valleys of the Chiltern hills, and an interesting experience is in store for the student of ethnology if he devotes a few days to a ramble up and down the great chalk-folds between Dunstable and Streatley-on-Thames. Even the most superficial

B

observation will give the traveller subject for remark
in the contrast between the fair-haired, ruddy, Mercian
rustic and the dark sallow dweller on and among the
heights.

The rough-and-ready method of those history-makers
who, in the manuals once used in the class-room,
represented the Saxon invasion as a tidal wave sweep-
ing every " Briton " into the mountains of Wales—
there to be penned up, we will suppose, until as draper
or dairyman they returned to their own in the City
of Lud—have led the majority of folk to think of the
English rustic as a pure-bred Anglo-Saxon. The
small number of invaders taking part in any one
descent would render any comprehensive corralling
movement impracticable, and the isolated accounts of
extermination, such as that which occurred at Anderida,
in the country which became that of the South Saxons,
is but an exception to the general rule of conquest
and vassalage. In fact, the Saxon inflicted upon the
mixture of races which he found on his arrival in
south-eastern Britain much the same fate as became
his own in 1066.

It is probable that a majority of the Romanized folk
whom we call Celts did retire westwards before the
heathen invader, taking their culture, almost intact,
with them ; to set up, in the western mountains, a
semi-independent, and always hostile, state, which
persisted for hundreds of years. But there was
another and far older race of men, remnants of which
are to this day scattered about the whole of the kingdom, who seem to have cared little for so-called
liberty, and were as averse to travelling as they were
to fighting, unless that happened to be a necessary
proceeding to win the daily meal ; whose chief ambi-

tion was to be left alone in their wattle huts, picking up a bare subsistence upon the wild things of the woods —coney and berry—bird and root. Sometimes, not generally, they worked for the thane who held the rich lands of the valley, and hugged to themselves the dark old religion which, in secret and strange ways, spread among their, ultimately Christian, lords, and which is the foundation of much of our everyday superstition.

The Watling Street, cutting its way through the heart of the Chiltern, perpetuates the Saxon name given to one of these tribes of wild aborigines—the Watlings and types of this ancient race are scattered over England from Kent to Devon, from Wessex to Northumbria, but in greater numbers and almost out-classing the later comers in the higher combes and hollows of the hill-countries. With dark eyes and hair and small stature, they are distinctly different from the conventional English rustic, whose " type," if we may use the expression, is found near London in a state of comparative purity in Essex, a district which was colonized early and with comparative ease, and which became a kingdom with outlying portions in what is now Hertfordshire and Middlesex. Beyond the Roding are very few representatives of that older folk who can claim " grandfather " to be a native of the land between that river and the sea. The task of picking out aborigines is very difficult south of the Thames for the reason already stated, though in that comparatively little visited district which was once the great forest of Windsor and which has its centre about Wokingham, the elderly peasant is often curi-ously un-Saxon in appearance.

Cockney speech has been claimed to be " Middle

English." This is an interesting conjecture, especially as the intonation and pronunciation of the Londoner seem to have altered very considerably during the last three-quarters of a century; but the tongue of the " Dials " is most certainly not that of Warwick or Stafford. That the ugly twang of the lower-class Londoner is spreading through the surrounding countryside, especially in the south and west, is a matter for very great regret. A variety of causes are at work. A minor one, doubtless, is the fact that large numbers of youngsters are sent from the slums every summer to spend a week or fortnight in the fresh air. All honour to the large-hearted philan- thropy responsible for this good work. The cottagers' children with whom the young townsmen stay may lose archaism and gain argot, but the balance will still be on the right side.

CHAPTER I

ON WESTERN ROADS

UNTIL the opening years of the present century, the countryside served by the Great Western Railway between Ealing and Slough was the most sparsely populated within twenty miles of London. A region of quiet lanes and lonely farms, with little traffic except on the Bath and Oxford roads, has now given place to ragged and second-rate suburbs, rendered additionally hideous by many factory buildings of gaunt and staring aspect near the banks of the Grand Junction Canal. With regretful memories of the once pleasant hedgerows of South Middlesex, we must therefore start our explorations at Slough—a place itself, indeed, of mushroom growth, for beyond one or two inns and a few private houses, the town is a creation of the railway and dates from the early fifties, before which period it was the Bath Road end of Upton-cum-Chalvey, a small village just off the road to Eton and Windsor. At the corner of this turning is one of the few ancient buildings in the town—the " Old Crown "—an inn which claims to have served the wayfarer for over six hundred years. The Upton portion of Slough is worth a brief visit for the sake of its church, which possesses a fine Norman doorway and a remarkable yew that may be almost as old as the door. On the right-hand side of the Eton road is a house once occupied by the astronomer, Sir William Herschel. He died here in 1822 in his eighty-ninth year. A Hanoverian by birth and a musician by profession, he found his true vocation in mathematics, a study leading to his famous discoveries in the skies.

The main street of Slough was once the great coach-way to Bath. It is to-day a scene of incessant motor traffic, which leaves one wondering as to the future of the iron road—the premier trunk line of England —which accompanies it closely for some distance. Before the commencement of the " Highflier " days, the ominous name undoubtedly indicated the character of the road hereabouts, and in the lesser by-ways of these fat meadow-lands walking, for two-thirds of the year, is unpleasantly hazardous for the pedestrian in shoes.

About a mile from the centre of the town is Salt-hill, once the scene of the Eton Montem procession. A little further, and to the south of the road, is Cip-penham, the site of a palace which existed in the days of the Angevin kings, and which was founded by the Saxon predecessors of those monarchs. Close to this small hamlet are the scanty remains of Burnham Abbey, now incorporated in the buildings of a farm. This religious house was founded by Richard, King of the Romans, about the middle of the thirteenth century. From hereabouts we may catch alluring glimpses of the romantic outline of " noble and lordly Windsor " across the Thames-side meads to the south.

But our chief purpose in coming to Slough was to get away from it, and the easiest method is to take the first road over the railway, to the west of the station, which goes past Stone House—used for the imprisonment of German " brass hats " during the Great War—and then brings us to the pleasant Stoke villages, of which one—Stoke Poges—is for ever immortalized by its association with the most perfect poem in the English tongue.

There is a possibility that Gray had more than one rural churchyard in his mind when writing the " Elegy." Upton certainly has the " yew tree's shade " and " ivy-mantled tower " and the church and its surroundings were well known to the poet,

STOKE POGES CHURCH.

but Stoke Poges will always be accepted as the correct place for literary pilgrimages, for here the poet was buried. Apart from Stratford-on-Avon, and the various shrines within the confines of London, this country churchyard attracts more visitors than any other locality with similar associations.

Approaching the church from the south-east, a dismal memorial to Gray is passed on the right. This consists of a lofty pedestal surmounted by a sarcophagus, erected by John Penn in 1799. The poet's grave is outside the east wall of the picturesque old church. Here he lies with his mother—Dorothy Gray, and his sister—Mary Antrobus. For a long period no record of his interment, other than that upon Penn's memorial, was to be seen.

The lofty spire, so familiar in photograph and painting, has lately disappeared. Though of no great age, it had become dangerous, and it is said that the present truncated steeple is a near copy of the " ivy-mantled " one which Gray knew.

Besides the Gray cenotaph, Penn erected a memorial to the great Elizabethan lawyer, Sir Edward Coke, who lived at Stoke Poges manor house, now connected with the church by a so-called cloister. The house is used for parish purposes and was for a time the studio of Sir Edwin Landseer. While in the possession of Coke, it was visited by Queen Elizabeth, who, besides being sumptuously entertained by her Attorney-General, was presented with jewels valued at over one thousand pounds. Coke was an East Anglian by birth, and a singularly difficult individual by all accounts. His harsh and arrogant attitude at the trial of Sir Walter Raleigh does not redound to his credit, though he had a reputation for rectitude which was not always a trait of his contemporaries in the law. An added interest attaches to the manor house in that Charles I was brought to it as a prisoner thirteen years after the great lawyer had died in the ill-odour consequent upon his attitude towards the Royalist cause.

John Penn, who was a grandson of the founder of Pennsylvania, rebuilt the house on a slightly different site. Here is deposited a portion of the historic elm under which the Indian treaty was signed by the great Quaker. John de Molyns, a subject of Edward III, appears to have been the original owner of the property and some of his descendants have memorials within the church. These include one to Lord Hastings and another to his son, the first Earl of Huntingdon. The piers of the nave are Norman, but there is a medley of styles in which the most pronounced is a strange debased Gothic mixed with some good Decorated work. The font is a plain example of the latter. A queer old gallery has fortunately escaped restoration. The curious room under the tower is used as the Stoke Park pew. The carved chairs within are said to have belonged to Thomas Penn.

The churchyard is, of course, the chief interest and, apart from its connexion with the "Elegy," it is worthy of a visit for the sake of the exquisite beauty of the beds of roses and the well-cared-for graves—no "mouldering heaps" in these days, but patterns of quiet comeliness for other rustic graveyards to copy. In regard to tidy churchyards, Buckinghamshire probably stands first among the home counties, though Kent is a good second, while Essex shows a large proportion of the neglected and melancholy type of the eighteenth century : rank jungles of nettle, thistle and dock, or a breast-high growth of seeding grasses.

The near-by villages of Farnham Royal and Burnham are now centres of "country house villadom," if one may use such a term, The new buildings scattered about the neighbourhood are not much in evidence from the roads ; usually a thick screen of trees keeps, for both the householder and the pedestrian, the amenities of the rural by-way. Farnham gets its title of "Royal," not from the residence of a far-off monarch, but through the Norman family of de Verdim, who had the privilege of presenting the King with a glove at the coronation and of supporting the royal arm, gloved and holding the sceptre, at that ceremony. If the church ever contained any memorials of this old-time family, they have long since disappeared, and the present building is practically a re-erection, so much has it been altered and restored. The chief interest is a brass of Eustace Mascoll, dated 1564, clerk of the works to Wolsey while the great Cardinal was engaged on his buildings at Oxford.

Burnham contains a few old houses in the main street and around the ancient church. The latter is of

BURNHAM BEECHES IN WINTER.

some archæological interest, for it contains very early Norman arches at the east end which have by some been ascribed to pre-Conquest builders. The monument to George Evelyn and his wife is a fine example of seventeenth-century sculpture ; and on the south side of the chancel, another, almost as good, of John Wright, vicar during the closing years of the preceding century, stands. This is a bust, with the full ruff and gown of the period. The late eighteenth-century bas-relief monument of Justice Willes bears a weeping figure of Justice which is more curious than beautiful. Certain brasses of the Eyre family are also worthy of inspection. The home of George Grote, the historian, was at East Burnham. To the north, approached by the official chars-à-bancs of the Great Western Railway and countless others all through the summer, lie the

famous Beeches, saved to the people for all time by
the public spirit of the City Fathers. The Druids' oak
is but a few minutes' walk from the village street, and
beyond it lie the best of the aged trees which give a
name to this delightful series of woods and commons.

Quiet roads go eastwards by the Alderbourne
Valley, in which lies the little hamlet of Fulmer,
toward Uxbridge, but the nearest way is by the more
frequented highway between the latter town and
Windsor. This passes Black Park, and a pathway
through the demesne takes the pedestrian by a romantic
pool surrounded by solemn and ancient trees of forest
growth. This park is famous for its grand timber
and, when seen from a distance, justifies its name.

Uxbridge can, alas ! no longer be termed a country
town ; the trams that clang and rattle along twelve
miles of the London–Aberystwyth road from Shep-
herd's Bush Green have seen to that ! A matter of
even greater regret is the spoliation by this urban
convenience of the once charming little village of
Hillingdon, the senior of Uxbridge ecclesiastically and
now its eastern suburb.

The Ux-*bridge* is that over the Colne, a small stream
that, after rising in southern Hertfordshire, forms
almost the entire western boundary of Middlesex.
Hereabouts it is a pleasant enough little river, often
confused by strangers with the adjacent canal. It
was this latter waterway which in the nineteenth
century gave the town a certain measure of prosperity,
greatly increased in other ways since the neighbourhood
became a place of residence for Londoners. Apart
from the eighteenth-century Market Hall and one or
two old houses, there is little of interest. Of these,
the best known is the Treaty House, so called as being

the place of meeting between the two bodies of Commissioners appointed by Charles and the Parliament to discuss some basis for agreement. The Republican Army was in possession of the town, half of which was given up to the Royalists for lodgings during the twenty days set aside for the futile negotiations. Only a portion of the old house remains. It now forms part of a hostelry, and is to be found at the lower end of the main street between the bridges. South of Uxbridge, leafy lanes lead to Cowley, Iver and Langley Marish. The two first are pleasant little villages in the flat meadows of the Colne, and both have churches of some antiquarian interest. Iver retains some portions of an Early Norman building, and a Jacobean memorial to a lady whose husband had the proud distinction of being carver to two kings! Langley Marish Church has a red brick tower, but the chancel dates from the twelfth century. Here are two sets of seventeenth-century almshouses, the Seymour and the Kederminster. The latter was established by a once important local family, whose great pew and collection of religious books are unusual features of the church.

That portion of the County of Middlesex lying between Uxbridge and Harrow was, until a few years ago, the most rural district within a radius of fifteen miles from Charing Cross; but as these pages are written, hedgerows are disappearing, fields are being intersected by new yellow roads, and the "superior detached residence" is springing up everywhere between the picturesque old villages of Ickenham and Ruislip and the rather shabby west-end of Harrow. And so we propose to go direct to Harrow by the electric railway, leaving these localities for the return

journey towards Uxbridge.   The once delightful lanes
of South Middlesex—at their leafy best between
Hayes and Northolt—are no more, and to attempt the
sorrowful task of identifying their course would result
in being stranded in some building contractor's Slough
of Despond.   Twenty years ago, an alluring path led
through fields and by hedgerows ablaze with blossom,
past Greenford Green to tiny Perivale—one of England's many " smallest churches " but—*but* this book
has set out to describe things as they are—at present !

The growth of the little town on " The Hill " to the
west thereof has reversed the usual order of urban
extension, and this side is distinctly not its best.   Only
in the neighbourhood immediately to the east, and
on the actual slopes leading up to Harrow church and
school, do the ancient amenities linger.   And although
the graceful outline of the twin hills—that to the
south being Sudbury—is very pleasing from the
meadows about Uxbridge, the only good near view of
the spire-crowned height is from the east, particularly
that from the windows of those trains which run on
the one-time North-Western Railway.   The new buildings and the school chapel line the brow of the hill
upon this side, and the church appears to rise from
among them.   Below are noble banks of trees and a
green declivity, though the foreground of hedgerow
and flat meadow-lands, vast stretches of white and
gold in the spring and early summer, will soon give
way to the ubiquitous builder.

The school is obviously the first consideration in any
brief account of Harrow, though it is by no means the
only excuse for a visit.   The church is as interesting
as its situation is picturesque.   Close to it there stood
until 1724 an ancient building, used as a workhouse

in its later days, which was the original Harrow School
and antedated the foundation of "Lyon of Preston,
Yeoman, John," by at least a century.   It was in 1571
that the wealthy gentleman farmer obtained a royal
charter for what was to be one of the most famous
preparatory schools in the world.

At close view, some of the new buildings have a
jejune appearance, and contrast unfavourably with
the mellow walls of the old schoolhouse erected in
1615, and which comprised the entire extent of the

school until the
early years of the
last century, when
extensions com-
menced with the
erection of a new
wing. In 1839 the
first chapel ap-
peared, to be fol-
lowed by the not
very successful
effort of Sir Gilbert

OLD SCHOOL, HARROW.

Scott in 1857.   The so-called new schools date from this
year, to be followed in turn by the Vaughan Library
and, twenty years later, by the Speech Room.

The roll of scholars includes some of the most famous
names in the later history of the nation.   In literature,
the list is headed by Byron and Sheridan.   Anthony
Trollope, Theodore Hook, Lord Lytton, John Addington Symonds, Calverley, James Morier, and Sir George
Trevelyan are only a few of the scholars who became
great men of letters.   Among statesmen may be
mentioned Sir Robert Peel, Spencer Perceval, Sidney
Herbert, Earl Spencer, and several of our present-day

politicians. Cardinal Manning was also an Harrovian, and the list of masters includes the great-grandfather of the author of *Vanity Fair*. Thomas Thackeray reigned for fourteen years from 1746. The most famous heads were perhaps Dr. Wordsworth and Dr. Vaughan, whose two masterships covered the period 1836-59.

The school experienced a mutiny in 1771, when a disappointed assistant-master, who had expected to be given supreme power, started an opposition establishment at Stanmore, and took practically the whole school with him. The rebellion was crushed, and Lord Wellesley, one of the ringleaders, was expelled for his share in it.

The Fourth Form room, in the western wing of the old schoolhouse, is the most interesting place in the whole range of buildings. Here may be seen, carved in the old panelling, the names of many of England's great ones. Another house adjoining the churchyard is noteworthy for its associations, though the present structure only dates from 1833, when a fire destroyed the earlier building. The house is now called the Grove, and was originally the Rectory. It housed Sheridan for a few years and was the residence of Edward Bowen, a famous Head, and author of *Harrow School Songs*. He bequeathed the house to the school. A number of other large and pleasant buildings in and about the town form part of the school housing scheme ; among others may be mentioned " The Park," " Druries," and " Byron House," where Matthew Arnold lived for five years.

Harrow church was founded by Lanfranc, and the older part dates from 1094, having been built during the archiepiscopate of his successor Anselm. To this period the lower portions of the tower may belong, though the west doorway was built about fifty years afterwards. The chancel arch may be dated 1200, and the arches of nave and transepts, with the north and south doorways, belong to a period of thirty or forty years later. The aisle windows and clerestory are Perpendicular. In the first years of Victoria's reign, the chancel was practically demolished by Gilbert Scott's restoration, the south wall only being original work.

The church contains many interesting brasses; the earliest is that of Sir John Flambard. It depicts the

HARROW CHURCH.

knight in armour with his hound at his feet. The chief interest, of course, centres in the brass of John Lyon, who died in 1592. Part of the inscription runs as follows: "he founded a free grammar schoole in this parish to have continuance for ever, and for maintainance thereof, and for releyfe of the poore and of some poore schollers in the Universityes, repayringe of highways and other good and charitable uses hath made conveyance of lands of good value to a corporation granted for that purpose."

Among other memorials in the church will be noticed several to Masters of Harrow School. Of the remaining details, mention must be made of the pulpit and its massive sounding-board, dating from 1727; and the clerestory windows, which give a pictorial history of the parish and school.

The majority of visitors wish to see "Byron's Tomb." This rather stupid appellation occasionally gives rise, among the ill-informed, to a perhaps natural mistake. The flat-topped grave is that of John Peachey, who died in 1780. Upon it, the poet used to recline and watch the sunset over the Thames Valley. He refers to the fact in one of his poems, and also in a letter to his publisher. In consequence of the depredations of relic-hunters, the grave had, many years ago, to be protected by iron railings, and no budding poet may now seek inspiration by using this hard couch.

The heavily buttressed tower is a noticeable feature of the church, and the spire above, composed of wood and lead, is perhaps the best known landmark in the country north-west of London ; and not in this direction alone, for on the clear Sunday evenings of summer it may be seen, silhouetted against the sunset sky, from the heights to the south-east of the Metropolis as well as from the hills of East Berkshire. The king " who never said a foolish thing " had probably seen its slender finger from the upper windows of Whitehall when he expressed his interpretation of the phrase— " the church visible."

Of the celebrated view from the churchyard, we can only say that as it has lost its beautiful foreground, half the charm has departed. The huge wireless masts near the aerodrome at Northolt have utterly ruined the prospect in that direction, but doubtless, before many years have elapsed, another method of transmitting and receiving will have rendered obsolete these gaunt steel towers.

During the period just prior to the Conquest, Harrow appears to have been called Hergest, but by the commencement of the fifteenth century it had become Harewe at Hill. It was once the property of the Archbishops of Canterbury, but at the Reformation

c

the manor passed to the Crown, and thence into private ownership. In 1524, while it was still the property of the Church, the Prior of St. Barthlomew's, Smithfield, made of the Hill a temporary retreat. Here he built a noble house, and came with all his retinue to escape a dreadful flood which, it was prophesied, would destroy London Town. The astrologer-prophet afterwards gave out that a miscalculation had resulted in an error of one hundred years! The town was one of the many refuges for the wealthy during the Great Plague, when the " King's Head " Inn, then a hundred and thirty years old, saw several noble visitors.

Headstone, which lies about half-way between the commonplace suburb called Wealdstone and Pinner village, is said to have been the residence of the Archbishops. The building now consists of a much mutilated fragment of an ancient mansion still containing one good room with a mullioned window, old panelling, and an iron fire-back bearing the arms of Philip of Spain. A broad moat surrounds the house, and heavy chimney-stacks give it a picturesque air of antiquity. It became a farm-house in the middle of the fifteenth century. Fifty years earlier, it was the probable retreat of Archbishop Arundel, who was banished for treason against the second Richard. In 1170 Thomas Becket came here and, finding the rector of his own Harrow to be a King's man, promptly excommunicated him.

Pinner evidently intends, at no distant date, to become connected with Harrow by continuous links of brick and mortar. When the writer first saw the village street, the Metropolitan Railway bridge which crosses it had been in position for only a few months, and the quiet thoroughfare was as drowsy, rural and unsophisticated as any to be found in remoter Wessex. Its picturesque character is still kept, and its many gabled old houses are unlikely to be demolished now that an era of conservation is with us. A particularly good specimen of the bygone architecture of Middlesex is preserved in the " Queen's Head," an inn dating from 1705.

The bridge at the foot of the street crosses the diminutive Pin, a stream that one would think had given its name to the village ; but a reversal of the usual order is likelier here. Pinner church crowns the vista in the opposite direction in most effective fashion, the plain and lofty cross of wood encased in lead which surmounts the tower being not the least striking item in the picture. The cross was placed in position in 1637, and in this country is an uncommon fea-ture in all but very modern

PINNER.

churches. The body of the building dated from the fourteenth century, but it has been much altered from its original simple cruciform plan by the addition of a special aisle, built about the middle of the last century, for the use of the Commercial Travellers' Schools, a fine institution at Hatch End. The church was originally erected in 1321, for the consecration deed, so dated, is to be seen at Lambeth Palace, to whose lord the parish was " peculiar." The interior is not of great interest. A tablet in the south aisle commemorates Pye, who was Poet Laureate in 1790. His verse deserved the obscurity that surrounds it, and he is only remembered as the precursor of two famous holders of the office—Southey and Wordsworth. Pye

was a member of Parliament for Berkshire, and retired
to Pinner, where he died in 1831.

A number of old wooden grave-boards surround the
church. They are common in the churchyards of
rural Middlesex, where stone in bygone days was
difficult to procure. One records the death in 1775
of a William Skenelsby at the age of 118.

In the neighbourhood of Pinner are a number of fine
houses, with associations of varied interest. Pinner
Place was once inhabited by a well-known Anglo-
Indian named Holwell, one of the survivors of the
Black Hole. Pinner Hill, now dotted with artistic
residences, was formerly the demesne surrounding the
home of Sir Bartholomew Shower, a famous seventeenth-century lawyer. The daughter of Lord Nelson
and Lady Hamilton lived at Woodridings for a short
time before her death. Bulwer Lytton stayed for a
brief season at an old cottage in Pinner Wood, and
there wrote *Eugene Aram*.

Hatch End is a district of pleasant modern villas
which have sprung up around one of the Pinner railway
stations. The name belongs to a small hamlet, now
almost obliterated, to the east of the railway, and
signifies a gateway to the wood which once covered
Pinner Park. The road to Hatch End continues to
Harrow Weald, still pleasant and unspoilt in its northern section towards Bushey. Here is a considerable
portion of the great wood or common which the name
perpetuates. At the crossing of the Bushey and Stanmore roads stands a fine modern church having a
conspicuous tower capped with red tiles. Not far
away, at "Grim's Dyke," lived W. S. Gilbert, the
great "Savoyard." The mysterious bank, after which
Gilbert named his house, passes near by, and may

readily be seen in the fields lying to the west of the station, and again to the north-east, on the other side of the railway which cuts right through the embankment. The work is ascribed variously to British tribes and to the Saxons. If Offa's Dyke in the Welsh borderland is actually the work of the great chief whose name it bears, there would be good reason to suppose that this was also a defensive undertaking of the Mercians.

Continuing by the north-western road from Pinner, we arrive three miles farther on at Northwood, an utterly commonplace town brought into being by the Metropolitan Railway. The rather mean rows of villas which go to make up the greater part of this " wen " are a lesson for town-planners of how not to do it. The original tiny hamlet received its name from the wood to the north of Ruislip, to which parish it belonged until 1854, when the small church upon the right of the Rickmansworth road was erected. Here, in the churchyard, there is a massive stone, sent from Russia by the Czar, and covering the grave of Sir Robert Morier, one-time ambassador to St. Petersburg. Here are also several memorials to the Grosvenors, including one to the first Lord Ebury, who lived at Moor Park, just across the Hertfordshire border. This estate has been partly cut up into " eligible sites," and its mansion is a glorified golf club-house. Outside the southern gates of the park is a common bordered with old houses, and called Batchworth Heath. In one of the largest and comeliest of these dwellings lived Sir Robert Morier. The Mount Vernon hospital for consumptives is a conspicuous building on the sunny slope of White Hill to the south of Batchworth.

A once quiet and bowery lane leads from the Heath

to Harefield and another, more frequented, and running through a better-looking extension of Northwood, leaves the main road near the hospital and goes to Ruislip. Both villages are worth a visit, though the first-named is likely to keep its character longest, for Ruislip is now served by two railways. Many new villas are springing up in the vicinity of the stations, and also between them and the old village street. A charming walk through Harefield to Ruislip, and back to Northwood, might be taken by those who can perform their seven miles or so without fatigue.

Harefield street is not particularly pretty, and a number of dreary cottages and small shops erected

MOOR HALL, HAREFIELD.

some years ago replaced several rather tumble-down wooden structures that were probably as insanitary as they were picturesque. It is in its delightful surroundings that the charm of Harefield consists, and the best of South Bucks seems to have here crept over the border into Middlesex. The main street follows a ridge above the eastern bank of the Colne. On the opposite side of the valley rise green and wooded slopes that are actually the commencement of those foothills so characteristic of the wrong side of all chalk ranges. They rise in ever increasing altitude until they culminate in the bold bluffs above the Vale of Aylesbury. Not even the tall chimneys of the factory where a well-known asbestos sheeting is made, or the untidy dustiness of the lime-works, entirely spoil this prettiest stretch of the Colne and its companion waterway—the Grand Junction Canal. The curious name of one of the inns—the " Mines Royal "—

is puzzling to the stranger. It is a reminder of certain copper mills, long disused, worked here by the Society of the Mines Royal.

Harefield church is below the south end of the ridge carrying the village street. Its chief interest, according to certain authorities, would seem to be in a curious memorial to a gamekeeper, placed upon the north wall in 1744 by the Ashby family, in whose service he was. The church, however, has other points, and should certainly be seen. The end of the north aisle is enclosed by a screen, and is usually known as the Breakspeare Chantry. Within are several brasses to the Ashbys, who lived at Breakspears, a fine mansion in a beautifully wooded park to the east of the church, and the traditional home of Nicholas Breakspeare, the English Pope of 1154, who occupied the Papal throne as Adrian IV.

It is in the Newdegate monuments that the interest chiefly centres. They not only crowd the Brackenbury Chapel, but are to be found all over the body of the church and in the chancel, where will be seen three large funeral urns to some eighteenth-century members of the family. The series commences in the chapel with a brass of Edetha Newdegate, dated 1444, and ends with that of General Sir Edward Newdigate-Newdegate in 1902.

Among other curiosities that will attract notice are the old-fashioned pulpit and reading-desk, the funeral armour, and the overpowering monument to a Countess of Derby who died in 1637. She had married Sir Thomas Egerton of Harefield Place, and there entertained Queen Elizabeth in 1602 with great magnificence. The festivities are said to have included the presentment of *Othello*, then lately written, by the

Lord Chamberlain's company. The manor had been
sold to Sir Thomas Egerton in 1585 by the Sir Roger
Newdegate, who founded the prize poem of that name.
Just ninety years later it was repurchased, and is
still in the possession of the ancient family. The
original mansion was burnt down in 1660 through the
accidental oversetting of a candle by which Sir Charles
Sedley was reading in bed. This notorious member
of the Court of Charles II held the estates by virtue of
his marriage with Lady Chandos, last but one of the
owners during the interregnum. The succeeding

building also dis-
appeared, and the
last Harefield Place
was built some dis-
tance away, between
Uxbridge and Icken-
ham.

RUISLIP.

The almshouses
are among the most picturesque in the county. That
Countess of Derby whose gorgeous tomb we have
seen was the foundress. About ten minutes' walk
to the south of the church are a couple of quaint
cottages with, close by, a small Early English
chapel. These constitute the scanty remnants of
Moor Hall, a one-time chapelry of the Knights of
St. John.

Ruislip is rather more than three miles to the south-
east, but the walk, partly by footpath, is delightful.
Nowhere do the wooded parklands and lanes of Middlesex show to better advantage, and the new red of
villadom is not in evidence until the explorer is close
to Ruislip. The fine sheet of water to the north of
the village is enclosed upon one side by the woodlands

that extend almost to Northwood. The lake was formed to feed the Grand Junction Canal.

The original pronunciation " Riselip " seems to be changing to the more vulgar " Rooslip." The derivation appears still to elude the investigator, but the name is doubtless connected with some far-off Saxon patronymic. The ancient houses closely surrounding the churchyard are perhaps more picturesque than pleasant to live in. The church itself is of much interest, though the restoration by Gilbert Scott in 1870 removed many quaint and old-fashioned things. The carved oak bread-cupboard just within the west end, from which loaves are distributed every Sunday, is an uncommon feature. The name of the benefactor—Jeremiah Bright, who died in 1697—is perpetuated by this very practical form of charity. Near by, is an ancient oak chest bound around with heavy iron bands. The hatchments on the wall above were allowed to remain at the restoration, although they were very properly removed from the chancel and nave which they once disfigured in a way familiar to us in those pictures of church interiors dating from the first two decades of the nineteenth century. The list of vicars starts in 1290, to which year the base of the pillars would probably belong. They are alternately round and octagonal, with pointed arches above. Wall paintings were brought to light in 1870, and that at the end of the north aisle, of an angel weighing souls, while the Blessed Virgin presses down the balance in the sinner's favour, is a good specimen of this kind of mediæval art.

The most interesting memorials are in the chancel, and commemorate several of the Hawtrey family, whose home was at Eastcote. The most famous

member was that Lady Banks whose heroic defence of
Corfe Castle is one of the outstanding incidents of the
Civil War. Her father was the Ralph Hawtrey whose
effigy, with that of his wife, is upon the chancel wall.

Ruislip was once the home of a body of French
monks attached to Bec, in Normandy. Their house
became in course of time an English priory belonging
to Okeburn, in Wiltshire. The fourth Henry did away
with this community, and from his heir the manor
came into the hands of the Collegians of Windsor—the
present owners. The manor farm, however, belongs
to King's College, Cambridge. Considerable remains
of the old building still exist, and part of the moat
may be traced by the curious. Ickenham, midway
between Ruislip and Uxbridge, stands yet unspoilt
and rural about its spacious green. " Development "
between the village and its station is proceeding apace,
though " Jerry " is not in evidence. Some quite
charming types of modern domestic architecture are to
be seen hereabouts, and the difference between the
appearance of the city man's home here and those a
few miles away beside the older railways that were the
first to tempt him into the country, is remarkable.

At the junction of the roads, amid masses of foliage,
stands Ickenham church, a small building of various
dates, but chiefly of the Decorated period. Within
are memorials of the Shorediches of Ickenham and the
Clarks of Swakeleys. The earliest brass is to a William
Saye who was Registrar to Queen Elizabeth, and died
in 1582. Of some interest are the records of a number
of faithful servants which appear on the gravestones in
the churchyard. Another, commemorating a rector's
servant, consists of a brass placed upon one of the
pillars within the church.

A footpath to Uxbridge leads past the fine Jacobean mansion called Swakeleys after a one-time owner—Robert Swaklyve—whose home, however, must have presented an appearance very different from the present pile, for he lived in the fourteenth century. The characteristic scrolled gables and fine chimney-stacks make this one of the best examples of the period to be seen near London. A short time ago, it became the temporary headquarters of the Young Women's Christian Association, while the members of that body were connected in various ways with the British Empire Exhibition at Wembley. It is to be hoped that this house will be saved for posterity. Efforts to this end have been made by the Society for the Protection of Ancient Buildings, but at the moment of writing the fate of Swakeleys is still uncertain. This Society, and, of course, the National Trust for Places of Historic Interest and National Beauty, deserve the grateful thanks and material support of all who "admire and reverence things ancient and things lovely."

OXFORD FROM MAGDALEN.

CHAPTER II

TOWARDS OXFORD

THE great West road, starting at the site of Tyburn, crosses the breadth of England and Wales until its course is arrested by the sea in Cardigan Bay. This is the true road to the West, and the first town of any real size and importance upon its broad way is the " city of dreaming spires," fifty-four miles from the Marble Arch. Our present chapter takes us along this artery and down some of its by-ways.

The double lines of thickly clustered telegraph wires must be left, about a mile and a half from the old " Swan and Bottle " at the Colne crossing in Uxbridge, for the pretty little village of Denham, which, for its size, contains more old houses than any other less than twenty miles from Charing Cross. Not only is its architecture pleasing, but the whole plan of the place is highly picturesque, from the striking situation of the church to the clear brooklet which trespasses upon the village street and the enormous wistaria decorating the front of the village inn. Yet until the advent of the railway, not so long ago, one seldom met a stranger here on those Saturday afternoons of summer when

exploring Londoners are afoot. The tram contingents
to Uxbridge seem to leave this by-way severely alone,
possibly because the broader road appears to lead to
more important things. But the half-mile or so of
detour will repay the wanderer, who will find an old
church dating from about 1350, and containing some
interesting monuments and several brasses. One of
the latter is to an Abbess of Sion—Agnes Jordan—
who died in 1544. An older brass in a modern frame
shows the effigy of Amphillis Peckham, dated 1445.
This was originally a memorial of a friar, and the
careful observer will notice how the brass has been
altered by the later worker. Another, dated 1494, is
to Walter Duredent and his wives, while a fourth
commemorates a priest in the sacred vestments. The
stone slab in the chancel, bearing the incised drawing
of a robed figure, is thought to be the work of an artist
in brass. Among other noteworthy objects are the
wall painting in the nave, and the fine monument of
Sir E. Peckham.

Hill House, near the inn before mentioned, is a good
late-Jacobean building, and near the Colne is a fine
old farm-house called "The Savoy." It contains a
quantity of panelling and some curious mural paintings
in an upper room. Denham Court was the home of
Sir W. Bowyer, friend and patron of Dryden, and here
the poet was a frequent visitor. The truly magnificent
avenue of limes which leads from Denham church to
the Court is alone worth turning aside to see. The
other great house of the neighbourhood—Denham
Place—is partly guarded from vulgar gaze by the
mellow old brick wall on the west of the village, but
the house can be seen to advantage from the road
leading to the station.

Resuming the main route, Gerrard's Cross is reached in four miles from Uxbridge. The straggling hamlet with its exotic and unlovely modern church is fast becoming another of London's residential suburbs, but few signs of this are visible from the breezy roadside common, around which are some old cottages. At the western extremity is the entrance to Bulstrode Park, through which the pedestrian has a pleasant alternative route towards Beaconsfield. Bulstrode is named after the family that once owned it. The present house dates from 1862, when the Duke of Somerset removed its predecessor, built by the infamous Judge Jeffreys in 1686, also, in its turn, a rebuilding. This was bought by Dutch William's minister, Bentinck, and continued to be the home of the Portland family until the early years of the last century. Here, among other treasures, the Portland vase was housed until its removal to the British Museum. The mansion was a notable meeting-place for the leading political lights of the latter half of the eighteenth century. A footpath runs across the park to Hedgerley, a secluded little place quite off the holiday-maker's track. The rebuilt church here preserves several old brasses, and a glass case contains a fragment of material said to be part of a cloak belonging to Charles II, who, finding the altar bare of cloth or frontal, took the covering from his shoulders and placed it thereon.

The scenery gradually improves as the altitude increases, and in the neighbourhood of Jordans, which lies to the north of the main road about two miles from Gerrard's Cross, it can well be described as beautiful. This tiny hamlet, as a place of pilgrimage, is unique. Here, in the course of a year, there come hundreds of Americans to see the resting-place of the

founder of a great New England State—William Penn.
The grave and beautiful simplicity of the Quaker is
surely exemplified in the place and its surroundings.
The calm quiet loveliness of the rustic scene—the
solemn trees overshadowing the dignified memorials of
the great dead—simple, lowly round-topped stones
in the short grass, marked merely with initials and
a date. There is nothing quite like it elsewhere in
England, and to the writer, apart from the trees and
hedgerows, which are purely English, there is something
in the air of the
place strangely
reminiscent of
New England.
Perhaps the con-
tinuous stream of
visitors from over-
sea have left be-
hind them a
Transatlantic
aura. At any
rate, the lines of

JORDANS.

the Meeting House, a combination of dwelling and
hall, are distinctly those of similar abodes of peace
in the Eastern States.

The courteous Friend who abides in the dwelling
allows the visitor to explore without hindrance, but
is ready at once with information or to interpret the
initials upon the gravestones. These include, besides
William Penn's, those of his six children, Gulielmo Penn,
Thomas Ellwood and Isaac Pennington. The widow of
the last-named left a legacy towards the building of the
Meeting House in 1688, though the land had belonged
to the Friends for some seventeen years prior to this.

The house on the outer side of the road has been
much altered and added to, but the older portion was
built by a London Quaker in 1691. A few years ago,
a movement was launched to found a colony of Friends
among these quiet meadows. The scheme includes a
hostel, not necessarily confined to members of the
denomination.

A delightful and leafy lane leads to Seer Green,
passing an old farm-house and one-time Quaker
property called Dean, and thence on to Chalfont St.
Giles; but this pleasant village must be left to a later
chapter.

The onward way brings us in two miles to Beaconsfield—usually " Bekkonsfield " to the native. Doubtless this is correct. There is no " beacon " hereabouts,
and the word is said to refer to the " bucken " or beech
trees which give the shire its name. The distance
can be shortened for pedestrians by taking a footpath
through Wilton Park, at the western end of which
commences the reputed widest High Street in England.
The claim is open to dispute, but possibly no other of
equal length can boast the spaciousness of this pleasant
and sunny thoroughfare. Of late years, since the
advent of the railway, its pavements have been
brightened by the appearance of smartly-dressed residents from the new suburb which has sprung up on the
north of the old town and around the railway station ;
a place of artistic villas set widely apart, but accompanying the rambler for several miles on the roads towards
Amersham and Penn, thus making a lately remote
country semi-suburban in character.

Many old and picturesque houses still grace the
Oxford road and the cross-road to Windsor. One of
these, the so-called Rectory House, belongs to the early

sixteenth century, and was once a priory of Burnham Abbey. It has been well and carefully restored, and forms a fine specimen of typical " English " architecture, an unusual feature being the turret staircase on the north side. The interior is remarkable in the quantity and solidity of the ancient timber used in its construction. The " Saracen's Head " inn is another ancient building, but its restoration, some years ago, was overdone.

The large church was almost rebuilt by the frenzied zeal of nineteenth-century restorers. The principal interest now lies in the memorials—for there are two —to Burke. These are both within the church, and consist of a simple contemporary slab, which was the only monument of the great statesman until 1898, when the rather florid modernity was added. The tomb of Edmund Waller is a close second as an object of pilgrimage to Beaconsfield, and is in the churchyard under a tree. It is a deplorably ugly erection in the worst style of its period. Waller lived at Hall Barn, now the residence of Lord Burnham. Burke's home was at Gregories, not far from the Penn road, but the site is lost among the roads and houses of the new suburb. The house was destroyed by fire in 1813. Besides memorials commemorating the Great War, is one to Lieutenant R. S. Grenfell, who was killed in the charge of the 21st Lancers at Khartoum in 1898. The young soldier's sword is preserved beneath the tablet.

A pleasant way of leaving Beaconsfield for the west is to take the road past the station, and then, after about a mile, to bear westwards to Penn. The latter part of the walk may be diversified by following a woodland path.

The interest of Penn centres in the church. Here are the brasses of the Penn family with which the great Quaker supposed himself to be connected; a doubtful claim which has never been satisfactorily settled. The first of these memorials is to John Penn and his wife Ursula, dated 1597; both effigies have the lower halves broken off. There are also figures of their children beneath. Other brasses of the Penns are—William and Martha; John and Sarah; Susan Drury, mother of Sarah Penn. These are all between 1635 and 1641. Roger Penn is commemorated by a stone slab dated 1731. He was the last of the family to hold the estates, for, dying unmarried, his sister, wife of Nathaniel Curzon, inherited. A stone in the nave covers the tomb of a child, one William Penn, grandson of the Quaker.

An interesting brass of 1540 to Elizabeth Rok represents the deceased in a shroud. Other noteworthy objects include a stone coffin and some quaint rhymes in the tower chamber, where we may also see the royal arms of Queen Anne hanging upon the wall.

Penn is a remarkably healthy place owing to its altitude. From certain points fine views to the hill country beyond the Thames may be obtained, but the height of 560 feet is not readily apparent. There is much wooded country to the north and north-west—falling and rising, but gradually lifting higher to the ridge of the Chiltern escarpment—which is still lonely and house-free, unless we drop right or left into the parallel valleys of the Misburn and Wye. Towards the latter we must now proceed. Shortly after leaving the village a meadow is passed, known locally as the " French School." This is the site of a house in which was the school founded by Burke in 1796 for the children of the exiled aristocrats. It is pleasant to think that this pious work was taken over at Burke's death by the British Government, who kept things going until 1820, when the small exiles all went home.

We join the Oxford road again at Wycombe Marsh, a mile or more above the paper mills at Loudwater, the chimneys of which do not add to the view up the valley of the Wye. Signs of the approach to a populous place in the form of new bungalows and miniature chicken farms line the roadside as we near the old, and still prosperous, centre of chair-making. Time was when wagons piled high with the produce of the beech woods to the north of Wycombe were a familiar sight in the early morning hours on the Bayswater Road and along Oxford Street and Holborn, bound for the wholesalers in

HIGH WYCOMBE.

that dreary region behind the City where such firms do congregate, but the gaily painted wagons have disappeared from the London streets and the chairs come to town by railway or motor-lorry. In those far-off Victorian days, Wycombe was a considerable journey from London, for the only communication by steam was over the roundabout route from Maidenhead and Bourne End to Thame and Oxford; but now the finely appointed expresses to Birmingham and the north-west thunder through the station, and several of them think Wycombe important enough for a brief pause in their career.

Only a very small portion of the town is of sufficient

interest to detain us, and that is the district around White Hart Street—where there are some quaint old houses and the church, which stands close to the railway station. It is the largest in the shire, and is more stately and imposing within than the exterior would lead us to expect.

At one time the tower stood at the junction of nave and chancel. It was rebuilt at the west end about 1505. The oldest portion of the building is a piece of the north aisle wall at the west end thereof. This is said to be a fragment of the original Early Norman church. The principal part of the chancel and the upper portions of nave and aisles are Perpendicular, but there are several reminders of the Early English building which succeeded the Norman. Of particular note is the fine south porch dating from that period. The principal monument is that of the first Earl of Shelburne, who lived at Wycombe Abbey, now a girls' school. The most remarkable is, perhaps, the flat stone in the pavement inscribed—" George Clewer is dead, March 19th, 1701."

The old building known as the Little Market House dates from 1604. The Town Hall, with its unique weather-vane—a gilded centaur—was built in 1757, and is in a style which seems to have been copied more or less closely by several towns in the home counties. It contains quite a collection of pictures, including a reputed Vandyck which is almost certainly a copy, and a painting of St. Paul preaching to British Druids, by an artist named Mortimer, which once formed the altar-piece of Wycombe church. It is the scene of the curious civic ceremony of " weighing in " the mayor and corporation upon the election of that body. The custom is said to be upwards of six hundred years old.

In the London Road are some old almshouses dated 1562, and opposite is the partly built Grammar School, still retaining certain Norman arches—remains of the ancient Hospital of St. John the Baptist. Another old building known as the Priory stands near the church. This list sums up briefly the attractions of Chipping Wycombe, which was, until 1867, a parliamentary borough. From the balcony of the "Red Lion" Disraeli made many orations to his followers in the street below. It has always been a larger town than either the old or new capitals of the county, and bids fair to grow still more—though rather as a commercial and self-centred place than as a residential appendage to London.

This cannot be said of the old village two miles farther on, now called West Wycombe, but once Haveringdon, where a number of attractive residences have lately appeared upon the surrounding slopes. The picturesque street of houses bordering the high road has altered but little during the last three hundred years and, except for the improvement of the roadway between them, the present aspect of the street is probably the same as it presented to the Ironside troopers when they jingled through its then muddy and uneven length on their way to defeat on Chalgrove Field.

A ball-topped obelisk stands at the parting of the ways to Reading and Oxford. It is an eighteenth-century signpost, and the distances carved upon its sides are at variance with the measured miles of the Ministry of Transport, displayed close by. Upon the knoll above the fork stands the extraordinary church. This landmark, once so well known to the regular occupants of the Oxford coach—as it now is to railway

travellers to Chester and North Wales—was built by
Sir Francis Dashwood in 1793 on the site of an ancient
building, scanty remains of which may be seen in the
base of the tower.   Within will be found some Grinling
Gibbons carving, and a brass from the older building,
dated 1683, and on the ceiling, a painting of the Last
Supper.   The mausoleum at the east end contains,
besides the bones of the builder, who died Lord de
Despencer, the heart of his friend, Paul Whitehead,
the dramatist.   The eccentric peer had a reputation,
or rather, lack of one, due chiefly to his responsibility
for founding the notorious Hell Fire Club at Medmen-
ham Abbey between Henley and Marlow.   The de-
pravity of the members was probably more legendary
than real, and the desire to be original led merely to
the usual result—absurdity.

The view of the Wye valley is very pleasing as seen
from the rim of the ancient camp which surrounds
the church.   Another prehistoric fortification, called
Desborough Castle, may be discerned upon the hill to
the left of the valley ;   this is usually spoken of as the
" Roundabout " by the rustic folk.   To the south of
the Wycombes stretches a delectable country which
gradually drops to the Thames, with many fine seats
and gracious parklands, but few villages of any size
or interest.   Marlow is only four miles across the hills,
and with this old riverside town as a half-way halting-
place, a most delightful day's ramble is possible, the
journey being continued by crossing the river at Marlow
Bridge to Cookham, and thence by Hedsor and Drop-
more to the Beaconsfield road.

The road from High Wycombe to Marlow goes past
the grounds of Wycombe Abbey, and then climbs by
the estate called Dawes Hill, the home of Earl Carring-

ton. Afterwards, passing the lonely inn at Handy
Cross, the summit of the uplands dividing the narrow
valley of the Wye from the wider vale of the Thames
is reached, and a far-spreading panorama extending
from the hills beyond Henley to the Hampshire woods
and commons unfolds itself.

Marlow, with its memories of Shelley—the house he
occupied is in West Street—is known to every oarsman,
and the road which climbs the rising ground by Cookham Dean to Cookham is equally familiar to those who
decide to stretch their limbs while their companions
volunteer to take the boat round the hook of Bourne
End, but the country to the north of the latter village
is comparatively unknown.

The picturesque and even romantic appearance of
Hedsor House, which crowns the summit of a hill, is
not warranted by its age or associations, though it
occupies the site of an old manor. Hedsor church
also is more effective as a picture than as a building
of antiquarian interest. It is situated within the
confines of the park, and is perched upon a low hill.

The most interesting place in this vicinity is Drop-
more, worthy of a special visit by anyone interested in
arboriculture. The magnificent collection of coniferous
trees were planted by Lord Grenville—Pitt's Foreign
Secretary—between the years 1792 and 1830. Of
particular size and beauty is the great cedar upon
the lawn, and the glorious masses of colour displayed
throughout the month of June in the rhododendron
thickets are not least of the sights of this pleasaunce.
A way is open for the pedestrian across the park, and
the Beaconsfield road may be taken from the eastern
lodge gates.

Another charming ramble from Wycombe is to the

Hughenden district. The manor house and church are less than two miles from the Market-place, and although the chief interest centres in the fact that the mansion was the home, and the churchyard the burial-place, of Lord Beaconsfield, the short journey is worth taking for the beauty of the way thither. Queen Victoria's favourite statesman lived at Hughenden from 1848 until his death in 1881. The pleasant, though quite unassuming, house lies high upon the hillside, and is surrounded by a well-wooded park. The church cannot be seen until the visitor is nearly upon it, so closely do the trees surround the building. It was restored in a drastic fashion about fifty years ago, so that very little remains of the original structure. The Beaconsfield tomb is outside the east end of the De Montfort chapel, and the memorial erected by " his grateful and affectionate Sovereign and friend " is in the chancel. A brass records the fact that the statesman used a near-by pew.

The " De Montfort " chapel contains a number of monuments which, with two exceptions, have been proved to be spurious. They appear to have been placed here in the early sixteenth century by a local family who desired to be identified with the descendants of the great Simon. Brasses of a vicar who died in 1493, and a small figure of a kneeling man commemorating John Lane who died in 1621, are of interest, as is also the fine font belonging to the Decorated period.

This short excursion might well be extended through the hamlet of Naphill to Bradenham, which lies on the main road from West Wycombe to Aylesbury. Bradenham is described under the name of " Hurstley " in *Endymion*, and the beauties of the surrounding country are several times referred to in these descriptions of

the author's early home. Isaac Disraeli leased Bradenham Manor in 1829, and resided there until his death
in 1848. The church is remarkable for its Early
Norman south doorway, which is of that archaic pattern
usually described as "Saxon" by early nineteenth-
century archæologists. The church contains a memorial
of Isaac Disraeli, and a brass to a priest of the church
—Richard Redeberd—who died in 1521. There is
also a fine late seventeenth-century monument to
Charles West. Bradenham village is extremely picturesque, with a congeries of old cottages and the imposing
gates of the manor-house
drive at the end of the
green—the whole picture
enclosed by the gently rolling tree-clad hills.

WATLINGTON.

We resume our main
route at West Wycombe,
where the great west road
makes its final climb to
the summit of the Chiltern
Hills, reached just past the village of Stokenchurch,
six miles from West Wycombe. The Oxfordshire
boundary zigzags about the top of the ridge for some
miles, and a comparatively level country stretches from
the foot of the escarpment towards the university
city eighteen miles away.

From the spur called Beacon Hill, which rises to
the left of the road nearly two miles from the village,
a wide champaign opens up before us. It is a country
signally innocent of any pursuit but that of agriculture,
though much broken up by woodlands and with many
fine seats and spacious parks scattered about the great
expanse. The trough of the Thames may be readily

followed by the practised eye, from its dim blue beginnings beyond Oxford, nearly due north-west from
where we stand, to its sweep into the narrower defile
at Streatley on the extreme left. Thame meanders
across the middle distance, though of course out of
sight, to join the Isis below the double-capped height
of Sinoudon.

The reason for bringing the reader thus far is to
introduce him to a short circular excursion, on foot
or by car, which will reveal a very beautiful and, comparatively, little-known country—that of south-east
Oxfordshire. The section of the Thames which seems
to belong more of right to Berkshire has been dealt
with in this series by a far more able pen, and the reader
must be referred to the volume concerned for that
portion of the Thames valley which lies below Henley.

We now purpose to descend from the hills by the
main road past Aston Rowant station, serving a little-
used branch of the Great Western Railway. Just
short of the line, a lane running left and right is part
of the ancient Icknield Way, which we shall cross or
follow several times in our wanderings. Its position
here upon the lower face of the escarpment is indicative
of its general course—below the tell-tale silhouette of the
summit, and above the dangers of the dense woodlands
that once spread away towards the centre of the island.

We leave the Oxford road at an inn standing at the
junction with the Icknield Way, and follow the latter
through Lewknor and Shirburn to Watlington. The
former village possesses an interesting church, partly
Transitional and partly Decorated, with much beautiful
detail within. The latter boasts a castle built in 1377
by Warine de l'Isle on the site of a Norman fortress.
It has been modernized, but the moat still surrounds

it on all sides. It is now the seat of the Earl of Maccles-
field, and is occasionally open for inspection.

The chief distinction of Watlington is that it is a
terminus of the Great Western Railway. True that
Bradshaw only shows a service of six trains each day,
and one meets the same " motor " with the same
attendants at all times. Another castle stood here
once, by the evidence
of a moat, and a
fine church has been
spoilt by injudicious
restoration. Of the
picturesque in the
little town there re-
mains but the Mar-
ket Hall, a brick
erection of 1664.

We now pass on to
Britwell Salome, one
of several " Bright-
well " villages here-
abouts. The name
indicates that in each
there is a clear spring
issuing from the

THE HOSPITAL CLOISTER, EWELME.

chalk. In Salome is a magnificent yew, and a Norman door to the church. Farther on, still going
south-west, we reach Ewelme, one of the most charming
of the hill villages with its own " bright well "—a large
pool called the " King's Pond "—picturesquely shaded
by trees, and with the cottages of the hamlet standing
around it. Above, on the hill side, is a fifteenth-
century church, almshouse and school—a remarkable
series of buildings erected by that Duke of Suffolk

who was minister to Henry VI, and who met with a tragic end while seeking to escape his traducers. Within the church is an interesting memorial, probably unique of its kind, to Colonel Martin of the Parliamentary Army, who, during the Civil War, saved the church from the fury of the soldiery. Here is also a fine wooden font cover, and the grand tomb of the widow of the founder. Another memorial of much interest is that of the parents of the Duchess—Thomas Chaucer and his lady. This Thomas is said to have been the son of the poet, but the evidence is not clear. The " hospital," as the almshouse is usually called, is approached from the west door of the church, and is a pleasant quadrangle of mellow red brick. The school buildings are in keeping with the rest, and altogether Ewelme is worthy of a visit for its own sake, and not merely as a place to spend half an hour for rest and refreshment on the way to somewhere else.

A short mile farther, and we leave the Icknield Way for Crowmarsh Gifford, which is merely the Oxfordshire suburb of Wallingford, but contains its own little Norman church. We cross the Thames here by a bridge commanding a good view up and down stream, and from which Wallingford appears as a very pleasant goal to a day's walk.

This ancient Berkshire town possesses a remarkable series of earth ramparts enclosing the settlement on all sides except that upon the river bank. They may be Saxon in origin, but are probably far older. The Normans built a stone castle upon the site of a Saxon stronghold close to the " ford," and of its poor remains we may still see fragments. It was valiantly defended for the King during the Civil War by Blagge, and was one of the last key positions to fall.

That the town was once of far greater importance is evident from the fact that no less than fourteen churches stood within the ramparts, together with four religious houses. Of the latter practically nothing remains, and of the churches there are but three, with little of interest to the tourist in any of them. St. Peter's is remarkable only as being the resting-place of Blackstone , whose *Commentaries on the Law of England* is a legal classic. The most pleasing building in Wallingford, which contains a great number of well-built and mellow old houses, is the Town Hall, erected in the seventeenth century and standing on pillars.

Leaving the town by the Dorchester road, we reach Shillingford Bridge a mile and a half farther on, and again cross the river into Oxfordshire. To the right, the high road to London via Henley passes through Benson, of great note in coaching days, when it was usually spelt Bensington.

WALLINGFORD.

Turning to the left we soon reach Dorchester, an ancient town rivalling in antiquity its larger namesake in the south. It was certainly Roman and as a settlement probably antedated the coming of the eagles. The " Dyke Hills," between the town, the Isis and the Thame, are prehistoric fortifications of once great strength and extent. The evidence of the Roman occupation is found in the base of the encircling walls, and in the various relics of that period which have been turned up from time to time by excavators. It was of great strategic value in Saxon days, and became a bone of contention between Wessex and Mercia. This, no doubt, had much to do with the transference of the Bishop's " stool " to a spot of greater quietude and peace. It was the cathedral city of Wessex until 707, when the Bishop removed to Winchester, taking with him the bones of St. Birinus—the first Saxon bishop. After Offa of Mercia had carried his southern boundary to the Thames side, the Bishop of Leicester removed his " cathedra " to Dorchester as a consequence of the capture of his see-town by the Danes. This was in 869, and the town continued to be a titular city for over two hundred years until the Norman Bishop Remigius departed in turn for distant Lincoln.

The ancient cathedral became an Abbey church in 1140, when Alexander of Lincoln instituted an Augustinian community here. It is conjectured that the lower part of the nave walls may be a portion of the original building, but the earliest architectural features to be readily recognized are Transitional, and the remainder are chiefly Decorated. Taken as a whole, this spacious and beautiful building is the finest church in Oxfordshire, not excepting the cathedral behind Tom Quad in Oxford itself. But there are certain features which are unusual and, to say the least, unsymmetrical. The disproportionate length of the nave with its monotonous wall, and the extraordinary stone partition on the south side between chancel aisle and nave aisle, spoil any general view of the interior. It is in the examination of the details that the understanding visitor will find much to enjoy. Apart from one or two ugly additions belonging to the seventeenth century, all are good, and most are beautiful, as one would expect in a church practically finished during the Decorated period.

The leaden font, of Norman workmanship, is rare hereabouts, and this one is a particularly good specimen.

The Jesse window is more famous than beautiful, but below it are perfect examples of sedelia and piscina. Of equal beauty is the arcade between chancel and aisle. Among the several interesting tombs are those of three abbots, and of the four altar tombs in the south chancel aisle, one is of an unknown bishop. Although this tomb is in the Decorated style, it is possible that the coffin of one of the early bishops was, during that period, transferred to this sumptuous receptacle.

Some remnants of the priory buildings persist in the schoolhouse near the west end of the Abbey; apart from this there are few mediæval relics in Dorchester. A house called Bishop's Court may have been built upon the site of the ancient palace of the bishops, but there is no evidence for this, apart

SINOUDON.

from the traditional name. The town consists principally of a single street terminating at the old bridge over the Thame, about a quarter of a mile before the union of that river with the Isis. And here be it noted that the use of this name for the stream above Dorchester is, in the writer's opinion, warranted only for purposes of convenience. The Thames is the *Thames* from the Cotswold downwards. " Thame-Isis " is a poetic fiction.

On the farther side of the river, and giving a distinction to the whole neighbourhood, are the well-known landmarks usually called Wittenham Clumps, but more correctly Sinoudon Hills—two rounded knolls each crowned with a group of trees. On the side nearest Shillingford is Sinoudon Camp, a prehistoric fortress which overlooks the meeting of the two rivers, and was once obviously of great importance and strategic value.

Our road now follows closely the Oxfordshire bank of the Thames to Clifton Hampden, where there is a fine brick bridge, and a Transitional church in a perfect situation above the waterway. Here the river bends away somewhat from the road, which goes almost directly west past Culham station to the village of that name. Here the route passes a "cut," and turns directly north to Abingdon on the Berkshire bank of the Thames.

Abingdon, originally Seovecchesham and then Abendon, is a town of many memories, and one that was once of greater comparative importance than it is at present, for it was the assize town of Berkshire before Reading had usurped that position. Like the latter, it was the home of one of the grandest of the English Benedictine Abbeys. Of the church not even the foundations can be traced, but the so-called Prior's House and Guest House, for long devoted to brewing, still remain, and are reached by an archway in the market-place.

Of the churches of St. Helen and St. Nicholas, the former must claim our attention. This has the spire which is a distinctive feature of all views of the town. It is noteworthy as possessing no less than five aisles covered by magnificent timber roofs, and it contains many curious and interesting monuments. The churchyard has almshouses upon three sides, and that farthest from the entrance is of uncommon charm and beauty. Its present name is Christ's Hospital, but

at one time it was the home of the " Gild of the Holy
Cross." This guild was responsible for several important local works, one of which, despite inevitable
reconstruction and restoration, we may still admire—
and marvel at the good workmanship which preserved
it in constant use from the time of Henry V until
quite lately—this is Abingdon Bridge. Another was
the causeway to Dorchester Abbey, and a third, one
of the aisles of St. Helen's. The beautiful old panelled
guild-hall and the covered passage in front of the
building are the most interesting relics of the past in
the town, which contains
many fine old houses of
sedate and distinguished
appearance, and not least,
a very dignified and im-
posing Town Hall ascribed
to Inigo Jones but act-
ually built shortly after
his death. It occupies
the site of Abingdon
Cross, erected in the reign

THE ABBEY GATEWAY,
ABINGDON.

of Mary I and destroyed by Waller, no doubt in consequence of its " papistical ornaments."

We may either proceed direct to Oxford by the road
which passes through Bagley Wood, or go by the riverside to Radley and Sandford, a route much to be preferred to the former. Radley village church is out of
the ordinary in possessing pillars of black oak, said
to be eighteenth-century ship timbers. Across the
river near Nuneham Courtnay is Nuneham Park, the
seat of the Harcourts. Permission is occasionally
given to pedestrians to cross the beautiful park, but
as our route is northwards, it is sufficient to note that

E

the house was built in the eighteenth century by the first Earl Harcourt, who transferred the village from its original position near the river to the Oxford-Wallingford road, and succeeded in rebuilding it in both a picturesque and substantial style.

The only part of Sandford worth seeing is that near the river, and this consists of a typically Thames-side village gay with flowers in spring and summer, neat and tidy at all times of the year. At Iffley, the last call before reaching Oxford, the famous Norman church is found high above the river, and embowered in thick foliage. It must always be considered as one of the sights of Oxford, from which it is distant about two miles.

The church was built between 1150 and 1180, and is one of the most beautiful examples of the later period of Norman architecture remaining in England. It is perhaps to be regretted that the east end of the chancel was remodelled in Early English times, and also later, when larger windows were inserted at different dates. If the central tower appears to be rather low, it is entirely in keeping with the massive appearance of the building itself. One of the glories of the church is the splendid west door, and the other doorways are almost equally fine. The west window is a modern restoration.

The general view of the interior shows in a remarkable way the great dissimilarity between the two styles, and the present east end is an effective contrast to the work of the earlier builders. We are told that the original termination was an apse, and so we cannot help regretting that the perfect model has not come down to us; but the details of the Early English bay are very fine, particularly in the sedilia and piscina, while again the square black marble font is a specimen of Norman work at its best.

After admiring the picturesque churchyard and rectory, we now, after paying the modest toll, cross to the Berkshire bank and proceed once more up stream. On the farther shore are moored a long string of house-boats, many bearing the badge, colour or name of the college to which it belongs. Some are ornately decorated, others comparatively quiet and demure. Behind them, across the flat Christchurch meadows, rise the towers and spires of the city.

Famous chiefly for its University, the rise of Oxford was due to quite different influences. Its situation on one of the best fords of the Thames, on the borderland between the ancient kingdoms of Mercia and Wessex, was bound to bring it into prominence in early days. Its early importance is proved by the Anglo-Saxon Chronicle, which says that in 912 Edward, son of Ethelred, took possession of London and Oxford and all the lands obedient to those cities. The Domesday record shows that a resistance was made to the Normans, for the Book has a list of reprisals which followed its occupation, and strong fortifications were erected by Robert D'Oili to keep the Saxon burgesses to heel. Not only are remains of these buildings to be traced in the present Castle, but also in parts of the churches of St. Michael, St. Peter in the East, and St. Cross. That warlike lady, the Empress Maud, was beseiged in Oxford Castle in 1142, but she was able to escape when the river became frozen over. The Provisions of Oxford, drawn up in 1258, were directly responsible for the Montfort Rebellion. The chief claim of the town, however, to a place in the secular history of the realm is, of course, due to its position as the Cavalier capital during the Civil War.

It will thus be seen that this town, containing the most wonderful and beautiful series of medieval and modern buildings devoted to learning in England—if not in Europe—has historic interests apart from that centring upon the University. This arose to importance about the beginning of the twelfth century, though its proper organization as a teaching c e n t r e did not take place for another hundred years. At the end of the thirteenth century the students were to be numbered by the thousand, and about 1320 its fame equalled, if it did not surpass, any other in Europe. As the University grew, so opposition increased between the secular townsmen and the scholars. Pitched battles often took place and "town and gown" feuds have survived until quite recently.

St. Mary's Porch, Oxford.

It would be presumptuous to attempt any description of Oxford in these pages. We must merely pass through the main streets, and leave the traveller to procure a local guide-book if he wishes to make a conscientious exploration. If, of late years, the senior University town has permitted a lamentable amount of jerry-building to mar its environs, we shall see but little of it upon entering the city by the Folly Bridge end of St. Aldate's—which we should call " St. Old's." A reconstruction of the buildings in the lower portion of this thoroughfare is proceeding while these lines are being written. On the right is Great Tom Tower, built by Wolsey and " domed " by Wren, which houses the great bell of Oxford. Beneath it is the entrance to Christ Church College, or " the House," the chapel of which is the Cathedral of the see of Oxford. The conception of the great Cardinal was never completed, but the quadrangle, the largest in the University, is imposing and dignified. On the farther side is the Cathedral—the Norman Church of St. Frideswide— much pulled about by Wolsey, who intended to rebuild it, but was prevented in this, as in other schemes of his, by a fickle fate. The roll of Christ Church includes Wesley and Pusey ; Robert Peel and Gladstone ; John Locke was expelled from this college for sedition, and William Penn for nonconformity. Across the street from Tom Tower is Pembroke, where Dr. Johnson was able to afford only part of his time as undergraduate. Passing upwards, we arrive at busy Carfax, " Quatre-voies "—usually presenting a scene very different from the preconceived idea of a University town as a place of cloisteral hush. To the left is the high road to the west, and, incidentally, to the Oxford railway stations. This way passes on the left the prison, which incorporates part of the Norman Castle. Straight ahead is Cornmarket Street—" The Corn " —leading to St. Giles, a wide thoroughfare in which stands the Martyrs' Memorial ; the cross in the roadway marks the site of the stake where Cranmer, Ridley and Latimer were burned. Part of Balliol, and the front of St. John's College, are close by. The buildings of Balliol are nearly all modern, and the house in which John Wycliffe was master no longer exists, but the quadrangles of St. John's are untouched ; those of the cloistered second part were built by its most famous member—Archbishop Laud. Worcester is at the far end of Beaumont Street. It has beautiful gardens and some ancient monastic houses attached. In Corn-market Street are the shops and chief hotels—the "Mitre" and the "Golden Cross"; the "Roebuck," another old hostelry, has lately disappeared.

MAGDALEN COLLEGE.

And now we turn into the Street which claims (with several others !) to be unique. The writer first saw its lovely curve as a lad—when he was the only being upon its pavements—at five o'clock on a Sunday morning in June. That first impression of its exquisite beauty can never be lost, just as it has never been wholly regained. It is useless to attempt description of the buildings that adorn it. Its chief glory is St. Mary's, or "University" Church, admirably set off by the totally different, but nevertheless dignified, eighteenth-century "City" Church of All Saints, at the corner of "the Turl." Within St. Mary's, the University Sermon has been preached by men whose names are those of the chief ecclesiastics of the

nineteenth and present centuries, and it has heard the
voices of leaders of religious thought of a far older
time. The strange yet beautiful porch with its image
of the Virgin reminds us of an early Anglo-Catholic
—Archbishop Laud, whose chaplain—Dr. Morgan
Owen—was its builder. West of St. Mary's is Brasenose—a name said to be derived from the brass lion's
head which served as a knocker on the door of the old
hall. Across the High Street new buildings, which in
a few years will gain a mellow weathering, hide from
us the beautiful groups of Merton, Oriel, and Corpus
Christi. These can be seen by turning down Oriel
Street. In the first-named, and oldest of the colleges,
Duns Scotus was educated. Sir Walter Raleigh and
Cecil Rhodes were both Oriel men, and Corpus Christi
numbered Hooker, Jewel and Keble among its sons,
On the left of the High Street, behind St. Mary's, is
the most characteristic group of buildings in Oxford,
composed of the Radcliffe Library, the old schools—
containing part of the Bodleian Library with its many
literary treasures, the Sheldonian Theatre—with its
nightmarish " masks "—built by Wren, and the
Divinity School, where the House of Commons met in
1625. West of these, down Brasenose Lane, are
Lincoln, Exeter and Jesus Colleges. In the first-
named John Wesley founded the " Society of Metho-
dists," and a memorial bust has lately been placed
above the main doorway. Now passing onwards by
All Souls, behind which is Hertford and New, we
reach the most perfect curve of High Street, commencing
at Queen's College, and soon the beautiful tower of
Magdalen comes into view upon the left. Across the
way from Queen's is University College, popularly
supposed to have been instituted by Alfred the Great,

but actually founded by an archdeacon of Durham in 1229. Then, on the same side, come the modern buildings of the New Schools.

The explorer with plenty of time will penetrate to those remote regions where are Wadham, Mansfield and Keble. He will be able to contrast the latter, a hideous nineteenth-century erection of red and yellow brick, with the lovely buildings of " Maudlen," sacred to the shades of both John Hampden and Prince Rupert, and he will marvel at the architectural kink that afflicted our immediate forefathers. We leave Oxford by what is considered its most effective approach— the Cherwell bridge. This would be even more effective could the dingy transpontine suburb of St. Clement's be eliminated. Instead of following the modern high road to London through Headington, we bear to the right through a rather dull and uninteresting neighbour-hood, and presently join a winding and climbing lane which was once the ancient way to the south-east. The ascent becomes more rugged still until at last we come out upon Shotover, and can turn and admire the retrospect of spires and domes, still very beautiful despite the outbreak of red on the nearer side of the Cherwell. The summit of Shotover Hill has been purchased by the University, otherwise we might see the wild common, over which our track runs, fringed by " desirable " villas and bungalows. In the earlier days of road travel, it was indeed a wild and fearsome place, and many are the tales of the robbers, footpads and highwaymen who plied their nefarious trade on the lonely height.

An interesting relic of the time when horsemen riding eastward remounted their steeds after walking them up the steep slope is found in the mounting-

block at the side of the road. Beneath the sandy top
of the hill is found that Headington stone of which so
many buildings in Oxford are, unfortunately, built, for
it is a stone that weathers badly and recently it has
been found necessary to reface several college fronts
with Portland stone. The Headington quarries are at
the bottom of the northern slope.

The traveller can make a pleasant departure from
the road on the east side of Shotover by taking a
path leading direct to Wheatley, a large village of
clean stone-built houses, pleasantly picturesque and
old-fashioned. Here is a station on the line to Thame
and Wycombe. After leaving this village by the main
road, another detour, adding very little to the distance,
may be made by keeping to the London road for a time,
instead of going direct to our next halt at Thame.
When the Studhampton–Thame crossing is reached,
we then take the latter road to the left, and in a little
over a mile pass Rycote Manor House, now consisting
of but a few fragmentary ruins, except for those
portions which have been turned into farm buildings.
This forlorn scene, a real example of change and decay,
is reached from the road by a rustic—and generally
muddy—track. In the once splendid mansion, the
Princess Elizabeth was in 1554 entertained by Lord
Williams—an ancestor of the present owner, Lord
Abingdon—on her way to a polite kind of imprisonment at Woodstock. She came here again as Queen
on more than one occasion, and Charles I was a visitor
during the early years of the Civil War.

Continuing by the road to the north-west, we soon
reach Thame, which bright little market town is best
avoided on Tuesdays, when its thronged streets are
almost impassable. The town is entered at the north-

west end of High Street close to the church, approached
through a very fine Decorated south porch with a
parvise chamber above. The building dates mainly
from 1240, with Decorated and Perpendicular additions.
The transepts and tower at the crossing belong to the
latter style. The chancel screen and stalls came from
Thame Abbey, a Cistercian house once standing in
the modern Thame Park. The tomb of that Lord
Williams of Rycote who was designated her " jailor "
by Queen Elizabeth is in the centre of the chancel,
and the building contains several other interesting
memorials and brasses.

Behind the church is the Prebendal House, which
is as old as the church, and incorporates a very fine
Early English chapel ; while on the side nearest to
High Street is the Old Grammar School founded by
Lord Williams, but erected about sixteen years after
his death. John Hampden was one of several famous
men who were educated in this school. He died at a
house in the town from the effects of the wound
received at Chalgrove Field.

We pass down the spacious High Street, the vista
of which is effectually broken by a group of buildings
that includes the Town Hall, and go forward by the
left-hand road through Kingsley. In front are fine
views of the Chilterns, with Whiteleafe Cross conspicuous upon the escarpment above Risborough.

WHITELEAFE CROSS.

CHAPTER III

THE CHILTERN COUNTRY

PRINCES RISBOROUGH is a pleasant little town of no great interest apart from its charming situation. The market house and a number of ancient dwellings near the church give it an old-world appearance, but the church itself has a furbished up air, due to a drastic restoration in 1867. The name of the town perpetuates the fact that it was royal property in the fourteenth century, and tradition tells that the Black Prince had a palace near the church.

Monks Risborough, which takes its name from the fact that it once belonged to the monks of Canterbury, is a mile away on the Aylesbury road. It is a really charming village with quaint half-timbered houses, and a church which should on no account be missed. The architecture is of many styles, though the first is only represented now by the Norman font, an excellent example of the period and with fine ornamentation. The outstanding merit of the building is the series of beautiful Perpendicular windows. Among other details, the fine brass of a priest, supposed to be that of Robert Blundell, Rector in 1360, will be noticed. The situation of the church is very delightful. On the east of the churchyard stands the picturesque Rectory House, and in a field near by is an ancient dovecot with a carved doorway. All around the thick foliage of elderly trees frames entrancing views, on one side, of the wide champaign towards Oxford, and on the other of the gracious lines of the hills.

The road to Wendover, just traversed, is part of the Icknield Way and the upper of the two tracks which bear that name. This ancient track hugs the north side of the Chilterns all the way from far-off Cambridgeshire to the pass of the Thames at Streatley. The Whiteleafe—possibly "Whitecliff"—Cross above Monks Risborough on the steep side of Green Holly Hill has already been noticed from the Thame road. After bearing for long a fictitious history as the memorial of a battle between Saxons and Danes a thousand years or so ago, it is now conjectured to be merely a landmark to indicate the crossing place of the ancient track by a road made about 1650, though some present-day medievalists have claimed it to be a monkish work intended as a guide for pilgrims, but to what shrine or holy place is not stated. Many of the designs cut in the chalk hills of southern England are probably of quite recent date, though two or three at least, such as the "Long Man" in Sussex and the "White Horse" above Uffington, are really old and probably prehistoric.

The road now winds under Pulpit Hill, and soon reaches Great Kimble, where there is a restored church of much historic interest, for it was the scene of John Hampden's refusal to pay the "ship-money" demanded by Charles I, an action which actually started the great slide ending in the final collapse of feudalism

in England. Though a picturesque object from the
surrounding hills, the building is of small archæological
value apart from its Norman font, but Little Kimble
church, a quarter-mile farther, is an old-world relic
quite untouched by the restorer and with truly delightful surroundings, largely due to nature, but partly
also to a piece of landscape and water gardening near
by. There are indications of mural paintings upon the
walls of the church, and in the chancel are some ancient
tiles with curious figures still descernible upon them.
Services are now held only at long intervals, and the
writer has found it no easy task to gain admittance;
but the custodian of the key is, or was lately, a neighbouring farmer, and it would be unreasonable to expect
a busy household to be always on the *qui vive* for a
chance visitor.

Kimble was anciently Chenebelle and it has been
sought to identify the name with that of Cymbeline,
or Cunobeline, a native British king; but we may regard this as no more than a pleasant romance. The
name is probably Saxon in origin. Cymbeline's Mount,
or Kimble Castle, is the appellation usually given to the
conical hill which rises with a picturesque abruptness
to the east of the village, its summit crowned by an
ancient fortification. On the farther side, backed by
the long wooded escarpment of Coombe Hill, is the
beautiful Chequers Court, one of the most fascinating
houses in England, and now, through the generosity
of Lord Lee of Fareham, the home, while in office, of
England's Prime Minister. The first owner of the
property was named Elias Chakers, but whether the
house got its name from this individual or *vice versa*
is a moot point. This was seven hundred years ago.
The present mansion is a fine example of a stately

home of the mid-sixteenth century. It is associated
in a second-hand way with the Great Protector, for his
youngest daughter, Frances, married into a family of
Russells, whose descendant eventually became owner
of the Court. This accounts for the Cromwellian relics
among the treasures of the great house. They include
several portraits of Cromwell and his family, and other
objects of artistic and historic interest.

The memory of John Hampden is responsible for
many pilgrimages to Great Hampden Church. This
may be conveniently visited from the neighbourhood
of Chequers, for it is barely two miles away by road
and field path, though the latter is not easily found.
It leaves the Missenden road about a mile from the
south lodge of the Court, and after crossing open
land on the right thereof, climbs through the skirts of
a wood to a point about 700 feet above sea level, and
then appears to invade the precincts of Hampden
House. Eventually a ha-ha fence will be found to
intervene between the pedestrian and the mansion.
The present building replaced the home of John Hampden in 1754. Here there is no village or even hamlet ;
the church is close to the house, and at the end of
an apparently private drive. The sole interest of the
building consists of two memorials, one a tablet upon
the wall to the memory of the patriot's wife and
inscribed in eulogistic terms by Hampden himself, and
the other, his own memorial, erected by a descendant
over one hundred years after his death. Another
monument to his memory—a cross—stands near
Honorend. As we have seen, John Hampden died
at Thame after receiving his death wound at Chalgrove
Field while fighting with the army of the Parliament,
and the body was brought here for burial.

The Hampdens were in possession of the property from the time of the Conqueror, and the line, through female heirs, still persists. In the older house, one of the family was host to Queen Elizabeth, who, it is said, suggested the long avenue which sweeps down the hill to the south, and is called the Queen's Gap. The bank of Grims Dyke, which crosses the path, was cut through in making the Gap.

Retracing our steps towards Chequers, we leave the road to Butler's Cross and the poetically named Vale of Velvet Lawn, and climb the steep side of Coombe Hill towering up on the right. From the ridge a remarkable prospect is obtained of the country we have just explored. Chequers Court seems just below us, and Cymbeline's Mount and its surroundings are seen to great advantage. A short walk northwards to the South African War Memorial, and, if the day is reasonably clear, a truly magnificent view of the Southern Midlands unfolds before us. The distant blue ridges almost directly north are the low hills of Northamptonshire, and the greater part of Oxfordshire undulates away to the left. Practically the whole of Bedfordshire is before us to the right front, and the end of Dunstable Down just appears to the extreme right. In the foreground is the Vale of Aylesbury, with the county capital discernible as a touch of red among the trees in the middle distance, and a pleasant gleam of sparkling water to the east marks the position of the canal reservoirs near Weston Turville. The chalky bridle-way to Wendover keeps slightly below the brow of the hill, and just misses a circular camp upon the height overlooking the town. It follows more or less closely the track of the " Upper," or actual, Icknield Way. The " Lower " Way—running at the foot of

the hills—is the later Via Iceni of the Roman period.
The opposing height of Boddington Hill with Halton
House, a modern home of the Rothschilds, placed con-
spicuously upon its slope, and the equally conspicuous
sheds of the Royal Air Force not far away, fill the forward view as we descend. Soon after passing some
commonplace villas, we cross the railway and gain
the main street of Buckinghamshire's most picturesque
town.

Wendover probably contains more old buildings, for
its size, than any other place within fifty miles of
London. And this despite the fact that we are within

WENDOVER.

the sphere of the best country train service in the
Home Counties. Several
quaint and apparently un-
restored medieval houses
stand in the High Street,
and cottages, smaller but
probably as ancient, are to
be found on the Tring road.
To the east of the London road, in a charming spot
upon the banks of a clear and sparkling stream, is the
church and, close by, the Manor House, surrounded by
fine trees and emerald sward. The only incongruous
note is the constant hooting of motor-horns upon the
busy highway we have just left. The interior of the
church has not very much of interest to detain the
visitor, but the brass of William Bradschawe should
be seen, and the capitals of the piers—on one side
animals, on the other flowers—call for notice.

In history Wendover has made but little mark. It
was represented in Parliament by John Hampden.
Burke also sat for the borough in 1768. It returned

two members until 1832. The manor formed part of the marriage settlement of Katherine of Aragon.

The high road to the north-west makes direct for Aylesbury—barely five miles from the crossing of the ways in Wendover. Stoke Mandeville is a pleasant and unspoilt little place about half-way. Here is a ruined church situated beyond some meadows at the Wendover end of the street. Its modern successor, which preserves some of the features of the older building, is at the Aylesbury extremity of the village. The street is not actually upon the Aylesbury high road, but the slight detour is certainly worth while for those who delight in the " quiet and unsophisticated hamlet of the shires."

We are now away from the chalk, and in the midst of the fertile dairy-farming region called the Vale of Aylesbury. The traditional ducks, white in colour, are as numerous here as are the buff hens of Orpington in that one-time retreat of Ruskin and modern outer suburb of to-day. There is little of the latter aspect about Aylesbury town, which is quite provincial, and proud of the fact.

Aylesbury superseded the titular county town as long ago as the reign of Henry VIII, and is as thriving and prosperous as Buckingham is quiet and sedate. Although there are few ancient houses here, the " Place " has a pleasant old-world air, especially upon market-day, when the Buckinghamshire farmers and their wives throng the pavements in front of the County Hall and Corn Exchange. The " Old King's Head " is as ancient as it looks, and possesses an exceedingly cosy interior with an old-world atmosphere very welcome to the traveller who has faced a north wind all the way from Wendover.

F

The spacious and handsome cruciform church is a successful restoration by Scott of a sadly marred and mutilated Early English building erected on the site of its small Saxon predecessor. For Aylesbury is a very ancient place, and was a fortified British town before the Saxons captured it in 571 and named it Eglesburg. Of the monuments in the church, the most interesting is that in the north transept to Lady Lee, dated 1584. It does not actually belong to this building, for it was brought from Quarrendon, nearly two miles north-west of the town, where a few pieces of broken masonry mark the site of the splendid home of the Lees and the church which was dependent upon the manor. Another monument, in alabaster, of a knight in armour was brought from a monastery chapel of the Grey Frairs which once stood in the town. Two ancient stone coffins are kept in the north aisle chapel, and an interesting detail is the extraordinary lock of the north vestry door. The Norman font is an exceedingly fine example of the period, and the old oak wardrobe for vestments should not be missed.

On the west side of the church is the Prebendal House. Here lived for a time that extraordinary character, John Wilkes, who obtained the property by marriage, and by virtue of his standing in the town became its representative at Westminster in 1757.

An excursion to Waddesdon, about five miles north-west, is a pleasant finish to a day in Aylesbury. The Manor House is the most striking specimen of French domestic architecture existing in England. It was built in 1880 for Baron Ferdinand de Rothschild. The grounds are open on certain weekdays in summer and are very beautiful. A well-built model village and an interesting church add to the attractions of

Waddesdon. Creswell Manor House, to the north-east, about six miles from Aylesbury, is a fine mansion, partly of fourteenth-century date, and said to be haunted by the ghost of Fair Rosamond ; but the legend is probably due to a misconception. A one-time owner was Lord Clifford of Chudleigh, one of the Cabal ministers. The lady belonged to a far older family —the de Cliffords. The ghost is " well authenticated," whoever it may represent.

Another pleasant walk may be taken by way of Hartwell to Stone. Hartwell House is the home of the Lees, and this old county family were hosts to Louis XVIII, who spent five years of his exile here. The house is one of the finest in the shire, and forms a museum of treasures from fossils to pictures by Vandyck and Reynolds. It has a splendid Elizabethan front with a grand avenue extending therefrom across the park. The church is an erection of the eighteenth century, and is said to have been inspired by the Chapter House of York Minster. Stone possesses a cruciform church in a charming situation. It is built upon a hillock affording a perfect view of the hills we have lately traversed. The fine Norman south doorway is enclosed by a porch of the Decorated period. The Norman font is noteworthy for its elaborate detail. It originally belonged to the Berkshire church of Hampstead Norris, and was brought here in 1845. The brass effigies, near the steps leading to the chancel, commemorate members of the Gorney family from 1472 to 1520. The reverse of the last dated brass is in memory of a Christopher Thorpe who died in 1514.

The old trackway called Akeman Street, which runs in a south-easterly direction from Bicester to Ayles-bury, proceeds from the latter town as the Tring road, and this we purpose to follow. The first village—Aston Clinton—has a fine and spacious Decorated church with beautiful sedilia and piscina therein. Near by is a modern mansion, another possession of the Rothschilds. Buckland, the next village, is practically a continuation of Aston to the east. Its much-restored church is not of great interest. The next village—Drayton Beauchamp—possesses a church which is decidedly worth seeing. The building is mainly Decorated, and contains a quantity of ancient glass, and also some good modern windows. The chancel is overshadowed by an enormous memorial to Lord Cheyne, who died in 1728. Of more interest, and less overpowering, are the brasses close to the altar. These represent Thomas Cheyne, 1368, who was squire to Edward III, and William Cheyne, 1375. There is also a brass, minus the head, which perpetuates the memory of Henry Fazakerley, Priest, who died in 1531. One of the rectors of this church was the "judicious" Hooker, who was here from 1553 to 1600.

A CHILTERN COTTAGE.

We now cross the county border into Hertfordshire, and soon arrive at Tring. This old town, called Treung in pre-Conquest days, has a market dating from the time of the second Edward, and is thus of much greater antiquity than its present appearance would lead one to suspect. To speak candidly, the unpicturesque appearance of the lesser streets borders upon the mean and shabby. The Perpendicular church, restored in 1882, does not contain very much of interest, but the windows are unusually good for the period, and the carvings of the corbels with their grotesque caricatures of monks are remarkable. The massive monument of Sir William Gore, Lord Mayor of London, who died in 1707, is the outstanding feature of the interior.

On the south of the town is the beautiful expanse of Tring Park, yet another seat of the Rothschilds. A museum, containing one of the finest zoological collections in the country, stands in Akeman Street on the confines of the park. The specimens were brought together by Lord Walter Rothschild, who, in the park itself, has collected a number of living animals capable of being acclimatized. The mansion has been much altered, but the older portions are the remains of a structure designed by Wren which Charles II is said to have used as a retreat from the formalities of Whitehall. An obelisk in the park, where two paths cross, is supposed to have been erected by Charles in memory of Nell Gwynn.

The hills around Tring are of great beauty, especially in autumn when the beeches, which form the majority of the trees, change colour. It is always difficult, and mostly invidious and unsatisfactory, in a well-defined country such as the Chilterns, to pick out any particular locality as more beautiful than another, and certain scenes west of Wendover, and east of Tring, are certainly more generally imposing, but the essential characteristics of the chalk hills at their best may be seen without going far from the latter town.

The road past the station, which is nearly two miles

away to the east, continues to Aldbury, a beautiful
little place in an equally lovely setting. It is placed
in a hollow between wooded bluffs, the hill rising to
the east being clothed by the thick woods of Ashridge
Park. The village green is accompanied by a pond
and stocks, and even a whipping-post, and is a typical
old-world English scene. The local powers appear to
appreciate the fact, for there are few villages so well
looked after. Here are no unsightly corners, rubbish
dumps or broken fences, but all is worthy of the
perfect setting. The church, though restored, is a fine
building with a priest's chamber over the porch. It
is noteworthy for some interesting monuments of the
Harcourt and Hide families, and for a chantry chapel
containing the monument of Sir Robert Whittingham,
who met his death at the battle of Tewkesbury. The
sixteenth-century lectern, the brass of John Davies
who died in 1478, and the Italian glass in one of the
north wall windows, are a few other items to be looked
for within the building. In the churchyard is an
ancient sundial, and here also is the grave of Mrs.
Humphry Ward, who, during the last years of her life,
resided at Stocks, a house on the left of the road leading
to Ivinghoe. Aldbury is the scene of one of her best-
known novels—*Bessie Costrell*—where it is called
" Clinton Magna." From near Stocks, one may well
be tempted to make an ascent of steep Moneybury,
the tree-clad hill in front, upon which the Aldbury
monument rears its pointed top. This granite obelisk
was erected to commemorate the Duke of Bridgewater
of canal-building fame.

As the road to Ivinghoe ascends, it deteriorates into
the typical flinty lane of the chalk hills, and eventually
emerges into a kind of amphitheatre formed by the

striking group of heights that include Pitstone Hill on the west and the Ivinghoe Hills to the east. This is certainly the most picturesque portion of the Chiltern range. From most aspects, the half-circle of broken summits is an effective piece of scenery, but from the Icknield Way, a short distance east of Ivinghoe, they have all the romance of a miniature group of mountains, especially under certain atmospheric conditions of late autumn. From Beacon Hill, the third and highest peak—it is just over the 800-feet contour line —a wide panorama unfolds, and although it is similar to that from Coombe Hill above Wendover, the scenic foreground here is much more effective. The chequered

pattern of small fields, interspersed with blocks of dark foliage, of this northern weald is very like the southward prospect we shall see from the Surrey

IVINGHOE BEACON.

Downs. Yet there is a subtle difference, only manifest after several, perhaps many, returns to these heights. Everyone with the seeing eye notes the fact, but few guess the riddle aright. All essentials are similar except the important one of light. Here the sun is behind the observer, and it matters not if the sky is overcast. A million minute differences in leaf and twig, and in the very grass blades that face the sun, make up a tone that tints the landscape the year through.

Ivinghoe is an ancient place and was once of some importance, though but few old buildings survive. The houses, it would seem, have been allowed to decay without being replaced and the town is obviously smaller at the present day than at any time in its later history. The fine and spacious church was built for a much larger congregation than could now be collected from the sleepy streets and outlying farms. It is a cruciform building of much elegance, mainly dating from the Decorated period, though the lesser portions were probably erected in the early thirteenth century. The striking appearance of the columns which support the tower, and the fine timber roofs, give an unusual air of distinction to the building. Ancient carvings of the fifteenth century have been preserved and fixed to the modern bench ends. Several brasses, all dated within the sixteenth century, will be seen in the chancel, together with a monument in a recess to an unknown cleric.

The traditional rhyme :—

> " Tring, Wing and Ivinghoe
> For striking of a blow
> Hampden did forego
> And glad he did escape so."

refers to the story than an ancestor of John Hampden lost the ownership of the places named through a sudden quarrel with the Black Prince while his partner at tennis, but it has been proved that the family never possessed either of the manors. It is said that Sir Walter Scott named his romance *Ivanhoe* under a misconception of the spelling and pronunciation of the name.

Little Gaddesdon village is of that variety usually termed " sweet " when the spectator first comes upon the masses of colour in the cottage gardens lining the road. Like Aldbury, it is well cared for, and the charming street in the height of summer is indeed a pleasant sight to tired town-dwellers. The inevitable war memorial takes on an unusual guise here, and a marble cross and fountain with an inviting seat for wayfarers commemorates Lady Marion Alford, whose name is remembered with affection by the country folk around. Little Gaddesdon church contains several monuments to the Bridgewater family, but is otherwise unremarkable.

The great house of the neighbourhood is Ashridge, until lately the seat of Earl Brownlow. It was built by the architect Wyatt for the first Earl of Bridgewater on the site of an ancient manor-house belonging to Edmund Crouchback, Earl of Cornwall, and which had as an appendage a monastery erected by the prince for a French religious order. The extraordinary sham Gothic palace of Wyatt is certainly imposing, especially the grand entrance, by far the most effective portion of the immense pile. The park covers a wide area upon the chalk downs, and contains many deer in its semi-wild glades. Here also is the landmark obelisk of the " father of inland navigation " which we saw from the way to Ivinghoe. A short time ago these pleasant sweeps of tree-clad down were in danger of coming within the clutch of the " real estate man," but thanks to public outcry and public spirit no great harm is now to be apprehended.

A lane running nearly south along the ridge eventually brings the wanderer to Nettleden, another delightful village having a small Perpendicular church. From this point, a short road to the left brings one to the less interesting Great Gaddesdon, actually a much smaller place than its " little " namesake. Here is a church containing so-called Roman bricks in the walling. The present building dates from the thirteenth century, however, and is not of great interest. On the east of the village is the fine estate of Gaddesdon Place, consisting of an eighteenth-century building erected in the Italian style in the midst of a beautiful and extensive park.

We are now on the main road to Hemel Hempstead, which lies about ten miles south of Ivinghoe by the lanes we have traversed. The high lead spire of the cruciform church—landmark for miles around—comes into sight as we near the beautiful stretch of Gades-bridge Park. The ancient township was of some importance in the days of the Mercian kings, and the name is said to be derived from the hemp fields which once extended over the hills to the east. The main street of the one-time " bailiwick " has the appearance of a flourishing, prosperous and self-contained agricultural centre. A town hall and corn exchange look down upon a busy scene on market day, but the old High Street is demure and peaceful through-out the rest of the week. The fact that Hempstead is upon a branch railway is doubtless responsible for its provincial air, and those residents who have business in London must be of the variety to whom time is no object ; though Marlowes, served by the main line station at Boxmoor, is a place of superior villas with almost a surburban air about it. The Londoner on his first visit to Hempstead will be amazed to find himself traversing " Cheapside " and " Cornhill." The church is very ancient, certain portions being nearly eight hundred years old, and the western doorway is a splendid example of Norman work. The effect of the massive masonry of the nave backed by the groined roof of the chancel beyond the crossing is admirable. The transept roof was originally of the fourteenth century ; it was restored nearly fifty years ago. The fine brass, dated 1480, to Robert and Margaret Albyn is worthy of note, and a tablet on the outside wall has an inscription of austere brevity: " Multum dilectus. Multum desideratus. After death the judgement." A monument to Sir Aston Paston Cooper reminds us that the famous surgeon made his home at Gadesbridge Park.

Hemel Hempstead is only a mile and a half from Boxmoor station on the old London and North-Western main line. The walk thither over the common is very pleasant. At Marlowes, about half-way, as well as at Boxmoor, evidences of urban growth are visible, and new houses dot the main road towards King's Langley on the south and Berkhampstead on the north-west. The latter is a considerable place, and is steadily growing. It once boasted a castle of some strength and importance, and its foundations are said to antedate the Conquest. Insignificant fragments remain close to the railway, though the moats and outline of the walls are well marked, and may readily be traced by the inexpert. Berkhampstead was one of the chief towns of Mercia, for it is fairly certain that the kings of Middle England resided in the ancient fortress ; but its chief historical interest lies in the fact that the Conqueror came here soon after Senlac, and received the submission of Edgar the Atheling and certain of the Saxon prelates and nobles, and that from the castle he proceeded to Westminster for his coronation. This palace-fortress appears to have been a favourite residence of Edward III, who gave it to his son, the Black Prince, and here the latter brought captive King John of France. During the reign of Richard II, Chaucer held an official position within its walls. According to Stukeley, the antiquary, the town stands upon the site once occupied by " Durocobrivis," but the claim is very conjectural indeed. The line of

Grims Dyke passes over Berkhampstead Common, and if this mysterious earth wall is older than Offa's reign, it might well have some connection with a pre-Roman settlement occupying the course of the broad valley.

Berkhampstead church is one of the largest in Hertfordshire. It dates from about 1220, and is built on a site once occupied by a Saxon church. The transepts have chantry chapels attached ; those on the north side with elaborately groined roofs. The east window is a memorial of the poet Cowper, who was a native of the town—his father was rector here. The poet's mother, Anne Cowper, is also commemorated by a wall tablet. Two large tombs call for notice ; one is of John Sayer, who was a cook in the service of Charles II. A brass tells that John Raven, esquire to the Black Prince, died while his master was staying as a guest at the castle. An unusual feature of the building is the curious timber pillar supporting the roof of St. John's Chapel. It is said to date from the fifteenth century.

The Grammar School, which is the next most important building in the town, was founded in 1541 by Dr. John Incent, afterwards Dean of St. Paul's. Cowper's birthplace, the old Rectory, has long since been pulled down, but the well-house, quite unaltered, is still called Cowper's Well.

Northchurch, or Berkhampstead St. Mary, is a continuation of the larger town. Here is another cruciform church, much restored, but perhaps retaining Saxon masonry, and usually visited by those interested in strange memorials for the sake of its brass commemorating " Peter the Wild Boy," a mysterious individual who was found roaming the forests of Hanover in 1725. Queen Caroline took an interest in the lad, and he was brought to England and given a home upon a farm at Broadway, where he died at an advanced age. A modern memorial tells of the remarkable record of a bell-ringer who performed his duties for a period of seventy years.

King's Langley and Abbot's Langley, respectively three and five miles south of Boxmoor, are interesting villages. The former is a considerable place, fast becoming a small residential town, though the old industry of straw plait making is still carried on, and there is an important paper-making works on the banks of the Gade. Langley Regis was the original name of this one-time royal manor, and the first king to hold it was Henry III. The fifth son of Edward III was named Edmund de Langley after his birthplace. The royal palace stood on the west of the churchyard, and the expert may be able to trace the site. The Perpendicular church contains the tomb in which Edmund and his wife—Isabel of Castile—were interred. This was brought from the chapel of a Dominican friary, finally dissolved in the reign of Elizabeth, which was connected with the palace. The tomb is now within a chapel at the side of the chancel, from which it is separated by a finely carved screen. Several other interesting monuments and brasses are to be seen within the building. It was at the friary that Piers Gaveston, over two years after his execution, was buried in 1315 in the presence of Edward II, his friend and too kind master, and the Archbishop of Canterbury.

Abbot's Langley is upon the high ground to the east, and gained its prefix from the fact that it became the property of the Abbey of St. Alban in the days of Edward Confessor. The church, of various styles, contains some ancient brasses and an imposing monument to Lord Chief Justice Raymond, who died in 1732, but the chief interest of the village lies in the fact that it was the birthplace of Pope Adrian IV, whose traditional connection with the neighbourhood of Harefield has already been noticed. Nicholas Breakspeare, as he then was, endeavoured to become a novice at St. Albans, but the great monastery would have none of him. Emigrating to France, he commenced his ecclesiastical career in Paris, and rapidly rose to the supreme position, when, by the irony of fate, or perhaps through the ironic humour of the

SARRATT.

king, the Abbot of St. Albans carried the compliments of Henry II to the new Pope.

From King's Langley, the lane running westwards takes us through delightfully undulating and unspoilt country to Chenies, which is just across the Chess in Buckinghamshire.

A mile past the hamlet of Chipperfield, two miles from King's Langley, a lane turns to the left, and brings us to Sarratt Green and Sarratt. A number of old houses stand around the spacious green with its oddly named inn—" The Old Boot "—but the church, over a mile away through winding lanes, is almost alone except for a few dwellings, an almshouse and a near-by farm. It is a cruciform Norman structure with a curious saddleback roof to the tower, and contains Early English double sediliæ and a piscina and aumbry of a date contemporary with the Norman building. A tradition is current that Richard Baxter once preached here. The pulpit from which the discourse would have been delivered still exists, for it is of the Jacobean period. Not far away is an old house mentioned by Mrs. Crowe in *The Night Side of Nature*. Its passages are said to be haunted by a headless man, dressed in a blue coat.

The lane continues past the church, and drops steeply to the clear chalk waters of the Chess. Over half a mile from the bridge it divides, the left-hand road leading to Chorley Wood and the new township which, thanks to the Metropolitan Railway, has sprung up around the once lonely common. Our road goes to the right, and soon reaches Chenies, one of the show places of the north-west countryside, and a favourite excursion for American visitors who take the village in the Jordans round. It is in a charming situation overlooking the valley of the Chess and very delightful in itself.

The present name of the place, for it was originally called Isenhampstead, is derived from the one-time lords of the manor—the Cheynes—who were in possession in the fifteenth century. Afterwards, it became the property of the Sapcotes and from them, by marriage, passed to the Russells. This was in the early sixteenth century, and the series of monuments in the Russell chapel commence in that period, and end in quite recent years. They are thus of great historical value, but, unfortunately, are not well seen from the body of the church. Permission to enter the chapel itself, which was added to the church in 1556, must be obtained from the Duke of Bedford's agents. A splendid altar tomb at the east end commemorates the first Earl of Bedford, who died in 1554. The last memorial, dated 1885, is in the form of a bronze candelabrum, and is to Lord Arthur Russell. Modern stained-glass windows have been placed in the chapel to commemorate those members of the family who are not otherwise represented.

Several interesting brasses are to be seen in the body of the church. Among others will be found one to Lady Agnes Cheyne, *circa*. 1480 ; Anna Phelip (1510) is shown holding a heart. Near the brass of Agnes Johnson (1511) is one of a priest in canonicals, and near the door a smith named John Walliston, *circa* 1470, is also commemorated in this fashion.

The leafy alley not far from the west end of the church, called the Monk's Walk, is firmly believed by the more unsophisticated villagers to be haunted by the shade of a cowled and rope-girdled religious. The beautiful old Manor House, dating from the middle of the sixteenth century, might well be another lurking-place for ghosts, but here clothed in doublet and hose. It was built by the first Duke of Bedford on the site of a royal castle.

A most delightful ramble up the valley of the Chess, passing on the way a foaming weir, brings us in less than half an hour to the charming little hamlet called Latimers. The Chess hereabouts winds through lush meadows at the foot of lofty wooded hills. The small collection of gabled houses around the green and its rustic seat is innocent of inn or shop, and the inhabitants themselves are not greatly in evidence. The scene is as peaceful and secluded as any within a hundred miles of London. Not far away are the ruins of old Flaunden church. That village itself, with a new church, is fully a mile and a half away in an upland valley to the north.

A short distance from Latimers, up the Chess valley is the seat of Lord Chesham, finely placed on a slope above the river. It is an Elizabethan mansion, and once housed Charles I as a prisoner and, later on, his son as a refugee. The road to Chesham, which we purpose to take, proceeds to climb the combe, passing near the site of a Roman villa at Dell Farm and then, leaving Chesham Bois high on the hill to the west, accompanies the branch line of the Metropolitan Railway to its terminus near the head of the valley.

Chesham, until the advent of this link with the Metropolis, was in a very quiet backwater, and was as rural in character as any small town in Dorset or Somerset; but the roads to the north-east in the direction of Berkhampstead, and to the south and Amersham, are now lined with villas, and the old streets in the centre have blossomed out with smart shops and stores. North-westwards, however, by a path starting close to the church, we may quickly reach a very secluded and lovely stretch of the nearer Chiltern range that is in great contrast to the commonplaces of Chesham, where there is little of interest apart from the church—a composite structure now containing few visible traces of the Norman building which originally stood upon the site. The parvise porch will be remarked, and also the sundials upon the southern buttresses, but though large, and a finely planned cruciform church, it has remarkably few details over which to linger and, at the time of writing, it is generally kept closed. A fine old house near by is a good example of the domestic architecture of the seventeenth century.

Leaving Chesham in a westerly direction, a road goes to Wendover by the top of the ridge, passing the hamlets of Hyde Heath and South Heath. The former borders a small but picturesque common, and has a remote and lost air not often seen nowadays

G

within a couple of miles of the Metropolitan Railway. South Heath, however, has become a residential locality served from Great Missenden station.

We now proceed by the Amersham road, and the modern residences of " Metroland " accompany us nearly all the way to the old town on the banks of the Misbourne. The road skirts the woods around Chesham Bois, which, however, does not gain its title from its environment, but from a family named de Bois who lived here in the thirteenth century. The finely placed but much restored church is some distance

AMERSHAM.

from the main road. It contains several good brasses, but the difficulty of approach hardly justifies the detour.

Amersham in the vale appears to ignore the fine new town upon the hill. This has its own shops and banks and is more or less independent of the old place. The main street remains practically unaltered from the days when it returned two members to Westminster, among whom, in 1624 and later, was Edmund Waller. A notice-board upon one of the old cottages at the south end of the town warns " common beggars and ballad singers " of their fate should they ply those callings in Amersham. The Market Hall was built by Sir William Drake in 1682. The family to which Sir William belonged have owned the near-by Shardelowes estate since 1605, and the church contains a special annexe for their memorials. The three by R. A. Bacon to members of the family deceased in 1796, 1810, and 1816 are much admired. The chancel and north aisle contain several interesting brasses, notably that to John Drake, who died in 1623. This bears the following lines :—

> Had he liv'd to be a man
> This inch had grown but to a span
> Now is hee past all feare of paine
> 'Twere sinn to wish him heere againe
> Vewe but the way by wch wee come
> Thou'l say hee's best that's first at home.

The old Grammar School, founded in 1624 by a Canon of Windsor, Dr. Chalmers, has been rebuilt near the town. The almshouses, which date from 1657, are a picturesque group of buildings at the north end of the main street, along which we continue to the open country, presently passing on the left the beautiful demesne of Shardeloes. The mansion is on a slope above the waters of the Misbourne that stretch for half a mile along the valley in a wide shallow lake. About two miles out of Amersham, a lane makes a slight divergence to Little Missenden. This side road is worth taking, for the village is a pleasant little place with a tiny old church, Early English in date, containing a quaint window in the roof. At Great Missenden, over two miles farther, new buildings are again in evidence, but in a much less degree than at Amersham. The scenery is of the best in the Chiltern country, and this may account for the banks of the Misbourne being chosen by some Augustinians in 1133 as their home, for this order seems to have had a *flair* for beautiful sites and fishful rivers ; though it cannot be said that nowadays there is much of the gentle sport to which the good brothers are supposed to have been addicted. As a matter of fact, in hot summers the little river is almost dry, except in certain artificially widened reaches. The site of the abbey is now occupied by a modern mansion. The last abbot was commemorated in the church by a stained-glass window, but this has disappeared together with certain other miscellaneous and ancient details. The building is more remarkable than its exterior would lead one to expect. It is a Decorated structure with some disproportionate Perpendicular windows, but there is good detail in the pillars and in the unusually fine arcade of the chancel. Two old brasses, both of women, are of interest, but the best thing about the church for the ordinary individual who is neither an amateur antiquary or a " pottering archæologist," is the really lovely view up and down the long valley.

MILTON'S COTTAGE, CHALFONT ST. GILES.

From either of the villages a glorious walk or drive of some eight miles can be taken through the lanes to the west of the high road, and parallel thereto, which would bring the explorer to Chalfont St. Giles without retracing any part of the route. This road, or rather, series of lanes, goes over the highlands between Misbourne and Wye, and passes through Kilmer Green, Great Kingshill, Penn Street and Coles Hill, where Edmund Waller was born at the Manor House.

Chalfont St. Giles was for a time the retreat of Milton, who came here for about nine months in July, 1665, when the Great Plague was nearing its height in London. It was in the old cottage which bears the poet's name that *Paradise Regained* was planned, and although it cannot be called his home it is of peculiar interest in that it is the only one now in existence of the several houses in which Milton lived. A small museum of relics connected with Milton is now installed in the little old house. Apart from the literary interest, however, Chalfont village is worth coming some way to see, for it is a delightful place, especially in spring, when the meadows surrounding it vie in colour with the gay gardens and red-roofed cottages. There are cottages here more picturesque than that occupied by Milton. One in particular, standing at the cross-roads, is quite delightful.

St. Giles' Church is approached by a sixteenth-century lych-gate between two ancient and picturesque dwellings. It is a patchwork of styles from Norman to Decorated. Some interesting details include a double piscina ; an altar tomb of William Gardyner, his wife and nine children, dated 1558 ; a wall painting ; ancient pews and alms box, and several brasses. Within the chancel are the effigies of Sir Thomas Fleetwood with his two wives and eighteen children, and the small figure of a priest. The chancel rails are said to have come from St. Paul's Cathedral, and to have been brought by Bishop Hare, an eighteenth-century Dean of St. Paul's.

Chalfont St. Peter is just two miles south of St. Giles, and though quite unlike its sister village, is equally picturesque. The modern church is well placed near the cross-roads, and preserves several brasses from the old building, together with a pewter communion set dating from the seventeenth century. The " Greyhound " inn, built during the Stuart period, is one of the best examples of the older village hostelry in Buckinghamshire. On the south of Chalfont, the rebuilt Grange marks the site of the home of Isaac

Pennington, Lord Mayor of London and a much-persecuted Quaker, whose house was a noted centre for the meeting of Friends until the dispersal of that body in 1665. Chalfont Park, which borders the road to Uxbridge, contains a mansion which is said to owe its "Gothic" ornament to Horace Walpole, whose sister lived here for some years. She was the wife of Charles Churchill, a nephew of the victor of Blenheim.

From Chalfont St. Peter an upland road wanders in rather an inconsequent fashion eastwards towards Rickmansworth. On the hillside, not far from the high road, is an institution for the care and employment of epileptics. This well-planned and remarkably successful colony is open to visitors.

The lane then descends to the Colne Valley, and joins the main road to Rickmansworth at Maple Cross, nearly two miles short of the town. The derivation of the name—"Rykemereswearth"—will at once be appreciated, for it signifies "fat water-meadows." Waterways and stretches of lush grasslands accompany us to the ancient town, and extend for several miles beyond. Many picturesque old houses remain in the narrow streets, which have not altered, nor has the town itself grown to any great extent during the last couple of decades, although it is served by the Baker Street, Marylebone and Euston railways. To the north and south, however, ancient and historic estates have lately been cut up and handed over to the builder.

The chimneys of paper mills, here as elsewhere in the Colne valley, tend to detract from the beauty of the countryside, and a fair-sized brewery also adds to the commercial side of the life of this pleasant Hertfordshire town. The church has been twice rebuilt during the last century, but it retains a few memorials from the original building. The vicarage, though partly restored, is an ancient and beautiful house. Another old dwelling in the High Street, called Basing House, was the residence for a time of Sir William Penn.

The remains of Rickmansworth Park accompany the west bank of the Chess in the direction of Chorley Wood, and the suburban amenities of Moor Park occupy the high ground across the Colne to the south. The latter estate was once the property of Cardinal Wolsey, and the original house was built by an Archbishop of York— George Nevil—in the reign of the fourth Edward. It eventually came into the hands of "King" Monmouth. The present mansion is to a great extent the erection of an eighteenth-century financier named Styles, who employed Sir

RICKMANSWORTH.

James Thornhill to decorate the great hall. The last owner to use it as a home was Lord Ebury; but those days are no more, and considerable portions of these still beautiful estates have recently been converted into building sites.

The Gade comes down from Hemel Hempstead and presently joins the Colne, and this little river, with the Chess, combine to make the lower Colne quite a con-

siderable stream. Their waters are accompanied at
a short distance by those of the Grand Junction
Canal, so that the broad flat valley, especially as viewed
from the railway embankment, has a watery appearance at most periods of the year. After a wet October,
the long vista of level meadow-land becomes an expanse
of silvery mere and, with the bronze and gold of late
autumn in the low wooded hills around, makes a
delightful picture in great contrast to the commonplaces of semi-suburban Middlesex to the south. In
the neighbourhood of Rickmansworth a large quantity of watercress is grown for the London market, and
the closely packed greenstuff in miniature crates is
generally in evidence upon the platforms of Euston
Station.

The Gade and the canal flow through the pleasant
glades of Cassiobury Park, and we may traverse part
of this delightful open space by turning off the Watford
road at Croxley Green, whence a lane leads to Water-
dell. The public path is struck a short distance
north of this point; then, going south-east, it
crosses a golf course and, afterwards, the two waterways at a picturesque spot not far from the great
mansion built by Wyatt in 1800, and until lately the
home of the Earls of Essex. Its close proximity to
the populous western suburb of Watford has no doubt
caused the abandonment of Cassiobury, and for some
years the southern part of the park has been in the
hands of the town authorities.

It must be confessed that the growth of Watford,
now the largest town in Hertfordshire, has not tended
in the direction of either beauty or even convenience,
for the main thoroughfare near the Town station is
ever in a state of chronic congestion, and the rows of

depressingly monotonous streets between the Rickmansworth road and High Street are reminiscent of
Tooting or Kilburn at their worst. But all this is a
sign of prosperity for which the great trunk line to the
North must be thanked, and which had commenced
long before the electric trains from Piccadilly began
their twenty minutes' service hitherwards.

Some old houses still remain in Watford, but in the
main street they are rapidly giving place to large and
ornate business premises. The Perpendicular church,
however, prevents any widening of the west side of
High Street. It is a spacious and interesting building
containing, in the Essex and Katherine chapels, a
large number of memorials too numerous to detail.
The altar tomb in the first-named annexe is that of
Bridget, Countess of Bedford, who founded the chapel
in 1595, dying five years later. Another imposing
tomb with a recumbent effigy is that of the wife of Sir
William Russell, who died in 1611. The Morison monuments are particularly fine, and were the work of the
celebrated sculptor—Nicholas Stone.

Watford is connected with the northern suburbs
by the ubiquitous motor-bus. Houses line the highway to Bushey and, except for the brief space afforded
by Bushey Heath and Stanmore Common, will soon
creep up to the older skirts of London. The once
lonely glades of Canons Park, near Edgeware, have
long since been invaded by bricks and mortar, and a
" tube " now unloads throngs of City workers in a
district which, a couple of decades ago, had not a
dozen houses that were not centenarians.

After passing the rebuilt Bushey Church, where Silas
Titus, the reputed author of *Killing No Murder*, was
buried, we cross the county boundary, and reach the

highest ground in Middlesex at Stanmore Heath.   The
trees upon its summit are over five hundred feet
above the sea, and are said to be visible on rare
occasions from the mouth of the Thames.   An old
writer mentions them as a mariner's mark, but that
was in those far-off days when the air surrounding
London was comparatively crystalline.

The extensive expanse of Bentley Priory Park sweeps
away to the south-west, the opposite extremity being
close to Harrow Weald church.   From no part of the
public roads surrounding it can a good view be obtained of the house.   The mansion has passed through
many vicissitudes, and was for a time a private hotel.
Here the exiled Louis XVIII was met upon his return
to France by the Prince Regent, the Czar and the
King of Prussia.   During the early years of the nineteenth century the house appears to have been a
rendezvous for many of the famous literary and
political lights of that day.   The small priory of
Augustinians was suppressed in the Great Dispersal,
and the original buildings disappeared when the present
house was built by Sir John Evans in the last decade
of the eighteenth century.

On the left, before descending the hill into Stanmore,
is The Grove, once the residence of Mrs. Brightwen,
the author of *Wild Nature Won by Kindness*, who conducted many interesting observations on the habits of
birds and the timid things of the woods in this once
unfrequented spot, doing much to render credible the
stories of Francis of Assisi in his dealings with his
" little brothers and sisters."

To the east of the Grove, on the footpath to Elstree,
is an obelisk erected in the days of those courageous
antiquaries who were quite unafraid in their guesses,

to mark the site of the Citadel of the Suellani who, under the great chief Cassivellaunus, defeated the Roman army.

Stanmore Hall was built by the Duke of Chandos as a retreat for his widow. The Duke also caused Belmont, the artificial mound in Stanmore Park, to be thrown up. This is a good view-point and over it a footpath goes to Harrow The house in Stanmore Park, now a school, was once the home of Andrew Drummond, a famous eighteenth-century banker. Later on Viscount Castlereagh lived here for a time.

The picturesque ivy-clad brick shell standing near the modern church was consecrated by Archbishop Laud, and it is difficult to understand why it was abandoned. Probably the craze for " Gothic " was the only reason. The ancient church of Stanmore Magna stood close to the railway, and the site may be identified by the solitary grave of a former vicar—Baptist Willoughby—who died in 1610. The new

THE FONT, STANMORE.

church contains a number of monuments removed from the Laudian building, and also an effigy of that Earl of Aberdeen who was Prime Minister in Queen Victoria's reign. His connection with Stanmore lay in the fact that his son was vicar of the parish.

Little Stanmore, usually called Whitchurch, is on the road to Edgeware, alongside which runs the boundary of the once ducal Canons Park. Originally an ecclesiastical property—hence its name—it came into the possession of the Duke of Chandos in 1710. He pulled down the old house and erected an imposing palace, so vast that his successor was unable to finance it. At the death of the second Duke, in 1747, Canons was disposed of by public auction at house-breakers' prices, and shortly afterwards a more suitable mansion was built upon part of the old site.

It is in the church and its memories of Handel that interest now centres. This building was set up by the first Duke, who employed the artists Verrio and Laguerre to decorate its walls with frescoes that now appear as stiff and rather dismal monotones. The ducal pew at the west end is embellished with a copy of Raphael's " Transfiguration." The Duke's monument is on the north of the chancel. He is accompanied by his two wives, and the whole conception is a remarkable example of the taste in memorials displayed by our forefathers in the mid-eighteenth century.

The most noteworthy object in the church is the organ upon which Handel played during the three years he spent here as organist, and upon which " Esther " and several other works were composed. It is in a curious position behind the altar. Perhaps next in popular interest is the grave of William Powell, the original of the *Harmonious Blacksmith*, who combined with his trade the duties of parish clerk.

Edgeware was, until quite recently, merely a long quiet village upon the Watling Street, served by the occasional trains of a branch railway, and not greatly altered in character by the electric trams which clang their way hither from Kilburn. But now that the long frontage of Canons is to be cut up into villa plots, and new houses are planned to cover the meadows between the village street and the heights of Mill Hill and Highwood Hill, the character of Edgeware is rapidly altering, for better or worse, according to point of view.

St. Albans Cathedral.

CHAPTER IV

ST. ALBANS AND THE NORTH

THE next tour—to St. Albans and the north thereof—may be made either by the Watling Street that, with but one half-turn to the right at Brockley Hill, makes direct for Verulam ; or we may take the crowded Holyhead road upon which the distances are reckoned from the one-time Hick's Hall, the London house of the seventeenth-century Lord Mayor Hicks who became Viscount Campden. This road goes through Barnet, and the frequent bus service to St. Albans gives its course a semi-suburban character. A third way, allowing us to make easy divergences to both first and second routes as occasion requires, leaves Hampstead North End, and passing through the smart suburb of Golder's Green—the " Grand Parade " was a lonely and delightful lane when the writer first walked this way—passes through Hendon Church End, a Hendon very different from and more inviting than that of the " Welsh Harp " and the railway sidings which border Watling Street. Here, from the church—standing high above the Brent and Silk streams—there is a fine view across the country we have already traversed, and over a goodly part of that to be journeyed through in this chapter. The foreground, alas ! is being slowly but surely covered by the red tide of Outer London.

Before leaving the hill, we might well spend a few moments within the church, which still conserves some quaintly ugly galleries—relics of the age when men, " from a sense of decency and order," covered the once picturesque outer walls with stucco. Among the several interesting memorials, there is one to remind us that Sir Stamford Raffles lived at Highwood Hill, over which eminence we shall presently pass. Another records that a nineteenth-century vicar was the famous Greek scholar—Dr. Scrivener. The Coutts have monuments here as well as members of two other families of banking fame—the Prescotts and Trotters.

Hendon, however, cannot be claimed as part of London's countryside nowadays, and we must pass on to Mill Hill, still retaining its picturesque main street with a pleasant strip of greensward down the centre. The chief interest here lies in the school, built in 1807 on the site of Ridgeway House, the home of a celebrated botanist named Collinson. It was founded for the sons of Dissenters, who were not then wanted at the public schools of England. It is now entirely unsectarian in character.

Mill Hill is also the home of several important Roman Catholic institutions, the most conspicuous being St. Joseph's College, marked by a lofty campanile surmounted by a gilt statue of its titular saint. The sisters of St. Vincent's Convent occupy an old house said to have been built by Charles II for Nell Gwynn. It was once called Littleberries, and still retains a handsome room decorated in the style of the Restoration.

The road northwards dips to a small green, and then rises to Highwood Hill, which commands lovely rural views to the north and west.   Here was once a chalybeate spring, and the residences of some famous people, including Wilberforce, the Emancipator, and, in later days, Mr. Sergeant Cox of the *Field* and *Queen*.

A lane leads eastwards by pleasant ways to Totterridge, a straggling village in Hertfordshire, lying upon a long ridge extending eastwards from the Mill Hill heights.   Though containing nothing of particular interest, the place has a certain charm difficult to describe.   The views from the ridge, framed in the foliage of ancient trees, are delightful, though they are mostly in the direction of London's northern heights.   A pond, and a pleasant stretch of flower-spangled greensward bordering a great part of the way to the village irself, are among the amenities of the ridge road. Copped Hall was the birthplace of Cardinal Manning in 1808.   It stands near the plain eighteenth-century church.

Resuming the northward way at Highwood Hill, we soon arrive at Arkley, a small and scattered hamlet with a modern church, whence fresh and extensive views again delight us.   Here the direct way to St. Albans deteriorates into a lane leading to Shenley, and the explorer in a car will desire the more obvious road by Elstree, a large village on the Watling Street beyond Brockley Hill.   Antiquaries are divided in opinion as to the site of the Roman Sulloniacæ, which was either at Brockley or Elstree.   The desired evidence of actual remains of the period is, at present, wanting, and the only noteworthy thing about Elstree is its fine and healthy situation, and the views towards the country beyond St. Albans and across the Aldenham or Elstree Reservoir. This picturesque sheet of water was formed to feed the Grand Junction Canal. The village after which it is officially named is some distance away to the north-west, beyond the seventeenth-century Aldenham House and upon a by-road connecting Radlett with Watford. Aldenham church is Perpendicular in date, with a very fine fifteenth-century oaken roof, a Norman font of Purbeck marble, and a remarkable muniment chest fashioned out of a single beam of oak.

A return must now be made to the lane connecting Arkley with Shenley that presently passes on the right the park of High Canons. On the farther side of the demesne is the straggling hamlet of Ridge, a breezy place with a small Perpendicular church. Beyond, and almost upon the main London road, is another and much more imposing church in the pleasant village of South Mimms.

Shenley boasts a village cage, a reminder of those days when the wrongdoer was in greater evidence than now; but the traveller should not rest content with this relic, but proceed to find the church at Shenleybury—nearly a mile away on the road to St. Albans. It contains the tomb of Nicholas Hawksmoor, the architect, who was responsible for several buildings popularly attributed to his master—Sir Christopher Wren. This church is now threatened with destruction. Its situation is, perhaps, inconvenient, but that is hardly an excuse for its demolition.

Two houses in the neighbourhood are of note. That of Porters, which stands in the park a short distance from the church, was the home of Lord Howe, the famous admiral ; while to the east is the fine Jacobean manor called Salisbury Hall. It stands upon the site of a home of the Montacutes.

Continuing northwards, we dip into the valley of the Colne, which is crossed by the main road to our right at the hamlet of London Colney. Then, rising again and passing the railway lines, we approach the ancient town and modern city of St. Alban near the ivied ruins usually referred to as Sopwell Nunnery, though they consist almost entirely of the remains of a mansion which took the place of the religious house soon after the Dissolution. The nunnery was founded by an abbot of St. Albans—Geoffrey de Gorham—about the middle of the thirteenth century, and according to Camden, it was here that Henry was married to Anne Boleyn.

The most effective entrance to the town, and towards the great church which dominates it, is by Holywell Hill—the approach from Watling Street and the west. From the slope of the hill and the bridge over the Ver at its foot, the long line of the roof, and square and massive central tower of the Cathedral, have an austere and solemn beauty. The picture would be perhaps more effective could we see the whole of the town grouped around its parent church, but the spires and roofs of St. Albans, seen on each end of the great edifice, are picturesque enough to please the most exacting. From this side, we are spared the view of the commonplace suburbs that have lately grown up around the city. The dignity of the Abbey gains enormously from the fact that the ground level is 320 feet above the sea—the highest site of any cathedral church in England.

A volume, or at least a chapter, would be necessary

H

to do any justice to a history and description of the
Cathedral and Abbey Church of St. Alban, and only
a few brief points in its past story and its present
appearance can be touched upon.

The " proto-martyr of Britain " was a converted
Roman soldier who had helped a Christian priest—
Amphibalus—to escape from imprisonment.   For his
act of mercy he suffered death, and upon or near the
spot a small church was erected soon after the martyr-

CHOIR, ST. ALBANS
CATHEDRAL.

dom. This building, practically destroyed during the Saxon
invasion, was restored at the
end of the eighth century by
Offa the Second of Mercia, who,
having discovered the bones of
St. Alban, placed them in the
new church, and founded a
monastery of Benedictines to
care for them.

The older portions of the
present structure date from
the end of the eleventh century, when Paul de Caen, the
fourteenth Abbot, used a great accumulation of
Roman bricks and other material from the ruins of
Verulam to build a new and imposing church, and these
characteristic flat tile-like bricks may be seen in the
central tower, the transepts, and other parts of the
Norman building. Although its length was not so
great—426 feet as compared with the present 550 feet—
Paul de Caen's church must have had an even grander
appearance than that of the great building we see
to-day, for it is believed that at the west end of the nave
two square battlemented towers once stood, of the same

character as that now at the crossing.   The Decorated architecture of the eastern part of the choir was commenced by John of Hertford in the thirteenth century. John of Wheathampstead, who was Abbot during the mid-fifteenth century, added greatly to the beauty of the details, and designed the great altar screen, though this is generally known by the name of his successor— William of Wallingford.

At some unknown date, a church dedicated to St. Andrew was built against the north wall of the nave at its western end.   This was for the use of the townspeople, who had no actual right of entry to the Abbey Church, though on great festivals they attended services in the nave.   St. Andrew's disappeared at the Dissolution, though the communicating doorway—now leading to a cupboard recess—is still to be seen.

The modern restoration was commenced in 1857 by Sir Gilbert Scott, but his operations were abandoned for want of funds.   It is to Lord Grimthorpe that we owe the present aspect of the western front as well as considerable rebuilding and alteration in various parts of the fabric.   There is much difference of opinion, both among the laity and those architectural experts who are qualified to pronounce, as to the success of these "improvements."   The most unfavourable body of critics are among those townspeople who remember their great church in its partly dilapidated state.   Credit must be given to Sir Gilbert Scott for removing the disfiguring plaster from the tower and making its magnificent Norman work, the finest of its kind in England, secure for many generations to come, and to the late Lord Grimthorpe for what is, after all, a very dignified, if unoriginal, west front.   It is in the sadly marred Norman transepts that the latter benefactor, who was unfortunately allowed a free hand on the principle that he who pays the piper calls the tune, failed to show any grasp of the essentials of true restoration. The poorly designed circular window of the north arm, and the utterly incongruous lancets, a fairly close copy of the well-known " Five Sisters " at York, on the south side, are the alterations most severely criticized. Apparently the idea was to give the Abbey the tallest lancet in England. It measures sixty feet in height. In the writer's opinion, the worst offence lies in the fact that these windows are, to some extent, shams. As seen from the exterior, they appear to light a space extending from floor to pointed roof. They, of course, finish at the same level as the flat inner roof, and the upper portions of the windows serve to light the roof story. In a sacred building this sort of architectural subterfuge seems peculiarly bad. No less a master than the great Wren himself was guilty of a fault which may be placed in the same category, for the walls above the aisles and in front of the clerestory of St. Paul's Cathedral are merely scenery ; though for that matter such glorious conceptions as the west front of Salisbury are also sins against the principles of good architecture.

To those who are old enough to recollect the rounded and battlemented turrets which once stood at each corner of the transepts, the square erections of Lord Grimthorpe look peculiarly mean and ugly. The former were doubtless as devoid of architectural merit as the latter are " correctly Norman," but the patchings of another age had a dignity and grace of their own.

The contrast between the Norman piers on the north of the nave and the Early English on the opposite side is very effective, and the rise of five steps just

within the western doors, and another of three at the
east end of the nave, give an unusual distinction to
this part of the Cathedral. It must be remembered
that this is the longest Gothic nave in the world.
The grandeur of the Norman arches supporting the
tower is perceived as the crossing is approached. An
extraordinary feature will be noticed in the Early
English arch imposed upon a Norman pier. Upon the
latter is a representation of the Crucifixion, as also
upon four other piers. It is thought that altars once
stood against the base of these, and that the paintings
took the place of a reredos. Other mural decorations
can be discerned upon the piers and arches, some
almost obliterated. All were until recent years
covered with whitewash. A modern painting by
F. O. Salisbury of the funeral procession of Queen
Eleanor will be noticed and admired.

Beyond the organ, which interferes with any complete view of the interior, is the choir, containing the
Bishop's Throne. This once stood in Rochester
Cathedral, and accompanied Bishop Claughton when
he left that see upon its division, for, strange as it seems
to us at this day, St. Albans until 1877 was within the
ecclesiastical jurisdiction of Rochester. The magnificent Wallingford screen, each niche filled with a
beautifully chiselled modern statue, fills in the east
end of the Presbytery for two-thirds of its height.
The statues of St. Alban and St. Amphibalus occupy
the spaces immediately left and right of the altar,
above which is a coloured altar-piece by Alfred Gilbert,
R.A. The mother-of-pearl in the angels' wings, the
crystal globe, and the curious brass scrollwork in front
of the figures, render the work quite unique in character. Upon one side of the sanctuary is the chantry

of Abbot John of Wheathampstead, containing a fine brass, and opposite is that of Thomas Ramryge, Abbot in 1492. This is a truly splendid specimen of Perpendicular ornamentation. Other abbots are buried beneath the floor of the Presbytery, and the cenotaph of the first Bishop of St. Albans is in the north transept.

The south arm has a very interesting pair of relics from the Saxon church. These are two baluster shafts which will be seen in the triforium on the east side. It is conjectured that they were turned upon a lathe, and the excellent condition of the stone proves that they came from the interior of the ancient building.

Beyond the High Altar is the Saints' Chapel, and on the way to it, in the south aisle, a fourteenth-century holy water stoup is passed. Beyond, on the opposite wall, is the quaint eighteenth-century figure of a mendicant, hat in hand, apparently asking for alms. The Saints' Chapel once contained the bones of St. Alban and St. Amphibalus, both enshrined in caskets covered with glowing colours, and studded with gems and precious metal. The sorting and putting together of the fragments of stonework once forming the base of the shrine was a miracle of patience and ingenuity, and reflects the greatest credit upon the late Mr. Chapple, who conducted the work. Although far from complete, a good idea of the appearance of the shrine can be gathered if one can exercise a little imagination. The watching loft, in which a constant guard was kept against the theft of relics and ornaments, is upon the north side, and opposite is the magnificent chantry of Humphrey, Duke of Gloucester, brother of Henry V. This is another fine example of characteristic Perpendicular carving and ornament. The fragmentary restoration of the shrine pedestal of

St. Amphibalus will be found in the north aisle of the
Saints' Chapel.   The Retro-choir, east of the latter,
was for many years after the Reformation a public
way or short cut.   The Lady Chapel beyond was used
as the town Grammar School until 1869, and in consequence suffered very rough usage.   Hence we are
not surprised to find here a great deal of modern work
—all, it is gratifying to add, of a very high order both
in design and execution.   The carvings of fruit and
flowers are beautiful, and the restraint shown by Sir
Gilbert Scott and Lord Grimthorpe in the general
restoration is beyond praise.   The style is Decorated,
and the east window is a noteworthy example of this
period.   On the south side is a vestry which was once
the Chapel of the Transfiguration.   That Duke of
Somerset who was grandson of John of Gaunt was
buried beneath the floor of the Lady Chapel.   His
corpse was found lying in the street without, after the
battle of St. Albans in 1455.   The Earl of Northumberland and Lord Clifford, slain in the same fight, were also
interred here.

The Grammar School was removed from the Lady
Chapel to the Abbey Gatehouse, which we have seen
below the west front of the church.   This building
dates from the time of Thomas de la Mare in the mid-
fourteenth century.   It was used as a joint prison for
refractory monks and errant townsmen—for the Abbot
had power to deal with laymen as well as the religious
in those far-off days.   It continued in use as a gaol
until 1868.   The school found a home within the old
walls not far from the spot where it first became known
to history.   It sets out to be the oldest in the land, and
how many years it was in existence before the earliest
authentic date—1119—can only be conjectured.

Another supposed gatehouse, so far as foundations are concerned, is the old " Round House," now the " Fighting Cocks " inn, which is said to have been the St. Germains Gate of the Abbey. It is a quaint structure not far from the River Ver, and declares itself to be the oldest inhabited house in England, a claim as impossible to substantiate as that of the several other structures demanding a similar fame.

The Cathedral—or Abbey, as it is always called by the townsfolk—and its immediate surroundings by no means exhaust the interest of St. Albans, though the majority of day visitors are content with the great church and its precincts. There are many ancient houses still left, and Fishpool Street retains several. To reach this thoroughfare we cross the open space called Romeland, where George Tankerville was burnt by order of Bonner during the reign of Mary I. Close to the market-place, and in the centre of the city, is the Clock Tower, built in the early fifteenth century to house the enormous curfew bell called " Gabriel." The tower was much restored in 1865, but it fortunately escaped a disastrous fire which destroyed several of the old dwellings in the market-place some years ago. Near by is a fountain marking the site of an " Eleanor " Cross. The body of Edward's beloved Queen rested before the High Altar in the Abbey on its way to Westminster. French Row, on the west side, keeps its ancient characteristics almost unimpaired ; it is said to have received its name after French

THE " FIGHTING COCKS "
INN.

troops had occupied it in 1216. On the left-hand side
of the way, at the corner of Dagnall Street, is the so-
called Moot House.

From the classic Town Hall, the tree-lined St. Peter's
Street continues towards Barnard's Heath. In the
broad roadway, the first Battle of St. Albans was
fought in 1455 between the forces of Lancaster and
York, resulting in victory for the latter, the wounded
Henry VI being taken prisoner to the Abbey. On
Barnard's Heath, six years later, the tables were turned;
the Earl of Warwick was defeated; and Henry and
Queen Margaret were conducted as victors to the Abbey
while the Abbot, John of Wheathampstead, changed
his colours.

In St. Peter's Street is the spacious Perpendicular
church which gives its name to the thoroughfare.
The tower appears to be in an odd position at the east
end, but the explanation is simple. The church was
originally cruciform, and has lost its chancel and
transepts. Though over-restored, the building retains
some old stained glass in the north windows. A brass
commemorates Roger Pemberton who died in 1627.
He founded the almshouses on the north-west side of
the church in consequence, it is said, of his misfortune
in accidentally killing a widow while shooting in the
woods. An interesting tomb in the north aisle is that
of Edward Strong, who, as master mason, was in charge
of St. Paul's Cathedral during the rebuilding. The
churchyard is the resting-place of many Yorkist and
Lancastrian warriors whose bodies were brought from
the street without.

The site of the original Roman city was upon the
far side of the Ver, and the visible ruins consist chiefly
of the walls. A footpath runs in front of the east wall,

and between it and the fosse or defensive ditch, now filled with bushes and undergrowth. A great mass of masonry known as Gorhambury Block probably marks the angle of the western wall. It is known that considerable remains of buildings, including a theatre with stage and auditorium, are buried beneath the greensward, which appears to the casual eye as ordinary as that of any other stretch of pleasant meadow. St. Michael's church was considered by Sir Gilbert Scott to stand on the site of the Basilica, even if the base of the walls is not actually part of the original building. Here again the flat Roman bricks will be seen built in

FISHPOOL STREET, ST. ALBANS.

with flints, but this church has lost much of its interest through over-restoration. The principal attraction is the celebrated monument to Lord Bacon, which consists of a life-like figure of the philosopher sitting in a high-backed chair. It must not be forgotten that the great Lord Chancellor's titles were Lord Verulam and Viscount St. Albans, and the ruins of the great porch of his home at Gorhambury are still in existence.

Some writers have depicted the fall of Verulam into speedy decay as a consequence of the population following the first British martyr to his resting-place on the hill beyond the Ver. Ultimately, of course, this migration by slow degrees did take place, and a new town sprang up around the church, the course of the Roman road being deflected to pass through it. But in Saxon days, Verulam was for many years a place of importance, when it was called successively Verlamceaster and Watlingceaster. As a matter of fact, the

city below the hill was largely rebuilt by the Saxons.
It had probably lain in a partly ruinous state for a
considerable time after its capture by Queen Boadicea.
It is to be hoped that when opportunity serves (or
shall we say before a garden city is planned to cover
the site ?) some systematic excavation of the foundations of Verulam will be attempted. It is probable
that the result would exceed in interest and importance both those at Silchester and the recent researches
in Monmouthshire.

St. Stephen's Church stands upon the Roman way
to London. It retains some Norman details and an
old brass, dated 1482, to a William Robins, who was
Clerk of the Signet. The brass lectern is said to have
been brought from Holyrood. From the church it
is a pleasant walk to Bricket Wood—beloved of picnic
parties and excursionists. The wood and a small
hamlet are about four miles along the Watford road,
and own a wayside railway station.

The straight highway to the north-west, with its
long and monotonous perspective of thickly wired
telegraph posts, rejoins the original track of the Watling Street nearly two miles from St. Albans market-
place, and then follows the Ver valley to Redbourn,
where St. Amphibalus was martyred. He was recap-
tured in Wales, whither he had fled after his escape
through the agency of St. Alban, and on the journey
back his captors, for some unknown reason, decided
upon his death when four miles from Verulam. Roger
of Wendover narrates that the bones of the saint were
discovered buried with those of two other men, and
that they were found through the miraculous inter-
vention of St. Alban, who appeared to the searchers
and led them to the spot.

Redbourn church contains a notable oak screen, and some remains of the original Norman building. The Easter sepulchre and sedilia, and two ancient brasses, are also of interest. The long street is quiet enough in the first part of the morning, before the heavy motor traffic of the day has started, but in the great days of the coaching era it was a scene of bustle and excitement, for this was the breakfast stage for travellers on the Holyhead mail.

Nearly three miles to the east, on the main Bedford road, is rapidly-growing Harpenden. Its situation on the edge of a large common is quite delightful, but the once sleepy village is now a semi-suburban town with smart and up-to-date shops. The church has been rebuilt, but the Norman font and some old brasses remain. Half-way from Redbourn is Rothampsted, a fine mansion originally erected in the fifteenth century, but largely rebuilt. This has been the scene of the famous " Rothampsted experiments " in the culture of cereals, which have proved of so much benefit to British farming.

The Watling street continues upon its original course for about two miles past Redbourn, and then the high road deviates slightly to the left for a long mile before entering Markyate Street. Just beyond the parting of the old and new ways, a lane leading uphill to the left brings us to Flamstead, a pleasant small village high above the Ver, hence the name—" Verlamstead." The Saunders Almshouses, built in 1669, form as quiet a retreat for worthy old people as may be found in the whole of our present travels. The petrol fumes and scurry of the great highway near by might be non-existent if the inmate's hearing is just pleasantly dull and he cannot be reminded of new-fangled ways by the raucous snorts and wails rising from the valley below. The spacious Decorated church has a large and dignified tower which, in a district where this part of the structure is usually commonplace, lends unusual distinction to the building. Inside will be found a chancel screen containing much original work. The vestry contains a piscina, proving that this was once a chapel with its own altar. An altar tomb, evidently of some important personage, has lost its inscription and cannot be identified ; but a brass of a priest in canonicals is readily identified as that of John Oudeby, who died in 1414.

Markyate Street, which borders the highway for some distance, is of literary interest as being the scene of part of Cowper's school-days. Just past the long village street, on the right hand, is Cell Park, wherein is a small church. The name perpetuates the memory of a Benedictine nunnery which once stood upon the site of the present Markyate Cell—a large mansion half a mile north of the village.

There is little to describe on the remainder of the Dunstable road, which gradually rises towards the pass between the hills on the south of that town. The highway forms a boundary between Herts and Bedfordshire for three-quarters of a mile, and then the long line of the Dunstable Downs comes into view on the left. These, and the bold swelling hills to the east, are the last efforts of the chalk to rise to a respectable altitude, and the Chilterns gradually diminish in height upon their march towards East Anglia, until they may be said to end in Henry Hill near Great Chesterford.

Dunstable is generally accepted as the site of the Roman Durocobrivæ, and it stands upon one of the most important ancient crossings in Britain. The Icknield Way was undoubtedly of great antiquity when the Romans made the new straight route from London and the Straits of Dover to Chester and the north-west ; and it is possible that a British settlement was in existence upon, or near, the spot before Durocobrivæ was built, for upon the hills around are many evidences of prehistoric man. The great earthwork

DUNSTABLE CHURCH.

called Maiden Bower, about a mile to the west, encloses nearly nine acres, and had b a n k s of extraordinary height and strength. The name is a corruption of Mai Dun, " great fort," and reminds us of Maiden Castle in Dorset—the largest and most remarkable of all prehistoric fortresses in Britain.

The Roman settlement here was not taken over by the Saxons as was Verulam. They destroyed the place, and it lay in utter desolation until the reign of the first Henry, who founded a great Augustinian Priory among the ruins. The nave of the Priory church is now the parish church of Dunstable. The choir and transepts, together with the tower which then stood at the crossing, disappeared soon after the Great Dispersal. The odd tower at the north-west corner is a Perpendicular addition, and to this period the battlemented parapet of the west front belongs. Just below this parapet comes Early English work, and the beautiful west door

is a fine specimen of Norman architecture at its best.
Upon entering, the imposing character of the Norman
piers will at once impress the visitor, who will not need
to be an archæologist to regret the loss of the eastern
part of this great church, much the finest in Bedfordshire. The east end is filled by a rood-screen which
once formed the boundary between nave and choir.
The wooden screen in front of the sanctuary is a Perpendicular work. Another at the side probably dates
from a century later. The east end was terminated
by a chapel in which the trial of Katherine of Aragon
took place. It will be remembered that the president
of the court which pronounced sentence was Cranmer.
A gateway and a few stones of the conventual buildings
still remain near the church.

Dunstable had an Eleanor Cross until the soldiers
of the Commonwealth considered it idolatrous, and
smashed it up. Few medieval relics exist, and we
must notice, therefore, the gateway of the "Anchor,"
next the Town Hall, which is good Tudor work, and
also the almshouses and school building of the Chew
Charity, on the London road, which date a century
later.

The trade of Dunstable, apart from the ordinary
channels of agriculture, is concerned with the making
of hats. The origin of the industry, which became
established about the time the second Charles came
into his own, was due to the fine quality of the straw
grown hereabouts. Nowadays, the straw is almost
entirely foreign, much of it coming from Japan.

A delightful walk of less than three miles over the
Dunstable Downs may be taken to Totternhoe, either
by Icknield Street or upon the smooth sward of the
bare rounded domes above. If the apparently low

altitude of the hills is at first disappointing, it must be remembered that Dunstable itself is five hundred feet above the river Ouse at Bedford, less than twenty miles to the north.

Totternhoe is a scattered place with its south end high upon the Downs, and its church in a hollow below the Icknield Way.   Half-way between these extremes is the great earthwork called Totternhoe Castle.   Once accredited to the Romans and then to the British, it is, in all probability, a Roman adaptation of a prehistoric work.   Below the " Castle," the scars in the hill side are the disused quarries of the famous Totternhoe stone.   It was formerly used in many of the churches and manor houses of this and the neighbouring shires.

A little over a mile south-east of the church, and just across the Buckinghamshire border, is Edlesborough.   Its conspicuous church stands high upon a mound which may not be merely a natural hummock of the chalk.   The building is worth a visit for its beautiful carved woodwork ;   that of the pulpit and sounding-board being particularly fine.   The stalls and rood screen also are uncommonly elaborate for an out-of-the-way village church.

The Icknield Way must now be followed eastwards out of Dunstable, and a bare and lonely country traversed all the way to Luton, the hilltops on the right becoming less imposing as we proceed.   Luton lies in the gap made by the Lea, here a very modest stream indeed, and the appearance of the place—a large and busy town—is not likely to tempt the searcher after the picturesque to make a long stay. Its architecture is almost entirely Victorian, and of a very utilitarian character.   Here, as at Dunstable, the principal industry is the manufacture of straw plait, though originally the actual work was done in the surrounding villages, Luton being a sort of " factor " town for the collection and forwarding of the native product.   Now there are modern workshops fitted with the latest power plant for this important industry. Hydraulic and other machinery works also tend to give Luton the appearance of a Midland rather than that of a Chiltern centre.

However, the traveller is justified in taking Luton on the way, even if any sort of industry is anathema, for the town possesses a remarkably fine cruciform church crowned by a handsome wes-tern tower. The building contains perhaps the most magnificent font, or rather font can-opy, in England. This consists of a six-sided Decorated

LUTON CHURCH.

enclosure with traceried gables terminating in richly carved pinnacles, the centre of the canopy being a groined stone roof covered with delicate carving. Abbot John Wheathampstead of St. Albans was responsible for the present chancel, which contains a finely carved sedilia.   On the north is the Wen-lock Chapel, holding the tomb of William Wenlock, Prebendary of St. Paul's.   An individual who was both Archbishop of York and Lord Chancellor of England—Thomas Rotheram—is also said to be buried here.   He died in 1500.   This chapel contains some ancient stained glass in the east window, and several brasses.   Others in the church are more or less

I

fragmentary in condition. Another chapel in the south transept is separated from the body of the building by a partition containing portions of the ancient rood screen.

The great house of the neighbourhood is Luton Hoo, two miles south of the town. This was the home of the Hoo's, after whom the south transept chapel in Luton church is usually named. The house was rebuilt by the Earl of Bute in 1762 from designs by one of the brothers Adam. An almost equally famous artist— " Capability " Brown—laid out the grounds. A disastrous fire in 1843 practically destroyed the mansion, but it was faithfully restored some six years later. Part of the north wing was afterwards converted into a private chapel, one of the most sumptuous in the kingdom. This was during the occupancy of the Leigh family. The estate now belongs to Sir Julius Wernher.

Luton is left by the road which passes near the railway station and makes for the village of Stopsley. To the north, the chalk hills extend for a considerable distance, capped by two heights over six hundred feet above the sea—Warden and Galley Hills. Near the latter, which rises just above the old course of the Icknield Way, is a large prehistoric camp commanding the country to the north and north-west.

The county boundary is now crossed and, passing the extensive park of Putteridge Bury, we soon reach Lilley, a village with a rebuilt church. Over a mile farther is Great Offley, said to be named after Offa of Mercia, who had one of his numerous palaces here. The church contains several interesting monuments, but it is in itself unremarkable.

The road gradually descends, and eight miles from Luton we reach Hitchin, a town that has greatly altered during the last couple of decades, but is still one of the pleasantest centres in Hertfordshire. Its history, by the evidence turned up at various times by pick and spade, goes back to Roman and pre-Roman days, and some picturesque houses of solidity and dignity show that it was a thriving market town hundreds of years before its modern neighbour—Letchworth—sent the throngs we may see in the wide Bancroft upon Saturday afternoons to make glad the hearts of the Hitchin tradesmen. The spacious church, which is said to be the largest in the county, points to a considerable population in the Middle Ages. The tower is extraordinarily low for its massive proportions, and it is only after entering by the beautiful south porch that the great size of the building becomes apparent. It has many things to interest the visitor,

HITCHIN CHURCH PORCH.

not least of which is an authentic Rubens, an Adoration of the Magi, once forming the altar-piece and now hanging over the north door. The beautiful mosaics behind the altar are no doubt more ornamental than this rather sombre old painting, but on the whole, its removal seems to have been an unnecessary proceeding. The mutilated condition of the font is said to be due to the zeal of Parliamentary soldiers in the Civil War, who are also blamed for the maltreatment of other portions of this fine old building. In the north aisle is an effigy of a de Baliol, and several other ancient memorials remain, including five brasses in a more or less battered condition.

To Free Churchmen, the Baptist Chapel in Tilehouse Street will be the first place of pilgrimage in Hitchin, for, although rebuilt, it stands on the exact site of the conventicle in which the great Dreamer preached. "Bunyan's Chair," which he gave to the chapel, was until lately a venerated object in the vestry of the present building. It is now preserved in the Town Museum.

The Biggin Almshouses, close to the church, incorporate part of the far older building of a Gilbertine nunnery dating back to the reign of the third Edward, but the age of the remains is not very apparent upon a superficial examination. The heavy wooden pillars and massive beams over the covered sides of the quadrangle are extremely picturesque.

In Golden Square, close by, lived Eugene Aram—he was, it will be remembered, usher at the Church House school—and at Mount Pleasant George Chapman, the translator of Homer, was born.

Little more than two miles north-east of Hitchin, and just over the county boundary in Bedfordshire, is the well-preserved Wilbury Hill Camp, probably a Roman adaptation of a more ancient fortress. It is actually upon the Icknield Way, which passes right through the walls. A mile to the east, and almost upon the Way, is the "Garden City" of Letchworth. An hour or so can well be spent in admiring—or deploring—the efforts of the domestic architect during the last twenty years or so, and, if there are certain examples of how not to do it, Letchworth is a very pleasant place with several industries of its own, con-

ducted upon admirable lines.   A small old Perpendicular church belonging to the original village should not
be forgotten.

The eastern extension of Letchworth now reaches
almost to the outskirts of Baldock, originally Baudoc,
an old town built around the junction of the Icknield
Way with the Great North Road.   This is one of the
several centres in the north-eastern quarter of London's
Countryside that we shall find devoted mainly to the
production of malt.   It is said that the soil in these
districts is better suited to the cultivation of the finer
varieties of barley than that of any other part of
England.   The large church and handsome modern
Town Hall, together with much picturesque domestic
architecture, make the little town an attractive place
for an hour or two of exploration.   Knights of the
Temple lie beneath the Decorated arches of the church,
and two deeds, displayed on the walls of a chantry,
are over six hundred years old.   It was here that the
cavalcade conveying the royal prisoner Charles I drew
up for rest and refreshment, and the rector, Josias
Bird, brought the communion chalice, filled with wine,
to the King's stirrup.   In thanking the priest, the
King is said to have attempted a show of lightearted-
ness—" We had not expected to find so good a bird
in Baldock."

From Baldock, the London road may be followed
to Stevenage, six miles to the south, passing on the
way Graveley, a delightfully unspoilt village with a restored Norman church in a district of gentle little hills
and peaceful valleys.   A long mile to the west, in the
direction of Hitchin, is Wymondley.   Here, in the
picturesque Delamere House on the south of the church,
lived Cardinal Wolsey.   Tradition has it that his royal

master once came here, and was suitably entertained.
A Roman villa was discovered near the village not a
great many years ago, and relics of the period are
turned up from time to time. The church is partly
Norman, but was much rebuilt during the restoring
mania of the last century.

The first little town on the way southwards is
Stevenage ; pleasant enough, but without anything of
outstanding interest apart from the large Early English
church. It was a more compact place before a great
fire destroyed the ancient houses, and now it straggles
along the North Road for a considerable distance, and
possesses a number of inns dating from the commencement of the coaching era. One of these—the " Castle "
—has a barn in which the coffin of a certain eccentric—
Henry Trigg—who died in 1724, rests upon the rafters
in accordance with instructions given in his will.

A turning to the right, rather more than a mile from
Stevenage, takes us from the London road to Knebworth, one of the show places of Hertfordshire, and
famous as the home of Bulwer Lytton. The house
stands in a beautiful situation upon one of the low chalk
hills which overlook the Beane Valley. It is built
upon the foundation of a sixteenth-century mansion
which in its turn replaced a Norman castle. The
present structure was not finished until 1883. It is
an extremely picturesque pile with countless turrets
and pinnacles in nineteenth-century Gothic, but nevertheless very splendid and imposing in its general effect.

A certain sixteenth-century owner named Roland
Lytton was knighted by Queen Elizabeth on one of
her several visits to Knebworth—a convenient lodging
upon her various journeys to and from the North.
The Great Hall is more or less as it was when Gloriana

dined in this noble apartment. It is stately with armour and old oak, some of the latter dating from Elizabeth's time, and some designed by Inigo Jones. The associations of Knebworth with Bulwer Lytton, however, outweigh those of its previous history. The beautiful gardens were visited and admired by almost all the novelist's literary contemporaries, and Dickens was a frequent guest, always enthusiastic in his praise of the splendid home of his friend.

The small church contains many memories of the family, including a fine brass of the before-mentioned Sir Roland. The monuments of several of his descendants are within the Lytton chapel at the side of the chancel. The mausoleum in the park was built by Bulwer Lytton's mother, who was the first of the family to be buried therein. The lines upon the exterior were written by the novelist peer.

Our way now lies through Codicote, an extensive village on the way to Welwyn, called " Wellin," which sleepy little town has lately blossomed into another important and thriving " Garden City." Old Welwyn is very quaint and picturesque with an ancient church —the scene of the ministry for thirty-five years of Dr. Young, the author of *Night Thoughts*. An avenue of limes in the Rectory garden is said to have been planted by him. At the end of the seventeenth century, when Spas were becoming the thing, Welwyn was found to possess " medicated waters," and their use was continued to the time of Young, who died in 1765. He described them as similar to those of Tunbridge, but no chalybeate spring appears to be existent in Welwyn to-day.

We may now continue by the main Hatfield road, with occasional fine views of the celebrated Welwyn railway viaduct, beyond which certain ominous splashes of colour show where new residences are springing up on the road to Tewin Green. Here is Queen Hoo Hall, a Tudor house that was for many years a farm, but is now restored to its original standing. It was the seat of the Botelers whose tombs are in Tewin church.

If the main road is deemed undesirable, we may make a pleasant detour through the village of Ayot St. Peter, which lies to the west, in a country of little wooded hills between the Maran and the Lea. In either case, we pass the spacious Brocket Park. Here the latter river is widened into a long narrow lake, and through this beautiful pleasaunce a ramble is permitted. Brocket Hall was the home of Lord Melbourne, who died here in 1865.

Three miles to the west of Lemsford, the small village at the south end of the park, is Wheathampstead, an exceedingly pleasant village on the banks of the upper Lea, a pellucid and lovely stream which it is difficult to believe can eventually become the river of Tottenham Marshes and Stratford-at-Bow. The large cruciform church contains a Saxon doorway leading into the Brocket Chapel, wherein is the altar tomb of Sir John Brocket and his lady, dated 1543. It is quite possible that this chapel, which contains a piscina, covers the site of the original small Saxon church. The parents of that Abbot of St. Albans called John of Wheathampstead are commemorated by a brass. Their names were Hugh and Margaret Bostock. Other memorials include the effigies of Sir John Garrard and his wife, and a marble tablet of 1558 to John Heyworth is of interest. Mackery End, immortalized by Lamb, is but a short two miles from Wheathampstead, and the old farm-house still stands, and probably has much

the same appearance that it had when Elia revisited
it over one hundred years ago.

From Lemsford, we continue to follow the Lea, and
soon reach Hatfield. Although this old town is not
" feudal," in the sense that Arundel is, it depends to
a large extent upon the great home of the Cecils for
both its fame and its fortune. The town, of course,
antedates the house by many hundreds of years, and
was chosen, as far back as 680, for the meeting of an
important church council presided over by Archbishop
Theodore. It was royal property in the days of the
Saxon kings, and afterwards belonged to the Bishops
of Ely. The palace of the prelates stood just south
of the church, where the gatehouse is still to be seen.
The Princess Elizabeth was held prisoner in this palace,
which had again become royal property in the reign of
her father. It was here that the Princess heard of the
death of her sister Mary.

During Elizabeth's reign the home of the Cecils
was at Theobalds, near Waltham Cross. Her successor
became greatly enamoured of that fine estate, and
persuaded Sir Robert Cecil to exchange it for the
Hatfield manor and a new and magnificent house ;
part of the reward being the title of Earl of Salisbury.

The house may well be called magnificent, and
though usually described as Jacobean in style, it is of
at least two distinct designs—mainly Elizabethan and
the later Anglicised Italian Renaissance. The effect
of this combination is both rich and full of dignity.
The interior is equally imposing, particularly the handsome apartment called King James' Room, which contains a bronze statue of that monarch over the fireplace. The greatest treasures are stored in the library—
where a priceless collection of manuscripts and auto-

graph letters are kept—and in the armoury, filled with
Armada relics and rare specimens of arms and armour.
Many fine pictures, chiefly portraits, adorn the walls
of nearly all the state rooms, and in the chapel are
specimens of beautiful French glass.

Not least of the charms of Hatfield is the park, nine
miles round, and traversed by magnificent avenues of
stately trees. Most visitors desire to see Queen
Elizabeth's Oak. This is now a sad ruin, and is carefully railed in from relic-hunters. The beautiful
gardens are laid out
with exquisite taste,
and one of the older
features of the grounds
surrounding the house
is an elaborate Maze.

Considering the past
of the manor, with its
royal and ecclesiastical
history, we should ex-
pect to find a large and
important church in

ENTRANCE GATES, HATFIELD.

Hatfield. Here we are not disappointed, even if the
drastic restoration of 1872 has, to a certain extent,
taken away some of the interest of the building, though
it brought to light the piscinæ in the chancel and
north transept.

The spacious cruciform church of St. Etheldreda is
of the Decorated period with a relic of an earlier
structure in the Norman arch of the south transept.
The chief interest is naturally in the Salisbury Chapel
on the left of the chancel, divided therefrom by an
ornate ironwork screen and an arcade upon classic
columns. The most imposing tomb in the church is

that of Sir Robert Cecil, Secretary of State and Lord High Treasurer of England under Walsingham. His effigy reposes upon a slab upheld by four kneeling figures. On the south of the chancel is the Brocket Chapel, in which are memorials of the former owners of Brocket Hall. The helmet of Sir John Brocket will be seen upon the wall above his tomb. The church possesses many fine modern details, and among these the reredos, of exceptional beauty, and the delicate marble shafts of the font, presented by the late March-ioness of Salisbury, call for special notice.

From Hatfield, a delightful ramble may be taken through leafy lanes in the direction of North Mimms, through a country beautiful enough in a quiet way to bear comparison with many better known districts of the Home Counties. This is a region of parklands, of which North Mimms Park is not the least, either in size or diversity of scenery. North Mimms village is quite charming, with a church to be described as a small museum of memorials, chiefly consisting of brasses, but including an elaborate erection in black marble to Lord Somers of Evesham, and the interesting Beresford altar tomb. Between the village and the main Hatfield–London highway is Brockmans Park, another extensive and delightful domain, of especial beauty in the fall of the year. Beyond the main road, a series of unfrequented lanes, more or less haphazard in direction, encircle the heights of Northaw and Cuffley, The latter, since the opening of the new loop-line rail-way to the north, is becoming rapidly built over ; but Northaw is still rural, and stands in a countryside that, considering its accessibility to moderate walkers, is strangely unknown to the townsman. For a brief space during the European War, however, these quiet

lanes were thronged with curious sightseers, who came
not only from the Metropolis, but from all parts of
England, to see the remains of a German airship,
brought down in flames upon one of these upland
meadows. The event is recorded upon a memorial,
erected at Cuffley through the instrumentality of a
well-known newspaper.

The busy London road continues through Potter's
Bar, another straggling village with new roads springing up between it and the railway station; and then,
skirting Wrotham Park, it crosses what was once
known as Gladmore Common, famous as the scene of
the Battle of Barnet and commemorated by an obelisk
called Hadley High Stone. Tradition says that at
this spot fell Warwick and his brother Montacute.
The engagement was fought on Easter Sunday, 1471,
and ended in victory for Edward IV after a stubborn
fight which lasted nearly all day.

Hadley Woods, a place of little solitude on holidays,
is close to the south-east of the common, and Monken
Hadley—to give the place its correct but little-used
name—is on the Enfield road in the western portion
of the wooded country once enclosed under the name
of Enfield Chase. The interesting church has an
ancient iron cresset fixed upon the lofty turret. This
was used upon dark nights to guide the wayfarer
through the wild thickets to the east. The old ruined
oak near the church was immortalized by Lytton in
The Last of the Barons. Another famous tree, now an
ivy-covered shell, stands near the road going south to
Cock Fosters. This is known as Latimer's Elm, and
tradition has it that the great reformer on occasion
preached beneath it. Before leaving Hadley, it must
be remembered that the grandfather of Thackeray

lived at the Grange, and was buried in the church-yard.

The large and populous town lying to the south-west of the woods is made up of High, or Chipping, Barnet and East Barnet. Both are ancient places with independent histories, and both are now joined by the suburban extension called New Barnet. Friern Barnet is over the county border in Middlesex, and is separated from the others by Whetstone. High Barnet was once ecclesiastically subject to its sister town upon the east and consisted, as its alternative name implies, of the market upon the high road. The church was probably founded in the thirteenth century as a chapel of ease, but little of this building remains, and a later enlargement of 1399 by Abbot John de la Monte of St. Albans, under whose manorial jurisdiction both town and church then stood, was largely improved away by a nineteenth-century restoration. At this time the present tower was built. The Ravenscroft Memorials are the chief interest apart from one or two noteworthy embellishments of recent date. One of these Ravens-crofts—James, who died in 1680—founded the Jesus Hospital in Wood Street, actually an almshouse of the usual type.

East Barnet church was also founded by an Abbot of St. Albans in the first years of the twelfth century. The building is very ancient, and the north wall is considered to be part of the first Norman building. In a house which stood near the church, and has long since disappeared, the Lady Arabella Stuart was kept prisoner. Another historic mansion called Mount Pleasant once stood upon the site of Belmont House. This was the home of Will Howard, Warden of the Marches, immortalized in *The Lay of the Last Minstrel*.

At the foot of Barnet Hill, we are within the sphere of influence of the electric trams which roar and rattle through Whetstone to Finchley and Highgate. To the east of this road is Friern Barnet, which gets its name from a one-time Friary of the Order of St. John of Jerusalem. Upon the site a mansion belonging to the descendants of Lord Bacon was erected. Some of this family were buried outside the church, a small building of several styles commencing with the Norman of the doorway. The Campe Almshouses, built by a London tradesman in 1612, are extremely picturesque, but every other vestige of the past is being rapidly overwhelmed by the advancing tide of London.

TRINITY COLLEGE, CAMBRIDGE.

CHAPTER V

TOWARDS CAMBRIDGE

THE fate of Friern Barnet, referred to in the closing words of the last chapter, is also that with which Southgate is threatened. The name of the latter village denotes that here was the southern approach to the great forest of Enfield, and remnants of the dense woodlands which extended over the stretch of country between the Lea Valley and the Barnet Hills are apparent in the many venerable trees and the number of enclosed parklands which still persist hereabouts. Of these, Arno's Grove and Grovelands are the finest, and both contain some grand timber. Isolated specimens of fine old trees may be found by the roadside all the way to Cock Fosters, where the conspicuous church spire rises high above the ridge running towards Hadley.

On the north side of Southgate, we reach a quiet stretch of open country traversed by the road going to Enfield; this we propose to take. It cannot be

said that the environs of this old town are anything
but suburban, though the market-place retains much
of its ancient character and the large thirteenth-century
church, drastically restored, is still interesting. It is
worth entering, if only to see the fine tomb of Lady
Tiptoft, who died in 1446. She is represented by a
brass effigy, and the curious in such matters may study
the details of her fifteenth-century costume. Two
seventeenth-century memorials of Sir Nicholas Raynton,
a Lord Mayor of London, and of Martha Palmer are
worthy of notice, and a tablet tells us that the famous
medico, Dr. Abernethy, died here in 1831.

TEMPLE BAR.

The so-called Enfield Palace,
on the south side of High
Street, is but a small portion
of the building erected, it is
said, by Edward VI to house
his half-sister Elizabeth. Vandals of the late eighteenth century pulled down most of the
centre block and the whole of the north wing of this
mansion.

We now go northwards past Forty Hall, a house
built by Inigo Jones in 1630, and then by Forty Hill.
Just beyond the latter is Myddleton House. This
perpetuates the name of the engineer of the New River,
which flows near our road on the right. Crossing the
county boundary into Hertfordshire, we soon arrive
at the confines of Theobalds—" Tibbles "—Park.
The present mansion was built about 1770, and the
site of the old manor house is in the north-western
corner of the park. The fact that the estate stood in
the midst of the finest chase in south-eastern England
led the " British Solomon " to arrange the exchange

with Lord Burleigh, for James, although puny and weak in person, was passionately fond of hunting, and from Theobalds he could range over many miles of woodland, from the slopes of Barnet Hill almost to the vale of the Roding. The King died here in 1625, and it would appear that this was the only place in England, or in Britain for that matter, where he lost, for a time, his nervous fear of assassination. The chief interest of Theobalds to-day lies in the fact that the western entrance is formed by the re-erected Temple Bar, purchased by the then owner of the estate in 1888, after the jumble of stonework had lain derelict behind a hoarding in Farringdon Street for several years. The City authorities have since endeavoured to regain their slighted " Port," but without success.

Our way now goes eastwards by a lane crossing the New River, and entering the Ware road just north of Waltham Cross. To the latter we will first make a brief visit. The Cross is now a terminus of tramways which come hither from the confines of the City at Smithfield and elsewhere. The quaint sign of the " Four Swans," just north of the Cross, still swings across the road just beyond the reach of the electric wires. The well-known Eleanor Cross, much restored, but probably very like the original, was one of the several erected by Edward I on the route taken by the funeral journey of his Queen. It is a graceful and beautiful work worthy of better surroundings than the present commonplace and semi-suburban village street, though the varieties of stone used in its restoration have given it an unfortunate appearance of haphazard patchwork.

Waltham Cross is less than two miles from Waltham

Abbey, which lies across the water-logged meadows of the Lea, hereabouts given up to miles of glass-houses devoted chiefly to the culture of tomatoes for the London market. A visit to the Abbey church can only result in a renewed sense of sorrow for all we have lost through the base materialism rampant during the years of England's so-called " golden age," for, of the splendid church that stood here when the " Defender of the Faith " gave an unfulfilled promise to change its status from an Abbey church to that of a cathedral for Essex, only seven bays of the Norman nave remain to indicate its once imposing proportions. The base of the walls must incorporate some portion of the very building to which Harold's body was brought after Senlac. Before riding south to his fate, he had spent the last hours before the high altar which, a few years previously, had been consecrated in the presence of Edward the Confessor. The building replaced an earlier church of more modest dimensions erected not long before to enshrine a miraculous cross discovered at Montacute in distant Somerset.

The chancel is modern, but a chapel and crypt on the south side belong to the fourteenth century, and among the older details will be seen a Norman font ; not, however, contemporary with the early building. The chief interest for amateur antiquaries appears to be connected with the old stocks and whipping-post, brought here from without the Abbey Gate. This picturesque survival forms almost the sole remaining portion of the conventual buildings.

We must now retrace our steps and follow the main road to the north through Cheshunt—by the evidence of its ancient name—" Cestrehunt "—a station on the Roman road, here called Ermine Street. At an inn near the station there is an undoubted Roman urn built into the wall, and this forms the " sign " of the hostelry. The urn was discovered near by in the early part of the last century.

Cheshunt church has many memorials and brasses of sufficient interest to warrant us in turning aside, and the building itself is a good specimen of early

WALTHAM ABBEY.

Perpendicular. Cheshunt College was founded in South Wales in 1768 by the Countess of Huntingdon, and removed here after the death of that exemplary peeress. Richard Cromwell, nonenity and son of the Protector, retired to Cheshunt at the Restoration and Cardinal Wolsey lived for a time in the village. It is now the home chiefly of those City men who are unconventional enough to chose a semi-rural retreat above the Lea Valley.

Wormley is a little over two miles farther on. It

possesses an ancient church at Wormley Bury, some distance to the west of the main road, in a pretty undulating district that extends from Goff's Oak—a hamlet to the south-west named after a once magnificent tree—to Little Berkhampstead, away to the north-west, where Bishop Ken was born. The latter place is better reached from Broxbourne, though the detour is hardly justified with so much of greater interest before us.

The tiny bourne, running into the Lea hereabouts, was once the haunt of brocks, or badgers, hence the name—Broxbourne. It is still a country village, though the banks of the river in the vicinity have of late years become popular as a summer bungalow resort. Of the blocks of cheap dwellings in the immediate vicinity, brought into being through the urgent need of accommodation for local workers, the less said the better. Nothing yet, however, has spoilt the charmingly quiet and restful scenery of the river towards Ware and Hertford, and the tranquil vale of the Stort, which opens out near Roydon to meet the Lea. There are few more effective pictures upon our home waterways than that of the Lea just above Broxbourne bridge. The church rises high above the river bank, and the surrounding foliage frames a graceful arch spanning the stream below. The Perpendicular building, now belonging to the much older tower, though severely restored, is interesting, and contains an archaic Norman font on eight columns and an early brass of a priest, besides several other ancient memorials and effigies.

It is pleasanter to walk by the river to Hoddesdon than to take the dusty and motor-crowded high road, and as we proceed the scenery is found to be rapidly improving. At Hoddesdon we are on the classic ground of the " Compleat Angler," though the house referred to by Izaak Walton is no longer in existence. The old " Bull Inn," immortalized by Prior, still remains, and with the fine seventeenth-century Rawdon House, now a convent, constitutes all there is of note in this pleasant town.

The main road now divides, that on the right hand going to Ware, Buntingford and the north, while the left-hand way leads by Haileybury to Hertford ; this route it is purposed to follow, but before doing so a glance must first be given to Rye House—little more than a mile from Hoddesdon on the road that goes through Roydon to Harlow.

To the excursionist, the Rye House Plot is of secondary interest to the Great Bed of Ware, but history must be briefly dealt with first. Rye House, originally a fortified manor in the reign of Henry VI, was in 1683 the property of a Colonel Rumbold who had commenced his military career in the army of the Parliament under Fairfax. Rumbold had never become reconciled to the Restoration, and the dissolute life of Charles and his court was, no doubt, an excuse in the minds of this old republican and his associates for the crime they contemplated. This was to waylay and kill the King and his brother on their return to town from Newmarket. The King failed to turn up to time, and the facts, and a good deal of fiction also, leaked out. Lord Russell of Chenies and Algernon Sidney were implicated and executed, while the real culprit escaped to the Continent. He was so ill-advised as to accompany the abortive expedition of Argyll, and was caught and hanged in Edinburgh.

The Great Bed of Ware is a super-couch almost quite square in shape, and capable of holding twelve persons. It is massively built of oak, curiously carved and ornamented, and was brought to its present home about sixty years ago. It is almost all there is of antiquity for visitors to see at Rye House, for the scanty remnants of the building in which the plot was hatched are not easily identified.

Haileybury, less than two miles from Hoddesdon and about the same distance from Hertford, was originally the training school of the East India Company. It is a fine and imposing pile, with a dome conspicuous from many distant parts of Hertfordshire and commanding equally extensive views. Haileybury has of late years risen to a high position among the great schools of England. In passing it, we shall notice the grand avenue of chestnuts leading up from the entrance gates and, if the hour is propitious, a visit to the beautiful school chapel will repay the traveller.

The road descends to the capital of Hertfordshire, which lies upon the south bank of the Lea, and *may* be the " Ford of the Hart " as the Borough arms have it, but is more probably the Herudsford—" red ford " —of the early chronicles. That a town of sorts stood here many years before the Saxons ascended the river valley is fairly certain; but its pages of authentic history open with the story of the first Council of the English Church, held here in 673, as told by the Venerable Bede, who also records that ingenious device of the great Alfred for defeating invaders who came by water. When the Danes sailed or rowed their sea-craft all the way from London River to the stockades of Herudsford, the brainy monarch diverted the course of the stream, and left the pirate navy high and dry, and entirely at the mercy of his pleased subjects.

Edward the Elder built a castle at Herudsford which was improved and enlarged by the Normans, and a few vestiges of this fortress may still be traced. Of the old church of All Saints barely as much remains, for it was destroyed by a disastrous fire in 1891. The fine modern building which replaces it is slightly larger than the original structure. Another new church—St. Andrew's—stands in the centre of the town close to the ugly Shire Hall. There is really little to see in this county centre, and it does not compare in interest with those other towns of Hertfordshire already visited. It is much less picturesque than its near neighbour— Ware—easily reached by a pleasant path along the river bank which passes

MALT HOUSES, WARE.

near the spot where the Lord Protector nipped the " Leveller " mutiny in the bud by shooting its leader. Another way is through Bengeo, on the low hills to the north. Here is an Early Norman church and several old cottages, and the Italianate mansion in Ware Park.

An idle hour may be spent in wandering through the by-ways of Ware—a place of pleasant odours, if the characteristic scent which hangs around malt houses can be so described. For Ware, despite these evil days of chemical beer, is still the centre of the industry of which the county capital has, or had, its full share. The golden days of the trade are no more ; machinery as well as other modern methods in the manufacture of malt liquors, have seen to this, but at one time it might have been said that at least every second adult in Ware was directly concerned in the conversion of barley into malt.

The town is not without interest to the antiquary. Its name is said to be derived from the great weir constructed by the Danes for their fleet " dock." The cruciform church is mainly of the Decorated period, with Perpendicular additions, much restored, but retaining a good carved screen between transept and Lady Chapel, and several ancient memorials. The tower is crowned by the characteristic small and slender spire of Hertfordshire and Essex, and it contains a tuneful chime. Near the church stood a priory of Franciscans. A few fragments of the ancient buildings are incorporated in the residence known as Ware Priory. Several medieval houses remain in the town, especially in the narrow streets turning off High Street. The old " Saracen's Head " was, for a time, the home of the Great Bed until that was spirited away to Rye House. It was originally housed at Ware Priory.

A pleasant round of some four or five miles through Amwell and Stanstead Abbots, or farther—to Hunsdon and Widford—might well be made before we continue the exploration to the north ; or better still, this digression can be made an original way of starting for Cambridge, of which it is intended to catch a flying glimpse.

Great Amwell is across the Lea, near the commencement of the New River. The hero of that undertaking stands upon an island in the stream not far from the village street—still as pleasant as when it was so described by Charles Lamb. The church forms a picturesque object among the fine trees which clothe the low hill behind it. Round the bend of the high road below we should look for the ghost of a famous rider. Gilpin's journey was as nearly finished as the horseman himself when his steed raced down the slope to Amwell End.

Passing the station of St. Margaret's, we cross the Lea again, and ascend the gentle slope crowned by the old flint-walled church of Stanstead. The pleasant village contains almshouses named after a famous local family—the Baeshes—who have their own chapel on the north side of the church. About two miles north-east of Stansted is Hunsdon, where there is another fine church dating from the fifteenth century and, not far away, the historic Hunsdon House, built on the site of a Tudor royal palace ; though the original building antedated that period, for it was erected by a Sir John Oldhall in the reign of the fourth Edward.

Widford, another haunt of Lamb, is but a short distance to the north. Here again is an interesting old church containing an east window commemorating a forgotten but once famous missionary pioneer and native of this village—John Eliot, who gave his best years to the natives of the American Colonies.

We may with profit proceed up the valley of the Ash to the ancient town of Much Hadham, for the scenery, though quiet and pastoral, is in places well above the average of that to be found in the country north-east of London. It becomes pleasantly undulating between Hadham and Buntingford, where the last low folds of the Chilterns retain much of their characteristic beauty.

Much Hadham church is in a pretty situation close to the river, and is well worth inspection. It is Early

English in style, with a fine south porch and several monuments of ancient date. Katherine Tudor, mother of Henry VI, lived for a time at Hadham House, and here a son was born, afterwards known as Edmund of Hadham. Standon, nearly three miles farther, and not far from the main road to the north which we left at Ware, is another ancient place with a church containing evidence—apparent only to the complete antiquary—of Saxon work. The structure is peculiar in plan, the tower being separate from the body of the building. A Roman Catholic college, first established at Twyford in Hampshire, flourishes at Standon.

The Old North Road is rejoined in the narrow village street of Puckeridge, where the Cambridge road debouches to the right and presently passes through Broughing—called "Braffing"—the site of a Roman station on the Ermine Street, and now a picturesque and old-fashioned village through which the little river Quin meanders among pleasant water-meadows at the foot of low hills. Our road is by the left-hand way, and we follow up another shallow valley—that of the Rib. Considerable parklands extend upon the western side thereof. This way soon brings us to Buntingford, over ten miles by the direct road from Ware, but considerably more by the roundabout route we have taken.

It is said that Buntingford contains more old houses than any other town in Hertfordshire of a similar size. This may well be accepted, even after the most casual stroll, for the little town is full of quaint corners and uneven gables ; but with all its old-world air, its history is quite uneventful. The church stands in the centre of the town and makes up for an almost total lack of interest by its commanding position. The structure dates only from the early years of the seventeenth century, for Buntingford was merely a roadside settlement, and the parish church was at Layston, nearly a mile distant. That church is now a ruin, and the village, if village there ever was, has entirely disappeared. We shall see the old town " pound " as we pass through the north end, and presently, on the right, the fine manor house called Corney Bury.

The route now traverses the almost perfectly straight course of the Ermine Street which rises steadily to Buckland, a small village with a restored Early English church. Thence across the chalk hills, here seldom rising above the contour line of four hundred feet, but imposing nevertheless in their bold rolling outlines, nothing is passed worthy of record until Royston, lying at the foot of a long descent on the northern side of the uplands, is entered. The town stands upon the junction of the ancient road we have been following with that still older trackway—the Icknield Way, and its foundations must therefore belong to a very remote past. It is a place of narrow and tortuous streets with many old buildings and ancient inns, of which the ' Plough " is the most noticeable, but the chief interest centres in the remarkable cave beneath the Market Place, to which a modern passage-way has been made. It is believed to be of prehistoric origin, and was accidentally rediscovered during the eighteenth century. Since then, it has been decorated by some very amateur craftsmen with a number of carvings in the chalk representing kings and other celebrities. One monarch —Louis XVIII of France—visited the cave in person, and the stranger in search of the curious should certainly see it.

Royston was once the home of a monastery founded

in the time of the second Henry, and the church is a remnant—much altered and enlarged—of that establishment.   It is a fine and spacious building containing some interesting brasses and the alabaster effigy of a knight.   The town was a resort of royalty in the early seventeenth century, for the poor remains of the Old Palace at Royston Heath mark the site of a hunting-box of James I, in which his unfortunate son was temporarily lodged while a prisoner in the hands of the Parliament.

Space will not allow any record of the villages between Royston and Cambridge, and, to be candid, there is little which calls for remark until the East Anglian University town is reached.   This we propose to do by rail, arriving at the busy railway junction, still retaining the curious anomaly of one platform for both "up" and "down" traffic.   Its extraordinary length is surely the bleakest waiting-place in England, for it is exposed to the full blast of the easterly gales which charge across the Fens with nothing but an occasional row of railway trucks to break their force.

The approach to the centre of Cambridge from the station is no more impressive than the mean street which leads from the Great Western Railway to Carfax in the city on the Isis.   Most towns in England present their least interesting side to the traveller who arrives by rail.   The majority of the London termini have depressing surroundings, while on the Continent these first impressions are usually well looked after, though few foreign towns can show a scene of such romantic beauty as that which greets one on emerging from the Waverley station in Edinburgh.   But this is a digression, and we may safely take taxi or bus along the commonplace Hills Road, with its conventional War

Memorial, if no further than its junction with the equally dingy Regent Street. Where these thorough-fares meet stands the magnificent and ornate Roman Catholic church. Needless to say, the building is always open during ordinary daylight hours. It is a really splendid example of modern Decorated Gothic, exceedingly dignified and imposing, and without the garish and tawdry ornaments which so often mar the interior of churches belonging to the Roman communion.

On the same side of Regent Street is Downing College, an uninteresting building in Classic style, but surrounded by wide lawns and brilliant flower-beds. On the right of the main street, and behind its houses, is the large and rather dull expanse of Parker's Piece —the town playground—which has the Borough gaol on its south and Cambridge Castle mound on its north side. This was the fortress erected in 1068 by William, and from which he directed the long opera-tions against Hereward the Wake in his Fenland stronghold. St. Andrew's Street continues the main artery at the point occupied by Emmanuel College. This is a structure in a variety of styles with a chapel designed by Wren. Farther on is Christ's College, in which Milton was educated. This once picturesque building has been spoilt by injudicious restoration. Here Hobson's Lane bears off to the right, and perpetu-ates the name of a noted Cambridge worthy—carrier and livery stableman—whose queer method of dealing out his horses in strict rotation gave rise to the phrase —" Hobson's choice."

We have now reached the best end of the town, and towers, pinnacles and gables of much architectural beauty appear over the lower house-tops, and close

the vista of each narrow lane. Sidney Street takes
us past the gimcrack Gothic of Sidney Sussex College,
in the original building of which Oliver Cromwell
failed to take a degree ; and then Jesus Lane leads
eastwards to Jesus College, where Archbishop Cranmer
was a student—a place of lovely old brickwork, picturesque quadrangles and a chapel which was once part
of the conventual church of a Benedictine convent.
Here, in the south transept, is some of the oldest
masonry in Cambridge, for in its walls is a part of the
original Norman structure.   In front of the entrance to
the college stands the fine modern church of All Saints.

Beyond Jesus Lane, the main thoroughfare becomes
Bridge Street. Upon the right-hand side is the
" Round Church," or St. Sephulchres, said to be the
oldest of the four round churches in England, or
which the Temple Church in London is the most
famous, as it is also the finest. Our way presently
crosses the Cam, upon the farther bank being Magdalen
a building very different in appearance to its namesake upon Thames-side. In the college garden is the
vallum of the Roman " chester." For the original
name of the town was Grantacaestir, a name perpetuated by a village two miles away. This becomes
Grantebrig when the fortress lost its importance, and
the modern name is merely a corruption of this. So
there is actually no river Cam. Already a laudable
tendency to revert to the original " Granta," a name of
great antiquity, is rife. Above the bridge, occupying
both banks, are the buildings of St. John's. The
modern chapel, with its great square tower, overshadow
St. John's Street, and is the most conspicuous building
in this part of the town. It is one of the best known
and most criticized works of Sir Gilbert Scott, but i

is impossible not to admire the vast interior with its overwhelming sense of space and height. The Great Hall, on the south of the chapel, is mainly old work of the sixteenth century, to which period most of the courts belong. If we may restrict our record to the mention of but one great name associated with the colleges passed, Wordsworth must be mentioned in connexion with St. John's.

We reach the " backs " by the " Bridge of Sighs," and so come to that outer aspect of Cambridge in which it may fairly chal-lenge Oxford, for if the East Anglian town has no superb street vista such as we have seen in the west, so Oxford has nothing upon its two rivers to com-pare with these exquisite lawns and avenues. In no other town in England can so much stately grace be found disposed in one spot.

BRIDGE OF SIGHS, ST. JOHN'S.

In the several bridges, the fine trees, the smooth green carpet and the clear waters of the stream beneath, there is not one incongruous note.

To cross the river by Trinity Bridge is to come to yet another imposing group of buildings. Here, in Trinity, Sir Isaac Newton took his degree. The hall dates from 1608, and the chapel is about fifty years older, though much of the interior is eighteenth-century work. The town is approached from this college by a magnificent gateway, begun in the reign of Edward IV and finished in the reign of that Henry whose rotund effigy so unmistakably adorns it. Across the way is the modern Whewells Hostel and, to the left of it, the Divinity Schools.

We now come to Gonville and Caius—colloquially " Keys." Here must be mentioned two names, those of Lord Thurlow and Judge Jeffreys, one a famous and the other an infamous representative of the law. The classic pile of the Senate House comes next, and then the University Library, where is housed one of the most famous of all books—the Codex Bezae, a sixth-century copy of the Gospels and Acts. Opposite the Senate House is the University Church—Great Saint Mary's, late Perpendicular, much restored, and not equal in beauty to its namesake in Oxford. To the east of St. Mary's are Market Hill, the Guildhall and the narrow street of shops called Petty Cury.

By way of Trinity Hall and Clare, we approach the best thing in Cambridge—Kings—and see on the way the river front of Clare and the beautiful Clare Bridge.

Much of the architecture of King's College is mediocre, and the new court compares favourably with the older buildings, in one of which were the rooms of Sir Horace Walpole ; but its chapel ranks among the finest ecclesiastical buildings in England. The magnificent vaulting and the glorious stained glass are superb. The latter dates principally from the early sixteenth century. The length of the building is that of a cathedral—316 feet, and from the roof ninety feet above the ground, a cathedral can be seen for on clear days the lantern of Ely is plainly visible fourteen miles away to the north.

To the antiquary, the most interesting object in the town is St. Benet's Church with its unmistakable Saxon tower. It is *possible* that the earliest portion o the building dates from the end of the sixth century

it is certainly not later than 650. The dim interior
has an overwhelming effect of age, and a brief visit
must on no account be omitted. A queer little churchyard hides itself away upon the south side, a place of
rank growths, and very eerie after twilight has fallen.

Our way now takes us along Trumpington Street,
in which is St. Catherine's, or " Cats," opposite Corpus
Christi, where Archbishop Parker was Master. The
square-pinnacled tower on the right is not that of a
church, but marks the Pitt Press, analogous to the
Clarendon Press at
Oxford. Queens',
down Silver Street
to the right, pos-
sesses one of the
most picturesque
courts in the Uni-
versity, and after
seeing it we may
cross the river again
to walk where once

TRUMPINGTON STREET.

Erasmus paced. He occupied rooms at Queens' during his Cambridge professorship.

There now remain but Pembroke, with its quaint
turret built by Wren, and Peterhouse, oldest of the
colleges, for it was founded in 1281. Here Archbishop
Whitgift, Cardinal Beaufort, Thomas Gray, and Lord
Kelvin were educated. Much new building, of stately
elevation, is proceeding as these lines are written.
Not only has Peterhouse a fine annexe, but additional
buildings are going up at Trinity Hall and King's.
Perhaps the best thing that has lately happened to
architectural Cambridge is the removal of the trees in
Tree Court, Caius.

L

The fine front of the Fitzwilliam Museum, irreverently "the Fitzwilly," is the last notable building. An hour or so could profitably be devoted to its galleries. Afterwards, the Botanic Gardens may be taken on the way back to the station.

On the return journey, and soon after leaving Cambridge, certain low "hills" on the left front will be seen. These are the celebrated "Gog and Magogs," which in any other locality than East Anglia would be entirely unnoticed. Soon Great Chesterford is reached, where the journey by road may be resumed. Chesterford was a Roman station, and an important native centre before that, for in the museum at Saffron Walden are a host of local relics, upturned by pick and spade, belonging to that long period which divides the days of the Eagles from those of Neolithic man. Ancient walls of defence stood around the town as lately as the sixteenth century, but now there is little of antiquity remaining. The church dates mainly from the years that saw the disappearance of the walls.

From Chesterford, the walk up the eastern side of the valley of the infant Cam, or Granta, is pleasant and picturesque. We pass close to Little Chesterford church, where there is a curious wooden sedilia and a Norman font. Then the road climbs over a hill partially covered with thick copse, and the scenery becomes really beautiful as the old town of Saffron Walden is approached. Low but well-wooded uplands surround the place on the west and north, and the gentle slopes towards the Cam and Audley End are reminiscent of the West Country.

Saffron Walden may well be described as the pleasantest town in Essex, as it is also one of the most interesting. The one-time cultivation of the crocus

in the immediate vicinity gave the place its name.
and the flower is emblazoned upon the borough arms,
The trade in saffron, both as condiment and dye, was
an important item between the years 1420–1700.
After that date its culture rapidly declined, though
Walden has continued to be a thriving agricultural
centre. Its position, somewhat off both the main line
of railway to Cambridge and the eastern of the trunk
roads to that town and beyond, has done much to
preserve its ancient character, for ancient it undoubtedly is. An earthwork of some strength near the
centre of the town points to a very early origin, and
upon Castle Hill is one of those mysterious cuttings
in the chalk known as a " maze," the use of which
has never been satisfactorily explained ; but it was
doubtless a parade ground for warriors. On this same
hill, the Normans erected a strong fortress upon the
site of a Saxon stronghold. The lower portions of
the keep still remain, but give little indication of the
former size of the Castle.

The magnificent church on the opposing hill to the
north is one of the finest in Essex, and its lofty spire
is a conspicuous landmark for miles around. The
architecture is entirely of Perpendicular date, and
though some of the details are of poor quality, the
nave would not disgrace a cathedral, so wonderful is
its air of space and dignity. The imposing appearance
of the interior has gained recently by the erection of a
large oak screen.

Some time may be spent in examining the exteriors
of the old houses which abound in the town. Several
remarkable examples of plaster work may be seen,
though most of them are obvious restorations. An
even longer time should be given to the Museum, than

which there is no better example in eastern England of how such an institution should be arranged and managed.

The beautiful park of Audley End is reached by Abbey Lane, passing a picturesque range of alms-houses originally founded in 1404 by a Bishop of London named Roger of Walden. To obtain a glimpse of the mansion, we take the public footpath through the park, and then descend to the old stone bridge across the Granta, after passing on the left the little hamlet of Audley End. The great house has been described as the most splendid in Essex. It might well be placed among the finest half-dozen in Britain. Like so many others, it occupies the site of a monastery of Benedictines. At the Suppression, the property of the church was granted to the Lord Chancellor, Sir Thomas Audley. Of the original monastic buildings, only the guest house—now a range of stables—remains, though the Abbey Farm, between the mansion and the town, still exists for a benevolent purpose. Audley End House was built in the early years of the seventeenth century, and was then apparently double the size of the pile we see to-day, for the enormous cost of keeping this great palace in repair led to the demolition of the western portion about 1750.

It is in the lovely surroundings of this grand specimen of Renaissance architecture that the principal charm of Audley End to the chance wayfarer consists. Strangers to the district will experience a surprise when the beauty of these East Anglian hills and dales are discovered within a county the name of which is to many a mere synonym for the tame and dull in scenery. Although only a few miles from the borders of Hertfordshire, it must be said that very few localities in the latter county—which, as we have seen, possesses some of the best scenery in the Chilterns—can surpass in beauty the twelve square miles or so around Walden.

From the town, a road running in a south-easterly direction traverses a sparsely populated country, passing only one small straggling hamlet called Howlett End on the long seven miles which will bring us to Thaxted. Until quite recently, this ancient one-time borough was quite cut off from communication with the outer world except by road; but now there is a light railway extension from the main Cambridge line at Elsenham, and a vehicle of the type that ignores all social distinctions—in other words, a "rail-motor" —makes the journey several times a day.

Thaxted, like Walden, enjoys the distinction of possessing one of the finest churches in Essex, and had the town been situated in a more convenient and accessible position, it would undoubtedly have been chosen as the cathedral of the Essex diocese. The exterior of the building is remarkable as being practically all in one style—fifteenth-century Perpendicular, though in the interior, especially on the south side, there is a certain amount of work dating from about 1320–60. The handsome tower and stone spire are in themselves unusual and noteworthy in East Anglia and it is in the fine exterior that this great church excels. The ornamental details—crockets, niches and gargoyles; the graceful buttresses of the spire; the pinnacles of the transepts—all come as a great surprise to the visitor who has hitherto had an acquaintance with only the generally small and plain village churches of Essex. It is surprising also that the medieval stone crucifixes in the gables of the east end and north porch have been retained. The interior is almost equally imposing, and it contains, apart from the elaborate modern furnishings, much medieval enrichment. The font cover and pulpit are particularly fine, and there is a beautiful reredos of clunch stone in the north transept.

Thaxted became a borough in the reign of Mary Tudor, and retained this status for little more than one hundred years. The old Guild Hall is now a parish room. It is an ancient timber building with an open space beneath the upper storey where the town market was once held. There are several old timber and plaster houses in the narrow streets.

THAXTED.

One, marked by the arms of Edward IV and possessing oriel windows, is a pleasing example of this style of domestic architecture.

Our next halting-place is to be Great D u n m o w—seven miles from Thaxted by the most direct road through a hamlet named Monk Street. A more interesting route, about ten miles in all, is through Broxted. This road takes us very near the once fine, but now much restored, old mansion called Horsham Hall, built in the reign of Henry VIII. It is about two miles from Thaxted, on the right of the Elsenham road. The house, which is of brick, was one of the temporary homes of Elizabeth during the reign of her half-sister, and it was the scene of a magnificent merrymaking of the sort that usually accompanied the tours of the great Queen when she revisited the Hall in 1571.

Our road winds through an undulating country interspersed with pleasant woodlands, and with every indication of successful farming. Presently we reach the villages of Chickney and Broxted, the former a little to the west of the road, with a church containing the remains of an earlier Saxon building. Broxted church is overmuch restored and uninteresting. Just beyond this village, we take the right-hand, though not the nearest, road to Dunmow, and after another three miles pass close to Easton Lodge—possibly best known as the scene of many of the social activities of the Countess of Warwick, who, quite recently, offered the house as a headquarters for the proposed Labour College. It was the property of the Maynards from the time of its erection in 1595 until the middle of the last century, when the Countess inherited the house and estates from the last of the line. Though the great mansion is picturesque and still retains much old work, certain portions are obviously Victorian restorations. This is, to a great extent, due to a disastrous fire in 1847, which gutted part of the building and destroyed a great quantity of its precious contents. An extensive park with fine timber surrounds the mansion, and within its confines stands the parish church of Little Easton, containing several memorials of the Maynards. Of particular interest is the splendid tomb of the first Earl and Countess of Essex with its effigies of enamelled brass. Another brass effigy of a priest, Robert Pyn, of the early fifteenth century, is also noteworthy. The church, though handsomely furnished, has a look of newness due to over-restoration.

At Great Easton, which lies some distance north of our road, is another restored church originally Norman.

Not far from the village is a mysterious mound surrounded by a moat. Its origin and purpose are unknown; it may be Roman work, or perhaps of even earlier date, but it is generally described as a small Saxon "burh."

We are now approaching Dunmow: like Thaxted, a decayed wool mart and one-time borough, a status lost in 1886. It was probably a station on the Roman road from St. Albans to Colchester, and is still marked "Caesaromagus" by the ordnance survey. The town is usually connected with the "Dunmow Flitch." The scene of this ancient ceremony was at Little Dunmow, nearly three miles to the east. Great Dunmow has but few old houses, and the town hall, erected in the time of Elizabeth, was so much altered and restored during the last century that it is now without any interest. The large Decorated church has also suffered in this way, but it contains a few medieval fittings, and possesses a good south porch.

Little Dunmow Church was once part of an Augustinian priory founded in 1104 by a lady of the locality named Baynard. Her effigy is still to be seen within the building, together with those of two Fitzwalters of the twelfth century. It was a member of this family who, in the reign of the third Henry, is said to have instituted the flitch of bacon competition for those who could take oath, in olden days before the Prior himself, that they were unrepentant of their marriage for a period of not less than a year and a day. The original Prior's Chair, which is kept in the chancel, was at one time used to "chair" the successful competitor. Latterly the rather vulgar celebration of this old custom has taken place at Ilford.

Those adventurers who desire to penetrate to the

more remote parts of north-eastern Essex will find
Dunmow a convenient place from which to extend
their journey. Braintree is eight miles by rail and
road on the way to Colchester. It is a very ancient
place on the Stane Street, and numberless relics of
prehistoric days have been discovered under the town,
while the remains of a " camp " in some private grounds
are said to be of Roman origin. Braintree church is
a large building of different periods, greatly restored,
but also of much interest to the antiquary. A short
distance north is the
fine church at Bock-
ing, a " peculiar " of
Canterbury and so
giving its incumbent
the title, puzzling
to the layman, of
" Dean of Bocking."
Six miles farther is
Coggeshall, on the
Blackwater, c e l e -
brated for the beauti-

St. Botolph's Priory Ruins,
Colchester.

ful Tudor mansion called Peaycocks House, and a handsome Perpendicular church. Across the river at Little
Coggeshall are the ruins of a Cistercian abbey, situated
close to a notable sixteenth-century house, and a little
old church that had for many years been used as a barn.

Colchester, nine miles from Coggeshall, is almost, if
not quite, the most interesting town in East Anglia,
though more for its past history than for its present
sights. The great Norman castle covers the remains
of Roman buildings, for this was the important centre
called Camulodunum. The greater part of the original
Roman walls still defy the centuries. In later days,

two great religious houses flourished in the town—the Benedictine Abbey of St. John Baptist, and the Augustinian Priory of St. Botolph. The ruins of the church belonging to the latter still exist, but of the abbey, only the gateway and a few fragments of wall remain. In addition, the town possesses a church—Holy Trinity—with a Saxon tower, and in this, as in several other of the eight churches, Roman brickwork and masonry have been built into the fabric.

From Colchester, railways and roads strike onward in several directions to the coast. One goes north-east for Manningtree, Dovercourt and Harwich at the mouths of the Stour and Orwell. Another goes east to those bracing little pleasure towns—Walton-on-the-Naze, Frinton, and Clacton ; and yet a third to less sophisticated Brightlingsea, at the mouth of the Essex Colne and opposite Mersea Island—not the "abode of desolation" it has been called, but worth visiting by the tourist in search of a district still quite remote from main roads and motors.

To the south of Dunmow is another little-known countryside—the region of the Roothings, or Rodings, and the Easters. The former string of villages follows the valley of the Roding River from High—to Beauchamp—Roding, a distance of about five miles. The Easters lie on the left of the vale, and are two in number—High and Good. At the former is a Saxon church built of Roman materials and with Perpendicular additions.

We may now, without losing much sightseeing, take the road or rail back to the Cambridge line at Bishop's Stortford. At Takeley, about half-way, there is another church showing Roman brickwork in the walling. It also possesses some finely carved bench ends. Here was once an alien priory, said to have been dedicated by the Normans to Saint Valery as a thank-offering for the saint's assistance in the matter of a favourable wind, when their fleet waited to descend upon the shores of Sussex. On the left of the road and railway are the remains of the ancient Hatfield Forest, and beyond this, over three miles from Takeley, is the old town of Hatfield Broad Oak. Here was another foreign " cell," and the interesting church once formed part of the priory.

Bishop's Stortford is a Hertfordshire town with suburbs in Essex. It is not impressive when first seen from the railway station, and for closer acquaintance one must penetrate to that portion of the town around and beyond the church. There still remain several quaint corners near the bridge over the Stort, but in the patchy rebuilding of the main street, much of the picturesque quality of the winding

THE " BLACK LION," BISHOPS STORT- FORD.

thoroughfare has been lost. The wide road north of the church is still unspoilt, and is lined with mellow old houses in great contrast to the lower part of the town. The Perpendicular church is of more interest than its rebuilt appearance would suggest. It is well placed upon the summit of Windhill, and many ancient dwellings line the narrow lanes climbing the south side of the Mount. Upon the opposite rising ground beyond the Stort once stood the Conqueror's castle of Waytemore, still marked by a moat and wall ; and some distance to the west of the town is the beautiful old manor house at Little Hadham. It has lofty hexagonal towers, and is one of the best specimens of the great country house in Hertfordshire. Lord Capel, the Caroline Royalist, lived here. He, it will be remembered, left his heart in a silver casket to be presented to Charles's heir, should he ever come to the throne. The casket was discovered fifty years after the Cavalier's death.

Of the other outstanding features of Stortford, we must not forget the celebrated Grammar School. Its most famous scholar was perhaps Cecil Rhodes, who was born in the town. The finest of the several old inns of Stortford is the " Black Lion," near the central bridge.

Road and railway now closely follow the river to Sawbridgeworth, which for some occult reason is occasionally called Sapsworth by the inhabitants. It is an ancient place, but has little of antiquity to show the visitor apart from the church, a Decorated structure containing several fine brasses and a handsome Perpendicular screen. Beyond the town, the road runs along the western boundary of Pishiobury Park. The house is one of Wyatt's grandiloquent erections.

We now cross the river and ascend the hill to Harlow, a small town in Essex, possessing a church—once Norman—built with Roman brick, and thus giving rise to interesting conjectures as to the early history of the place. The building has been so maltreated by various " restorers," who have followed up the damage caused by an eighteenth-century fire, that it is now of little interest. The almshouses, dated 1630, are picturesque and well preserved, and with the small farm building to the north of the church, known as Harlowbury Chapel, form the only noteworthy objects in the town. The latter is undoubtedly a Norman structure, and is said to be have been used by the abbots of St. Edmundsbury on their journeys to and from the metropolis.

The quietly beautiful Stort valley is seen at its best between Harlow and Roydon. The gentle slopes on either side of the river are pleasantly wooded, and the quality of the scenery of this corner of Essex is again a pleasant surprise to the uninitiated. Roydon, standing high above the river, is not the " King's Hill," for it was once called Woodredon, and was a much larger place and possessed a weekly market. The church is a well-proportioned Perpendicular building which has suffered from a mid-Victorian restoration. It re-tains several sixteenth-century brasses, and one to Thomas and Joan Colte dated 1471. This has the inscription " Edwardi regis consul honorificus." Here also is a thirteenth-century font, and a restored fourteenth-century rood screen. The

THE STORT AT ROYDON.

massive tower looks down upon a pleasant village green with ancient stocks and lock-up, and also the inevitable stone cross, " 1914–1918." But Roydon has also another and better memorial which takes the form of the village club—a pattern institution of its kind—on the Harlow road. Once a town, the village —for it had dwindled to that status during the nine-teenth century—has lately obtained renewed prosperity as a residential locality of the better sort. The whole of this countryside was at one time remarkable for its fine country seats. Many of these remain, but a large number in West Essex have been allowed to fall

into ruin, and of several the very site is conjectural.
Roydon possessed one of these in Nether Hall, a
fifteenth-century mansion of splendid proportions.   All
that remains of this is a fine entrance gateway with a
semi-hexagonal tower bearing the arms of the Coltes
supported by two colts.   A member of this family
was the first wife of Sir Thomas More, Chancellor of
England in the reign of Henry VIII.

Roydon is left by the Epping road, and presently
we are within a network of lanes connecting a number
of small hamlets, of which the chief are Great Parndon
and Nazeing.   The route passes through Epping Upland, where the much maltreated church was once the
mother-church of Epping—two miles away.   The
town now possesses its own handsome modern church
in the main street.   Epping is a pleasant and prosperous place standing upon high ground at the northern
extremity of the great forest of Waltham, now known
in its curtailed state as Epping Forest, one of London's
most popular as well as most beautiful playgrounds;
though certain portions of the Forest near Chingford,
where the carefully gravelled paths around Connaught
Water strike an incongruous note, have been spoilt
by a too-careful garnishing.   Within a few minutes'
walk, however, are woodlands of perfect beauty containing grand forest trees.   The district farthest from
town, and therefore in the neighbourhood of Epping,
has smaller timber, but on Sundays and holidays the
day excursionist is less in evidence.   Perhaps the
best portion of the Forest is that to the west of Theydon
Bois.   Here, and southwards near Loughton, the
woodlands, especially in autumn, are as beautiful as
anything of the kind in the Home Counties.

The visitor of an antiquarian turn of mind has

two ancient camps to explore in the Forest. One, near Loughton, is undoubtedly prehistoric, but the better known Amesbury Banks near the Epping–Woodford high road is usually ascribed to Boadicea. It is quite possible that the British queen utilized and repaired an old camp on this site for the last stand against the Roman forces.

The southern end of the Forest is now surrounded by suburban London-over-the-Border. The best known of these urban districts is Chingford, situated

CHINGFORD OLD CHURCH.

on the usual approach to the Forest from London. Chingford Mount, high above the Lea, preserves the picturesque ruins of the old church, abandoned, for some inexplicable reason, in 1844 in favour of an ugly new building at Chingford Green. Close to the Royal Forest Hotel is the half-timbered " Hunting Lodge of Queen Elizabeth," preserved by the City Fathers, to whom, needless to add, we owe the Forest itself, for with a commendable sense of public spirit, the Corporation fought for the right of the commonalty to this great open space—a fight which cost the City a sum of upwards of a quarter of a million.

CHAPTER VI

THROUGH ESSEX BY-WAYS

THE first stretch of real country in the valley of the Roding commences at Chigwell, though how long the old village will retain its rural character is a matter for anxious conjecture. It is a place of pilgrimage for all lovers of Charles Dickens, who, in *Barnaby Rudge*, makes the elder Willett landlord of the " Old King's Head," a picturesque hostelry erected in the seventeenth century. The inn figures in this historical romance as the " Maypole," and its later landlords must have been strong-minded individuals to resist the temptation to thus re-name the old house. The church that Dickens portrayed is now but the south aisle of the present building. A noticeable feature of the exterior is the Norman doorway, and within is a brass of great interest to ecclesiologists, for it depicts an Archbishop of York, Samuel Harsnett, who died in 1631, robed in pre-Reformation vestments. He was a vicar of Chigwell and an Essex man.

It is pleasant to walk by the high road through Abridge, for this is a way not greatly favoured by fast traffic, though motor-buses come so far on the Ongar road. A mile to the south of the hamlet is the small

Norman church at Lambourne, which contains some interesting German painted glass. A monument to Thomas Winnife records the fact that this seventeenth-century rector became Bishop of Lincoln.

The Roding is crossed nearly three miles from Abridge, leaving on the south of the stream the estate called Albyns, where there is a fine mansion designed by Inigo Jones. Continuing up the north side of the Roding valley, there is little of interest to record, and we turn to the left in another three miles to Stanford Rivers, where we find a Norman church, much altered in the fourteenth century, and containing several interesting brasses. The wooden belfry here is a curious fifteenth-century addition. From near the church, a lane leads us in two miles to one of the most remarkable of the churches of Essex. This is the famous wooden building at Greenstead. The walls of the nave are constructed of split oaken logs with the flat face inside, and, except for a few new logs inserted during a necessary restoration in 1848, these are the actual walls of the shrine which sheltered the body of the martyred Edmund on its way from London to St. Edmundsbury in 1013. How long the church had been standing before that date is unknown. The logs, of varying width, are about six feet in height. Wooden pegs were used to fasten them to the plates supporting the roof. This was probably of thatch. A chancel was added in Norman times, but was much altered with fifteenth-century brickwork, whilst the wooden tower was probably erected about a hundred years earlier.

Greenstead is only a mile from Chipping Ongar, and the ancient market town is approached by a leafy avenue leading into the main street. The town is

M

supposed to have been the site of a fortified Saxon burh. Remains of considerable earthworks still exist, and it is conjectured that the Normans erected a strong fortress upon part of the earlier works in 1162. Only a few fragments of a later building which replaced this stronghold in the sixteenth century now remain, though the great mound itself still towers above the ancient church.

GREENSTEAD CHURCH.

The walls of this building contain a quantity of Roman material, and it is likely that the lower portions a r e o f Saxon workmanship. An interesting chamber in the wall of the chancel is supposed to have been the cell of an anchorite, and in the floor is the g r a v e of Jane Cromwell, a cousin of the Protector. One of the most striking objects in the church is the massive framework of timber in the nave; this supports the belfry and spire.

On the far side of the Roding, and approached by a mile of footpath, is High Ongar. This village possesses a restored Norman church with an interesting south doorway of that period. From this point to Chelmsford, the direct road is a long and dull nine miles, to be made longer, but perhaps more interesting, by turning in one mile to the right hand for Blackmore. This small village is rather more than two miles off the main road. As we approach, an extraordinary tower, almost oriental in outline, is seen in front. This is the three-storied timber belfry of Blackmore Church, once forming part of a priory of Augustinians founded about 1190. It is still largely a Norman structure with later insertions and alterations, but it is in the medieval timber-work of the tower, and the fine north porch, that interest chiefly centres. On the south of the churchyard is the old Jericho Priory, used as a place of retreat by Henry VIII. It is supposed that the phrase " Go to Jericho " originated among members of the Court when their master was bent upon one of these seclusions.

From Blackmore, a pleasant side road traverses the high ground between Wid and Roding. This, after passing through Highwood and Edney Common, eventually rejoins the main road at Writtle, a small town that was once considerably larger, even rivalling its near neighbour—Chelmsford. The size of the church would alone be sufficient evidence of this fact. Beyond the fine Norman font and some old carved pew-ends, there is little of interest remaining in the much restored structure. Near the Dunmow road is a moated site supposed to be one of the many " lodges " of that restless monarch, King John.

We now approach the ancient county town, which contests with Colchester the honour of being the natural and historical centre of Essex. This was assured to Chelmsford, however, when, in 1914, it was chosen as the see town of the Essex diocese. St. Mary's Cathedral—the old parish church—is almost its only building of interest, if we except the Museum in Market

Street, where there is a good collection of local curiosities. Chelmsford, if it has few old houses, is clean and pleasant, and its busy main streets, characteristic of a flourishing shire-town, give little indication of the important industries which thrive within its borders. These range from brewing and gun-making to motor factories and electrical works—Chelmsford was the first town in England to make public use of the electric light. Tindal Square is named after a son of the town who was a Lord Chief Justice. His seated figure adorns the open space. The re-built Grammar School in Duke street was founded in 1551 to take the place of several schools swept away when the chantries that supported them fell in the suppression of religious houses.

BLACKMORE CHURCH.

The Cathedral is in many ways a remarkable building, though it has not the grace or proportions of the churches at either Thaxted or Saffron Walden. Much has already been done to add to the dignity of the building since it attained its present rank, and in the near future the fabric is likely to be much enlarged. Erected in the fifteenth century, it was practically rebuilt in 1800 after the sudden collapse of the nave through the faulty excavation of an old vault. Much of the restoration was carried out in a kind of terra-cotta, and the work was remarkably successful for the period in which it was done. The most interesting features of the interior are the curious arch enclosing two other pointed arches on the north of the chancel the great lockers intended for banners, under the tower and the memorials of Thomas and Avice Mildmay, dated 1557, and of Matthew Rudd—the latter a rather gruesome effort of a local sculptor in 1615.

The exterior of the church has a stately and picturesque appearance as viewed from the south. The fine porch with the room above containing the Knightsbridge library is a good example of flint work, and the tower—crowned by a slender flèche erected in 1749—is probably more effective than when it was surmounted by the original spire.

Although it is true that Chelmsford has little of antiquity to show the visitor, it is undoubtedly a very ancient place, and the Cathedral occupies the site of a building which probably antedated the Conquest. This in turn may have stood where once a Roman fort guarded the way from Camulodunum to the Thames crossing ; for that Chelmsford, and not Dunmow, was the station called Cæsaromagus is now well established. The fortunes of the medieval town were made in 1100 by Maurice, Bishop of London, who caused the Chelmer to be bridged, and so diverted traffic from the ford leading to Writtle.

Great Baddow and Widford are practically suburbs of Chelmsford ; the former has a fine fourteenth-century church with later brickwork built into the upper portions of the walls and chancel chapels. The village is worth a visit, and may be taken as the start of a pleasant excursion to Maldon on the estuary of the Blackwater, nine miles by road but nearly twice that distance by railway via Witham, an ancient Saxon burh on the great high road to Colchester and Ipswich. Going by road, and after passing Baddow, we leave Sandon slightly off the main road to the right. This is another pleasant village built around a green. It has an old church still retaining much Norman work, with Roman bricks and tiles in the walling. The sixteenth-century brickwork of the tower and roof is supposed to be due to Cardinal Wolsey, who was Lord of the Manor. A fine " linenfold " carved pulpit, and a brass of " Parson " Patrick Fearne and his wife, dated 1587, are interesting, but the most noteworthy object in the interior is the altar-rail of beaten iron-work. This is a modern addition, and was made by the village blacksmith.

Danbury is about half-way to Maldon, and is a remarkably interesting place well known by sight, if only as a distant object, to half Essex ; for the hill upon which stands the church is 365 feet above the sea, and commands an extensive, if monotonous, view to-wards the desolate waters

CHELMSFORD CATHEDRAL.

and sandbanks between the estuaries of the Crouch and Blackwater. A pleasant prospect opens up to the west and north, and on clear days the range for so moderate a height is remarkable ; though we must remember that in the whole of this large county of wide spaces only High Beech on the western borders of Epping Forest, and Langdon Hill in the south, are higher than Danbury. The name is possibly connected with the Danish occupation of the great prehistoric earthwork surrounding the church. Danbury Palace, so-called because it was for a time the residence of the Bishop of Rochester when Essex was in that diocese, stands in a beautiful park on the west side of the hill.

The fine tower and spire of the church make a useful seamark for mariners far out upon the North Sea. The building is mostly of ˹fourteenth-century date, but the whole fabric has been several times repaired and restored : on two occasions when the church was struck by lightning, in 1402 and 1750. The chief interset of the interior centres around the three " Danbury knights "—wooden crossed-legged effigies belonging to the thirteenth century—and, according to Mr. A. C. Fryer, in all probability members of the St. Clere family. Essex has several of these wooden effigies ; two others are not far away, at Little Baddow, a small village close to the Chelmer. They represent a franklin and a female figure—possibly his wife.

Other interesting objects in Danbury church include the old altar-rails, of the pattern usually associated with Archbishop Laud, which have been removed to the tower gallery ; the modern alabaster reredos ; the east window, the latter the gift of Bishop Claughton ; the deep " squint " in the wall of the north aisle, and the Mildmay helm hanging upon the wall.

The way now passes through the village of Woodham Mortimer, a pleasant little place containing a rebuilt Norman church and an oak tree famous throughout East Essex for its great size ; but the sister village of Woodham Walter, which lies some distance away in the Chelmer valley to the north, is much more picturesque, and possesses one of the few churches built in the reign of Elizabeth. This is in the later Tudor style with stepped gables. It is, however, in its domestic architecture—set off by the banked masses of some fine trees—that Woodham Walter excels, and the " Old Bell " inn is one of the best examples of an original sixteenth-century hostelry in Essex. The beams and barge-boards are carved with leaf patterns, and the interior is a perfect picture of old-fashioned comfort.

As we near Maldon, we pass within a mile of the Praemonstratensian Beeleigh Abbey. The chapter-house remains, together with portions of the domestic buildings, now converted into a residence. The site is between the angle formed by the railway and the Chelmer just before the meeting of the latter with the Blackwater.

Like other towns upon our smaller estuaries, Maldon

THE "OLD BELL" INN, WOODHAM WALTER.

is a much pleasanter place at high tide than when the black mud of alluvial Essex is exposed to eyes and nose. It is an ancient town, but with very little evidence of antiquity on the surface. It certainly dates from 913, when the Saxon Chronicle states that a "burh" was here constructed, if it is not older still. Of this earthwork it is said that a few remnants can still be traced. The Battle of Malden, between Saxons and Danes in 991, resulted in a victory for the invaders. After that date, the history of the town is an uneventful one. It contributed a ship and crew to the fleet summoned to repel the Armada of Spain, and found £80—four times as much as Harwich—as its offering towards the "ship-money" of Charles I. The former size and importance of the town is evident from the fact that it consists of three parishes, though only two churches now exist. The municipal life of Maldon goes back to the reign of Henry II, and the

Town Hall was built in the fifteenth century by a member of the local D'Arcy family. The building is of old mellow brickwork, and is usually called the " D'Arcy Tower."

All Saints' Church has an extraordinary tower, the like of which it would be difficult to find elsewhere. To fit the angle of the streets meeting at its west end, the plan is triangular instead of square. The spire above is hexagonal and was restored with contributions from America and dedicated as a memorial to Washington. In other respects the church is of no great interest, except for the fine Decorated arcading in the south wall of the Holy Trinity Guild Chapel. In St. Mary's Church, near the river, Roman tiles are again in evidence in what may be Saxon walling. The third church was destroyed, with the exception of the tower, to make way for the Plume Library in 1703. This was a gift to Maldon by one of its sons—Dr. Plume, Archdeacon of Rochester. The only other noteworthy relics of the past are the " Spital," some fragments of the old walls of the one-time leper-hospital, and the " Blue Boar " inn, where a goodly portion of the fabric dates from the sixteenth century.

The road from Maldon to Southminster is one of the dullest ten miles of road in Essex, though as we take the slight descent into the Crouch valley, a detour may be made to visit Althorne, somewhat to the south of the road. The quiet little hamlet contains a Perpendicular church built of flints. Within is a brass to William Hyklott, dated 1508. This commemorates the benefactor who paid for the walls of the fabric. Another brass is to Margaret Hyklott, who died in 1502.

Besides the cruciform church of St. Leonard at

Southminster, there is little in the small town to detain the visitor. "Day-trip" tickets are issued from London to Southminster station, and it is difficult to imagine what the excursionists do with themselves in the eight hours or so at their disposal, unless they walk by lonely lanes to the sea, five miles away at Dengie Flats, and there perform melancholy picnicking rites. Perhaps those with a taste for antiquities go as far as the solitary chapel of St. Peter at the Wall, now a barn, which may be the actual structure erected by St. Cedd in the seventh century. Nearly the whole of this remote district is devoted to sheep-farming, and it is a weird experience, in the early days of spring, to take the eastward road from Southminster towards a horizon fringed by masts and sails that appear moving along the far edge of an

BEELEIGH ABBEY.

enormous field, while the ear is assailed by the voices of some thousands of young lambs mingled with the deeper diapason of the ewes.

Southminster church is a large building with some traces of Norman architecture in the nave. A partial rebuilding in the early part of the last century must have greatly altered the character of the structure. The massive battlemented tower is dignified and well proportioned, but the nave has a gaunt appearance through the absence of aisles. The Perpendicular north porch with its parvise is, architecturally, the best part of the church. The oak screens separating the transepts and chancel from the nave are good modern work ; otherwise, the interior is featureless and bare.

From Southminster, it is barely three miles to Burnham-on-Crouch, famous for oysters and yachting, and with some slight pretensions to being a salt-water resort, though it is quite five miles to the sea between Holywell Point and Foulness, and the only practicable way there is by water, or by the narrow embankment path on the edge of the river. The quay is a pleasant lounging-place on a hot summer's day, and there are less satisfying pleasures than pulling down to the northern edge of the Maplin Sands and coming back with the tide. We have already passed the large Perpendicular church, which contains a Purbeck marble font of Norman date, and there is nothing more to keep us on the north side of the Crouch, crossed by a ferry to the west of the town. This ferry gives entrance to various devious ways across the Roach Valley, through either Great or Little Stambridge to Rochford. The former village has a large church standing high above the river. Its Transitional tower is dignified and well-proportioned, and some traces of a former Saxon building are to be found in the north wall of the nave. Rochford is not on either of the main roads to Southend, but indications of the proximity of a large pleasure town are apparent in the number of new residences on the outskirts of this old market town. Rochford church has a handsome Perpendicular brick tower, and not far away is the picturesque Hall, famous as the home of Anne Boleyn, figuring in most guides to Southend as one of the town's attractions.

Two miles north of Rochford is Ashingdon, the probable site of the battle between Edmund and Canute in 1016. The church, which has plentiful evidence of its original pre-Norman builders, may be identified with the thank-offering erected by the Emperor of the North four years afterwards. The name—Canewdon—borne by a small village to the east, is said to commemorate that of the victor.

The Prittlewell road passes near Eastwood, where there is another old church containing two good Norman doorways and a fine font of the same period. Prittlewell itself is now merely a suburb of the place that was once its own " south end."

MALDON MILL.

It is a very ancient little town, and a certain old doorway in the church, built of Roman tiles, is undoubtedly of Saxon workmanship. The fabric is mostly Perpendicular, and is a handsome specimen of that style in flint and stone. Here was once a cell of Cluniacs from Lewes, founded early in the twelfth century. A few scanty remains of the buildings are incorporated in the house known as the Priory. Another, and more ancient, relic of times long past is an encampment, covering about eight acres, in the fields near by, and probably of British origin.

The most remarkable fact about Southend is its phenomenal growth. Since the first year of the present century its inhabitants have nearly quadrupled. But much of this population is suburban in character ; in other words, a great number of City men are able to make the western end of the town—Westcliff—their

permanent home, thanks to the railway facilities.
Like several other resorts, the fortunes of Southend,
commenced with a Royal visit. The benefactors were
Queen Caroline and the Princess Charlotte, who came
here for a brief stay in 1804.

The garden front of residential Westcliff is a healthy
and sunny promenade, and the pleasant new extension
eastwards called Thorpe Bay is becoming the popular
quarter for holiday-makers—needless to say, neither
of these two ends of the town know one another.
Perhaps the best thing about Southend is its pier,
which stretches for a third of the way to the Isle of
Grain and the Kentish coast, and the pedestrian who
walks to the end and back has covered three miles.

To continue eastwards past Thorpe Bay brings us
in a few minutes to " Cambridge Town," an offshoot
of Shoebury, having all the usual arid dreariness of a
military station. The actual point of Shoeburyness,
where the Thames estuary gives way to the North
Sea, cannot be turned by the pedestrian. The War
Office people have seen to that, for they have covered
the Ness with batteries and barracks, built partly
on the site of a Danish earthwork that was probably
some distance from the sea at the time of its erection.
The small church of St. Andrew at Shoebury belonged
at one time to Prittlewell Priory. It retains the original
Norman chancel arch.

Westwards from Westcliff is the once tiny fishing
town of Leigh, which lately consisted of a single street
on the creek called Hadleigh Ray, but is now striving
to emulate its big neighbour by putting out feelers
of brick and roughcast. The much-restored church
has an imposing square west tower with a stair turret.
Within the building will be found a few old brasses,

but there is little else of interest.   Leigh is close to the
entrance to Benfleet Creek, which separates another
growing resort from the mainland.   This is Canvey
Island, usually approached from South Benfleet by
a raised causeway, practicable at low tide.   The flat
meadows of Canvey are being converted into bungalow
plots, and the smart little dwellings erected thereon
have a distinctly attractive appearance from the deck
of the steamer making London River.   Canvey was
embanked in 1623 by one Croppenburgh, who had
learned the art in his native Netherlands.   Forty-four
years afterwards, his compatriots were ill-mannered
enough to sail past the Nore and burn Canvey church,
of which fragmentary ruins are seen near its small and
quite modern successor.

The handsome wooden porch at South Benfleet
dates from the later fifteenth century, and is the only
remarkable thing about the church.   The village is
said to have been the scene of a battle between Alfred
and the Danes, who had a strong fort on the Creek
side.   A quantity of wrecked and burnt war-craft was
found embedded in the mud of the Creek by the workmen constructing the Southend railway.   These were
probably the remains of the Danish fleet, in the
destruction of which the citizens of London took a not
unworthy part.

From South Benfleet, a road runs north-east to
Hadleigh, where the gaunt ruins of a castle first built
in the thirteenth century by Hubert de Burgh look
across the flat lands to Canvey.   These old ivied walls
are still of sufficient extent to show us how fine a
building Hadleigh had become, with its later accretions
and additions, before it was abandoned during Elizabeth's reign.   The small Norman church has been

but little altered during the centuries that have passed over it, except for the erection of the wooden tower. The carved figure of an ecclesiastic on a window in the nave is identified as that of Becket, and the inscription —*Beatus Tomas*—points to its being made before 1173, when the murdered Archbishop was canonized.

Between Hadleigh and Rayleigh, we note the spire of Thundersley church on its hill to the left. We then pass over the new trunk road to Southend and ascend to Rayleigh, where the marshes are left behind, and we are again among those low hills that give the lie to the flat Essex legend. Rayleigh is a place of great antiquity, for its foundations are to be traced in a large earthwork upon the top of the hill, up the slopes of which the town is built. The church is a spacious Perpendicular building with a prominent tower. It should be entered for the sake of seeing the curious timber arch on the south of the chancel. Another item of interest is a strong box made out of a single oak block three feet long.

We leave Rayleigh by the Brentwood road and descend to the river Crouch at Wickford, where there is nothing to detain us. The road then proceeds up the gentle slope of Crays Hill, and on the farther side, to the left of our direct road, is Great Burstead. Here is an interesting old church in a variety of styles from Norman to Perpendicular.

At Billericay, the scenery approaches that of the Essex we explored in the last chapter. Wooded country, gently undulating, surrounds this clean and pleasant, though unremarkable, little market town, which has grown considerably since one of the railways to Southend passed through it. It has a modern church attached to an old brick tower, but there is little of quaintness about the place except its name—usually mispronounced. To please the native it should be called "Billricky." The neighbourhood obtained a great notoriety during the Great War, when a German Zeppelin was brought down close to the town.

We now turn away from the uninteresting London road, and bear northwards past the station to Stock, about three miles away. This small but picturesque village has a church forming one of an interesting group. All are remarkable for their timber work. Dating mostly from the end of the Decorated period, the timbers belong to that time and to the early fifteenth century. The tower at Stock is a remarkable example of buttressed wood, and the spire above, of the same material, is as graceful and satisfying as any similar work in stone. The south porch is another good illustration of the successful use of wood in architecture, though time has left its mark to the detriment of the fabric. Within will be found some "poppyhead" bench-ends, and a fine brass of Richard Twedye, who died in 1574 after a strenuous life as a soldier—as set forth in quaint rhyme beneath his effigy.

The decayed old tree known as Edward's Oak, said to have been planted by Edward VI, and the ancient "Ship" inn are at the top of the hill on the Chelmsford road, but we turn to the left by a lane that first drops to the Wid, and then rises again to Margaretting Church; a building of an interest almost equal to that at Stock, though unhappily furbished up at a time when the true art of restoration seems to have been little understood. Here again is a timber tower, spire and porches, the former of exceptional solidity and fine proportions. The stone-work is undoubtedly Norman at the base of the walls, but the upper parts

are Early English, and the chancel is of Perpendicular
date, The east window is a good example of medieval
stained glass, and illustrates the Tree of Jesse ; more
old glass may be seen in the nave, but the best thing
about Margaretting church is the beautiful north porch,
sketched and photographed times out of number.
The font is of fine design and curious detail ; it dates
from the fifteenth century.

The way now enters the London–Colchester high
road—which forms the main street of Margaretting.
We turn from the village towards the south-west and
quickly arrive at Ingatestone, a small town also bordering the highway for some
distance. In the angle of
the road leading to Buttesbury and Stock is the
church of St. Mary, pos-
sessing an imposing tower
with diaper work of black
bricks in the middle story.
Within will be found sev-
eral monuments to the celebrated Petre family, who
lived at Ingatestone Hall; this is an Elizabethan
mansion near the Wid, and is now devoted to benevolent purposes connected with the Roman Church.
The estate once belonged to Barking Abbey, and
was handed by Henry VIII to the Sir William Petre
whose alabaster effigy adorns the church. The Hall
is said to be the scene of *Lady Audley's Secret*, a novel
having a wide popularity half a century ago.

MARGARETTING CHURCH.

We are now in the midst of the district already
referred to as of so much interest to archæologists for
the peculiarities of construction and material used in
its village churches. A good example of these is found

N

by turning aside to Fryerning. This is north-west of Ingatestone, and is a Norman structure with Roman materials in the walls and a remarkably fine brick tower. Or we might go south-eastwards to Buttesbury, already mentioned, where would be seen a small building badly maltreated, but with several unusual details. It is proposed, however, to keep still to the main road which leads to Mountnessing. Here is a church which was practically rebuilt nearly forty years ago, but still retaining much of interest. The massive wooden frame upholding the tower and spire rises from within the nave in the manner so common in these parts. The chancel is a brick addition of the eighteenth century, but the upper portion of the west end was built over a hundred years earlier, in 1653, A curious item among the several objects shown to the visitor is the rib of a mammoth discovered by workmen in medieval times; another is an old chest of enormous proportions, requiring two men to lift the lid. The graveyard, with its beautiful flower-beds, and the general surroundings of Mountnessing church are delightful and will repay an hour spent in exploration.

The road rises and falls with nothing upon its borders calling for remark until we come to Shenfield, over two miles away. Here again the timber work of the church calls for more than passing notice. Huge shafts of oak, with carved capitals and clustered columns, separate the body of the church from the aisle and chapel. Moulded timbers of immense size support the tower and lead-covered spire. The trees from which these great baulks were cut must have been magnificent, not only for their size, but for their perfect shape and growth. But when we remember that the greater part of this countryside was covered with woodland at the time these churches were erected, we can guess that the task of the builders in choosing their material was not an arduous one.

Brentwood is but a mile farther on the way to London, and even here, eighteen miles from the City, there are suburban signs. The town is built high above the main railway line that has accompanied our path from Margaretting. It has a spacious and pleasant High Street, shaded here and there by fine trees. The Martyrs' memorial at the cross-roads calls for notice. It commemorates a dark old deed in the bad times of the sixteenth century. Another memorial, upon an oak tree, tells of a more stirring event in 1916, when a Zeppelin on its way to work havoc in the great city was brought down and destroyed in the meadows beyond the town. The ancient " White Hart " inn, dating from 1480, is reminiscent of the palmy days of the great east road ; after nearly a century of somnolence, it has entered upon still more bustling hours. An out-of-the-way honour was conferred upon this old town when it was chosen to give a territorial title to the Latin Bishop of Essex.

South-east of Brentwood, the Ingrave road penetrates well-wooded country with the wide stretch of Thorndon Park to the right. Ingrave village calls for little remark ; the church, more curious than beautiful, was built by a Lord Petre in 1735. It contains some brass effigies from the demolished sanctuary at West Horndon. Nearly two miles farther on this road is East Horndon church, a brick structure with a late Perpendicular tower, but retaining an archaic Norman font from the old building that once stood upon the site. The strange upper chambers over the aisles are supposed to have been for the use of the chantry priests. A large table-tomb against the wall of the south aisle is traditionally said to have contained the heart of Anne Boleyn. The monuments of the Tyrell family in the side chapel are many and various; the most noteworthy is that to Lady Alice Tyrell, dated 1422.

Soon after leaving Horndon, one of the beauty spots of Essex comes into view upon the left. This is Langdon Hill, and in a long two miles a lane is found making direct for the mount which rises boldly above the flat lands of the Thames. The Langdon, or Laindon, Hills are a resort of artists as well as holiday-makers, and both are attracted by the magnificent views to the south, and up and down the great river. To the mariner and those familiar with the waterway of the lower Thames, the tower of the modern church upon the hill-top is a well-known landmark.

Horndon-on-the-Hill is another lofty village breaking the southward view from Langdon, and approached by pleasant by-ways from the latter. Here we find an Early English church with another wooden tower and spire rising from within the nave. Still farther to the south-east is Stanford-le-Hope, a large village with numbers of new houses and a much-restored church, mainly Early English and Decorated in style and possessing a handsome Perpendicular tower. This is on the old Barking–Southend road, which busy thoroughfare must be taken as far as the " Cock " inn, where we turn leftwards to West Tilbury, a small village built on one of the many creeks which drain the Essex marshes. The busy docks and warehouses of Tilbury are two miles away at Tilbury Fort, opposite Gravesend, and connected therewith by a ferry ; so that we may, if tired of Essex, plunge straight across the Thames into Kent and our next chapter.

Tilbury Fort was one of the many block-houses set up by Henry VIII for the defence of the coast, and the locality is for ever associated with his great daughter and her stirring speech at the review of the army which had flocked to her standard when the intentions of Philip of Spain became known.

To finish the exploration of rural Essex, we must turn north-west and pass through East Thurrock, where there is a small over-restored church still retaining a Norman arch between nave and chancel. Not far away are the best known of the " Dene Holes " to be found in several localities in the chalk districts of south-eastern England, the true use of which has never been satisfactorily explained. They consist of narrow perpendicular shafts, of depths varying from sixty to ninety feet, with chambers at the bottom, sometimes over twenty feet long and nearly as high. The latest opinions on the vexed question of their origin point to the chalk-mine theory as being the most probable, but many antiquaries still hold to the older conjecture—that they were storehouses for grain in times of invasion.

Winding ways, trending north-westwards, bring us to Stifford, on a low hill above Mar-dyke. Old houses abound in this pleasant and out-of-the-way place, which has also a church retaining many ancient features, from the Norman arch of the south entrance to the seventeenth-century pulpit with its hour-glass stand.

From Stifford, a straight road goes northwards through South and North Ockendon. To the left, about a mile away and near Aveley, is the fine Tudor mansion and park of Belhus. In this house Queen Elizabeth is said to have slept before the review at

Tilbury. The first of the Ockendons is a straggling village with a Norman church having a round tower —an unusual design in this part of England. The north doorway is a very fine example of Norman moulding, and is worth turning aside to inspect. North Ockendon, two miles farther on, also boasts a similar door on the south side of the church, which, though partially rebuilt, is interesting. This small village is upon rising ground, overlooking those still unspoilt fields and hedgerows towards Upminster which will probably become London-over-the-Border at no distant date. To reach Upminster, a pleasantly wooded route is by way of the small hamlet called Corbets Tye, passing the parklands of Stubbers and Gaynes. Upminster church was originally Norman, but it has been much altered, and the once quiet village street has lost its old-world character for the smartness and modernity which must cater for a growing suburban population. Upminster Hall, on the Brentwood road above the valley of the Ingrebourne, is a picturesque old mansion of the early sixteenth century. It stands close to the road, and with its many gables and quaint chimneys, forms a delightful picture.

Upminster is stretching out to reach Hornchurch, its near neighbour on the west, and the fields towards Dagenham on the south and Romford on the north will not remain green for very much longer. At Hornchurch is the site of a priory that was founded by Henry II in 1159, connected with the Alpine Hospice of St. Bernard. The little town has a greater number of old houses and is more picturesque in character than Upminster. It appears to thrive upon its one industry—the manufacture of beer. The fine church is remarkable for the height of its tower and spire, and also for a curious badge in the chancel gable consisting of a bull's head with copper horns. It is conjectural as to whether this is a play upon the name of the church or on the ancient trade of the village—the preparation of the skins of cattle for the leather-sellers of Romford. It formerly went under the name of " Pelt Street " as a consequence of this fact.

Romford is on the great high road we have traversed here and there on our peregrinations. Though busy and uninteresting, it is an ancient place, and held an important position in days gone by. It was the chief centre of the Liberty of Havering-atte-Bower, a curious territorial division that included both Hornchurch and Havering, the latter being three miles north of Romford. The original charter of this " liberty," having its own magistrates and sessions, was granted by Edward Confessor, and persisted until 1892. Edward had a royal residence at Pyrgo, near Havering-atte-Bower, and the parklands surrounding that village are remnants of the eastern portions of the great Forest of Hainault. The row of ancient cottages called Elizabeth Row remind us that the great Queen stayed also at Pyrgo on her way to Tilbury.

THE HEART OF KENT.

CHAPTER VII

TO THE HEART OF KENT

WE should have to travel many miles down-stream from London Bridge nowadays before finding any real country on the Thames bank, and it is hardly practicable, while Londoners treat their river so cavalierly, to make a short journey by water—to Gravesend, for instance. To this once popular Cockney resort several steamers came daily during the summers of our grandfathers, and those of us who are merely middle-aged may have made the pleasant trip in person. If most of the beauties of London River have disappeared, the voyage is still full of the interest and romance that always surround the way to far horizons.

The magnificence of Greenwich, that can only be properly seen from the water, has long since been taken from Kent. Its ancient boundaries in Deptford have gone, and official London extends to beyond Plumstead and Eltham; the former a mere appanage of Woolwich, and the latter, since the advent of the tramcar, an ordinary suburb. It is happily certain, however, that the amenities immediately surrounding the historic Palace at Eltham are to be preserved.

The ancient way that we have crossed and traversed so many times in our journeyings upon the north-west side of the Metropolis is again found, now striding with Roman directness over the hills of North Kent on its way to Canterbury and the narrow seas at Dover. It cannot be said that the Kentish section of the Watling Street is remarkable for beauty, and a certain air of dinginess pervades its immediate surroundings for the greater portion of the forty miles between Shooter's Hill and Faversham. The wooded crest of the former, crowned by a water-tower, is a landmark throughout south-western Essex and a great part of north Kent. Over this crest runs the great high road. It then drops abruptly to Welling—the first village in Kent—and passes through dreary Bexley Heath to Crayford and Dartford. From Welling to Gravesend and beyond the way is rendered doubly commonplace by tram-lines, with the ugly accompaniment of gaunt iron standards and overhead wires. A far more pleasant way of reaching Crayford is by the road leaving Eltham at the eastern end of the High Street. This, after passing the beautiful public park at Avery Hill, brings us to Bexley, an old-fashioned village still, despite its proximity to its namesake of the heath. The surroundings of the church, with its curious shingled spire, are quite rural and picturesque, and the village makes a good starting-place for the exploration of the Crays, which lie to the south ; these, however, must be left for a later page.

Crayford, nearly a mile and a half from Bexley, still retains the old houses of a steep little High Street, climbing from the bridge and clear river at its foot to the church. This is worthy of a visit if only to see the curious and very unusual ground plan. The nave consists of two aisles and the chancel of three; as both portions of the building are of the same width, the arches of the nave are in a line with the centre of the chancel arch. A thirteenth-century church at Hannington in Northamptonshire has a similar arrangement, and the wooden arcade at Wingfield in Berkshire is also centred on the altar.

From the church we may continue northwards to Erith, a Thames-side town of some historic interest, though there is very little of the past now visible. Here, in 1178, the once famous Lesnes Abbey was founded by Henry de Lucy while he was Viceroy of England. To this retreat he came soon after Henry II took up the reins of government. It was a monastery of Austin canons, and reached a high status in the Middle Ages, but was suppressed by Wolsey in 1526. Only very scanty fragments of the buildings remain, though it is said that much of the fabric of Erith church, especially in the inserted tracery of the windows, consists of stonework from the ruins.

Somewhere in the neighbourhood of the Cray ford, or on Dartford Heath between that ford and the other on the Darent, is the site of a great battle between the Saxons, under that half-mythical person Hengist, and the British—resulting in the defeat of the latter and the abandonment of Kentland to the invader.

The busy main street of Dartford, with its noisy trams and open-air market, is part of the Roman road where that thoroughfare plunged down to, and through, the Darent. From the bridge to the Thames the little river becomes Dartford Creek, and is wholly given over to industrialism. Above the town, the valley is comparatively unspoilt, and above Farningham con-

tains scenes which rank among the fairest in the
" Garden of England."

Dartford was the home of a Priory of Augustinian
nuns founded by Edward I, whose property was converted by Henry to his own personal uses at the
Dispersal. The Tudor gatehouse and some scanty
portions of the walls remain, but the church is the only
building worth seeing. Its massive tower is said to
have been built for the defence of the ford. A curious
painting of St. George slaying the Dragon is to be
found near the altar, but the most interesting medieval
features are the quarters of the chantry priest, consisting of two rooms reached by a stone stairway. Several
fifteenth-century brasses are noteworthy, and also
the monument to Sir John Spielman, jeweller and
papermaker, who founded the first of the Dartford
mills, and so started the town on that prosperous
career of paper-making which still persists. The
most famous son of Dartford belonged to another trade.
He was a tiler named Wat, and he occupies a conspicuous place in the nation's history as the foremost
leader in the Peasants' Revolt.

Like the Beauty of Camberwell among lepidoptera,
the little bird called the Dartford Warbler is now
unknown in the locality which gave it a name. This
extremely rare little songster is occasionally heard in
the more remote parts of Shropshire, though it is
practically unknown among the country folk there,
who probably confuse it with another bird. It was
first recorded as a habitant of North Kent in 1773.

The most interesting place in the neighbourhood of
Dartford is Stone, about two miles away on the
Gravesend road. Here is a fine Early English church
of uncommon beauty, both in its general aspect and

plan and in the splendour of its ornamental detail. Near the church is an ancient manor house called Stone Castle, which retains a tower that belonged to the original fortress. Farther on, towards Gravesend, lie Greenhithe and Ingress Abbey. The latter is now a residence, built with the stones of demolished London Bridge on the site of a priory belonging to Dartford.

A detour to the south-east of Dartford town enables the traveller to escape for a time from the busy Dover highway, and also to visit another interesting church. This route goes first by the west bank of the river past Sutton at Hone, and then crosses the stream to tiny Darenth. Here, some years ago, were discovered the foundations of a large Roman building, or series of buildings, miscalled " the Roman Villa," but probably used as a textile factory. The site is about fifteen minutes' walk south of the church—an ancient structure with a curious upper chamber in the chancel. The lower portions of the walls are undoubtedly Saxon, and were built with material brought from the near-by Roman ruins. The archaic font may be even earlier in date than the Norman period to which it is usually assigned.

From Darenth, a lane goes by Longfield, where there is a small ancient church of varying dates from Norman onwards, and a large, ugly and scattered village with some pretensions to being residential. Close by, to the south, are the narrow valleys in which lie Fawkham and Hartley. Here are two other little old churches in quiet by-ways, peaceful and secluded. Our route however, bears north-east to Southfleet. This is a large village a short distance south of the Watling Street. A Decorated church containing many memorials, chiefly brasses, is the only thing of interest

Northfleet, on the Thames-side, has another old church, and a sixteenth-century clergy-house, but this is rather off our route, and we may make directly for Gravesend without losing very much.

Gravesend is no longer a " resort," but there are many so-called pleasure towns that might well envy this old Kentish borough its water panorama. It has, on a much broader scale, the same characteristic vistas up and down stream that are seen at Greenwich. Unfortunately, the Essex shore opposite—at Tilbury —cannot be called either pleasant or picturesque in these utilitarian days. If we ascend the mound called Windmill Hill, the prospect is widened out to include the green hills of Essex, and a long view of the great waterway unfolds.

Of actual antiquities in the town there are but few, and the church was rebuilt in the eighteenth century, but Gravesend, between the railway and the river, contains many pleasant and mellow old houses. Its streets have the mysterious but essential air of a salt-water port, and with good reason, for it is the boarding-place both for His Majesty's Customs officers and for the Thames pilots, who see outgoing ships safely through the sandy mazes off the Kentish coast. The wife of John Rolfe, the pioneer tobacco-grower of Virginia, is buried in Gravesend churchyard. She is better known under her picturesque title—Princess Pocahontas. A short time ago endeavours were made to identify the actual place of sepulture, but, it is believed, without success.

A most interesting little tour may be made from Gravesend through a countryside that is associated to a much greater extent than any other with the immortal memory of Charles Dickens. For a brief survey of this corner of Kent, we may walk in a south-easterly direction from near Windmill Hill to the hamlet of Singlewell, once noted for a very strong ale, brewed locally. From this point, a winding lane leads to Cobham, which possesses four " lions," and each separately would be worth the journey from Gravesend. The church is a building of much beauty, both in plan and in detail. It is in the Decorated and Perpendicular styles, and contains a remarkable series of brasses, chiefly commemorating members of the Cobham family, whose splendid home in the near-by park is one of the finest mansions in Kent. Cobham College, situated behind the church, was founded by John de Cobham in 1362 as a chantry-house of five priests, afterwards increased to seven. The present buildings date from the last years of the sixteenth century, and are used as almshouses. They form the most pictur-esque group devoted to such a purpose in the county, and include the ancient hall of the original foundation, famous for its fine stone chimney-breast enriched with heraldic ornament.

The village inn attracts crowds of visitors every summer, and of these a goodly proportion are Americans who desire to see the retreat of the love-lorn Tupman. His room is hung with pictures of characters from the pages of Dickens' novels, and the series invades both bar and coffee-room of the " Leather Bottle," where one may see also several actual relics of the great novelist. Mr. Pickwick's celebrated antiquarian dis-covery took place in the village street, probably at the corner of the lane by which we entered it.

The oldest part of Cobham Hall, in which Charles I and his queen spent honeymoon days, dates from about 1585, but large portions of the building were erected by Inigo Jones. Apart from the stately magnificence of the design, it is celebrated for the collection of old masters housed within its walls. These are not generally shown, and we must be content with the beautiful walk through the park towards the Valley of the Medway and Rochester. Within the demesne is the chalet brought here from Gad's Hill. It was used as a retreat by Dickens while writing, and was presented to Lord Cobham by the novelist's family.

As the path descends through pleasant woods to the hop-fields, we have a view of the opposite shores of the Medway, and presently of the smoky haze which hangs above the densely populated districts on the south side of

ROCHESTER CASTLE.

the estuary. The square mass of Rochester Castle—most impressive of all existing Norman fortresses—rising above the stream, with the spire of the Cathedral beyond, forms a romantic picture, not easily matched in the south of England. The transpontine suburb of Strood, through which we pass to cross the river, is not very prepossessing at first sight, but the church is large and interesting. Within it will be found a large number of memorials of local families, both of ancient and recent times.

We now pass over the bridge into the " ceaster " of the Jutish chieftain Hrof, and from the territory of the Kentish Men into that of the Men of Kent— all the country east of the Medway. The view downstream from the bridge is practically non-existent ; the ugly railway bridge blocks the vista most effectually ; but all that is worth seeing is on the right

front, where the curtain wall of the Castle rises directly from the river bank, and the great square keep rears its massive and imposing bulk above the dependent city. Its most remarkable feature consists in the unusual number of window openings. The well-proportioned corner turrets add greatly to the dignity and symmetry of this fine example of a Norman fortress. When the walls are approached by way of the pleasant public gardens that occupy the space within the curtain, the sense of majesty is increased, and the superiority of the architecture to that of the more famous White Tower below London Bridge is readily apparent. For many years Gundulf, the builder of the latter, was supposed to be responsible for Rochester, but recent clues credit another churchman—Archbishop Corbeil, who lived in the first half of the twelfth century— with its erection. The Castle, however, was already in existence before this later keep was built.

INTERIOR, ROCHESTER CASTLE.

Very scanty fragments of the Castle buildings, as distinguished from the keep, now exist. It is probable that certain eighteenth-century vandals, fired by a desire for a cheap and convenient quarry, caused their disappearance ; but we may be thankful that the quality of the masonry in the inner fortress rendered pick-work futile, while gunpowder would have been both costly and dangerous.

The first outstanding event in the history of the Castle was its seizure, after the death of the Conqueror, by Bishop Odo of Bayeaux on behalf of Robert of Normandy, and its subsequent surrender to Rufus. In 1202 it passed into the hands of the Barons, but fell to King John after a twelve months' siege. Sixty years later, subsequent to the defeat of Henry III at the battle of Lewes, the Castle passed for a short time into the possession of De Montfort's followers.

If it were not for the Castle, the Cathedral at Rochester would take a more important place in the estimation of tourist sightseers. Though not to be compared with the other Kentish cathedral, either in historical importance or in architectural grandeur, it has its own particular charm and interest. Here was the " chair " of the second bishopric founded by Augustine on his missionary journey, and the earliest portions of the building are fragments of a small Saxon church upon which Bishop Gundulf reared the first Norman cathedral. This was replaced by the present nave, dating from 1130. The most admired portion of this work is the fine west door with its elaborate and characteristic carving. Through this portal we obtain an imposing vista of the interior— heavy and massive, but well-proportioned. The Early English choir is of much beauty, enriched with Petworth marble and other ornamental stone. Its solid walls were built in consequence of one of those

strange and petty quarrels between monks and townspeople which disgrace medieval church history. The
crypt is one of the finest in England. So light is it,
and so graceful in the combination of Norman and
Early English, that it is difficult to believe we are below
ground.

For those who are interested in memorials of the
dead, a remarkable series of ancient tombs—of bishops,
priors and laymen—are to be seen. One in particular,

dated 1360, of Bishop
John of Sheppey, is
a splendid example
of the decorative
work of the period.
Another is that of
Bishop de Merton,
who founded Merton
College. Of the once
famous shrine of St.
William, a Scots pil-
grim who was mur-
dered just outside the
city walls in the early
thirteenth century,
no vestige remains.

ROCHESTER CATHEDRAL.

Listen to Dickens' summary, through the lips of Mr.
Alfred Jingle—" Old Cathedral—earthy smell—pilgrims' feet worn away the old steps—little Saxon
doors—confessionals like money-takers' boxes ' at
theatres—queer customers those monks—Popes, and
Lord Treasurers, and all sorts of old fellows, with
great red faces, and broken noses, turning up every
day—buff jerkins too—match-locks—sarcophagus—
fine place—old legends too—strange stories—capital."

Among the modern memorials are those to Dean Hole, whose memory is dear to all lovers of the national flower; to Charles Dickens; and to Richard Watts, whose charity has been immortalized by the novelist. Before leaving the Cathedral, mention must be made of the Lady Chapel. Its position to the south of the nave is most unusual, if not unique.

The exterior of the building, never particularly imposing, suffered severely from a drastic furbishing in the early nineteenth century. The modern short spire and central tower add to the dignity and general effect, especially when the great mass of the Castle is contained in the same view. The pinnacled tower known to Dickens, and described by him in Jasper's opium dream, was singularly dull and devoid of character, and the restorations of Sir Gilbert Scott quarrel with all the original work. It is in the precincts that the chief interest and beauty of out-of-doors Rochester lies, and the scenes depicted in *Edwin Drood* are but little altered since those unfinished chapters were written. On the south side is the fine Priors' Gate, and close to this is a small portion of the old city wall. Near by, are the modern buildings of the King's School, founded by Henry VIII. Perhaps the finest of the old houses in the city is the lodging " on the way to his throne " of Charles II, called Restoration House. This is a Tudor mansion of much beauty and dignity. Another notable building of Elizabethan date, now a museum, is Eastgate House in the street of that name. It figures as " the Nun's House " in *Edwin Drood*. The High Street, though much altered in recent years, retains many mellow old brick houses, and " a queer old clock, as if Time carried on business there." The Watts Charity for " six poor travellers "

—not *seven*—is a quaint gabled building founded in 1579. The pious benefactor, who was so severe upon " proctors," lived in the third of the famous mansions of Rochester. This is known as Satis House, and it stands on Boley Hill.

The beginnings of this ancient city go back to, at least, the days of the Roman occupation. It was then called Durobrivæ, and a well-preserved fragment of the original wall of this settlement may be seen behind a chapel in the Maidstone road. The origin of the place was doubtless due to a convenient ford that had probably been in use for ages before the paved way, afterwards known as the Watling Street, was laid by the Latin conquerors. The city is now the smallest member of a group of towns brought into being chiefly by the fine harbourage in the Medway, and the choice —originally made by Henry VIII—of the locality as a combined military and naval station. This has latterly developed into one of the most important in the south of the island, and had become of some consequence even in the reign of Charles II, for the Dutch Admiral de Ruyter thought it worth while to sail up the Medway in 1667 and burn some English ships, a feat which caused much discomfort of spirit and some natural anxiety to the citizens of London. Here are the Chatham Royal Dockyard, extending for three miles along the river bank, and endless barrack buildings for seamen and soldiers. The famous " Lines " are now surmounted by a splendid memorial to those from Chatham and elsewhere who fell in the Great War.

Brompton and Gillingham—the latter a separate borough of over fifty thousand inhabitants—form part of the extension of Chatham on the east bank of the Medway, and call for no remark. They are distinctly uninteresting to the tourist, and not much can be said in praise of the scenery around the estuary of the river, which ends where the forts of Sheerness —another rather dingy town of soldiers and sailors, lately threatened with the loss of some of its importance —command the fairway of both Thames and Medway. The east end of Sheerness has colourable pretensions to being a seaside resort, and bungalows are springing up on the north shore of Sheppey Isle in the direction of Minster and Leysdown. The firstnamed village contains the ancient abbey church of SS. Mary and Sexburga. The latter saint was the widow of King Ecombyrt of Kent, and was foundress of the abbey. The present building—mainly Early English—is but a portion of the original structure. It contains the tomb of Sir Robert de Shurland and a remarkable brass to Sir Roger de Northwood, who died about 1330. The former knight is the subject of one of the *Ingoldsby Legends*.

On the main road from Rochester to Gravesend, rather more than two miles from the bridge, is Gad's Hill, to which Shakespeare, in *Henry IV*, Part I, brings Sir John Falstaff—as we are reminded by the inn sign. The story of Dickens, in his youthful days of poverty, longing to possess the old house, with its wonderful view over the Cooling marshes, is well known. Here Dickens died in 1870, after owning the property for thirteen years. The Wilderness Gardens, where he did most of his work, is on the north of the road, and is reached from the house by a subway.

The original Falstaff is supposed to have been Sir John Oldcastle, who lived at Cooling Castle. This was built from patriotic motives by John of Cobham, above the marshes between the chalk hills and the Thames, as a defensive measure against foreign warships sailing up the river and bent upon plunder. Considerable portions of this fortress remain. It was erected towards the end of the fourteenth century, and is a fine example of that period, being composed to a large extent of chalk faced with Kentish ragstone and, in certain portions, with flints. Readers of *Great Expectations* will remember that beyond these lonely marshes were moored the "hulks," and hereabouts Pip had his adventure with the convict.

WESTERN TOWERS, CANTERBURY.

From Rochester, the old way to the Continent is followed more or less closely all the way by the railway, and both end within a few yards of each other under the heights of Dover. Both run through Sittingbourne and Faversham, though the last-named town is slightly to the north of the Watling Street. Neither of these ancient places is of sufficient interest to warrant an excursion, but they are on the direct route to Canterbury; and however out of place it may seem, especially to patriotic men of Kent, to mention the historic centre of the Kingdom of Kent in a work dealing with the country of the Londoner, a few lines must be written to accompany that individual so far to the south-east, certainly not with any thought of placing the ancient city within the sphere of the "wen."

Apart from its unique status as the seat of the Anglican Metropolitan, and apart from the splendid church that is its crowning glory, Canterbury is a fascinating place, and ranks with Chester, York and Lincoln in the number and variety of its medieval relics, for it must not be forgotten that the city has a secular as well as a church history. It was doubtless an important centre during the period prior to the Roman occupation. It was certainly an important commercial post on the Old Road that was developed and improved by the legionaries, who also planned and built auxiliary ways from Lympne and Richborough to join the great artery at this point. The Roman town was named Durovernum. As the capital of the King of Kent, it afterwards became Cantwarabyrig—the Kent-man's borough.

It is usual to speak of St. Martin's at Canterbury as the Mother-Church of England, because a building on the same site is known to have been used for Christian worship by Ethelbert's queen before that petty kinglet was converted by the missionary Augustine. But it is highly improbable that the heathen had quenched the light throughout the whole country east of the Severn, and more than possible that several otherwise unremarkable village churches contain within their structure actual remnants dating from the era of Romano-British Christianity. In one respect St. Martin's may be unique, for its font is said to incorporate part of the original vessel in which Ethelbert was baptized by Augustine.

As the scene of the martyrdom of Becket, a fame as wide as Christendom became attached to the Cathedral Church of Christ in Canterbury. The Old Road experienced a metamorphosis, and became *par excellence* the Pilgrims' Way. Blazing with jewels and precious metals, the shrine of the new saint and martyr became the goal also of foreign travellers bent on compounding for their sins in one of the pleasantest of ways—even at that far-off period. From the pilgrims—rich and poor, and St. Thomas was popular with the commonalty, for his martyrdom seemed to be the result of outfacing the arrogance of power—pious offerings were poured forth

GREY FRIARS, CANTERBURY.

for nearly four centuries to enrich and glorify the tomb of the Archbishop, to be confiscated and turned to base use by England's first official " defender of the faith " ! But the splendid casket remains.

Though not by any means the largest of our cathedrals, and eclipsed by both Lincoln and York in majesty of conception, in historic interest Canterbury is surpassed only by Westminster Abbey. The central, or Bell Harry, tower is accepted as the finest example we possess of Perpendicular. To this style the western part of the building belongs. The choir and eastern portions are Transitional and Norman, both of a very rare, rich, and peculiar type. No church in England has so splendid and suggestive an interior effect as seen from the west door. The choir screen, instead of destroying the vista, accentuates the beauty and mystery of the holy place beyond.

To attempt an enumeration, in these pages, of only the outstanding objects in the Cathedral would be merely to compile a bald catalogue, without life or interest. The place that held the remains of two such churchmen as Dunstan and Becket, and the tomb of a warrior whose name became the synonym for the perfect knight—the Black Prince—was also the coveted resting-place of lesser priests and princes. These include the figures of Stephen Langton, Cardinal Pole and Henry IV. But there are other things here besides tombs. The Chair of Augustine *may* date from Saxon days. It is of great antiquity, and is naturally one of the most prized material possessions of the English Church, for upon it, for a thousand years, the Metropolitan has been enthroned. Of the wealth of carved work, beautiful old glass, chantry and chapel, relics of the original Saxon Church, and of the modern enrichments and adornments, nothing can be said here. Canterbury is unique : merely to walk around the exterior of the closed building is to have a new experience. In the beams of a rosy dawn the walls glow with an unearthly light. At all times their tints are beautiful and ever-changing, and, as far as colour is concerned, the Cathedral is unmatched in England.

St. Augustine's College occupies the site of the monastery founded by the missionary saint, and incorporates some fragments of the original buildings. It was a notable Benedictine house, second to none in England, and with few peers among those on the Continent. It was the burial-place of its founder and of his convert—Ethelbert, as well as of the Primates of England who followed Augustine. Recent excavations have revealed several of these tombs, and the debris of centuries has been cleared away from the base of

the beautiful Norman stairs leading to the hall of what
is now the King's School.

Any description of the city is impossible also in the
limited space of this chapter. Its many old houses
and several churches ; the glimpses into hidden court
and waterway ; the vestiges of the Roman occupation,
and of Norman military works—all have been ade-
quately dealt with in several admirable monographs
and guides. The West Gate still stands, a dignified and
imposing entrance to the city, upon the London Road.

THE WEAVERS, CANTERBURY.

Five other gates
have disappeared,
together with much
of the medieval
town. The Castle
is a coal-merchant's
warehouse. The
mysterious " Dane
John " is merely a
mound of earth, so
that has escaped
destruction.

Many and various are the places of historic interest
and natural beauty within a short distance. These
include Fordwich, with a queer little timbered town
hall and quaint church ; a tiny place, but once the
" port " of Canterbury. Then there is Harbledown,
where everyone goes for the famous view of the
Cathedral, if not for the delightful village itself crowning the hill.

Herne Bay and Whitstable are popular resorts easily
reached from Canterbury, and the former is as smart
as the latter is quaint and fishy, for here is the home
of the celebrated " native " so dear to epicures. From

the bungalows of Sea Salter to the twin towers of Reculver, nearly ten miles away to the east, little of the Kentish shore is free of red brick. Herne, the mother-village of Herne Bay, is a delightful place with a fine and spacious Early English church, well worthy of being the goal of the five-mile tramp or drive from Canterbury.

Up to the present, our wanderings south of the Thames have revealed little of the " Garden of England," a phrase so often appearing in the advertisements of passenger transport hitherwards. Kent in its garden aspect is perhaps best seen between the Upper Stour towards Ashford and the Upper Medway beyond Maidstone. In this delectable country are no populous centres other than Ashford, which owes its rather shabby prosperity to the railway depot, and Maidstone, the bright and busy capital. The road from Canterbury to the latter town passes Chartham, where there is a handsome fifteenth-century church, and leaves the Stour valley at Chilham, where the road, almost identical with the track of the Pilgrims' Way, crosses the low but densely wooded hills to Charing, ten miles away in the very centre of the county. Chilham has the ruins of a castle, the history of which is long and remarkable. Tradition says that the foundation dates from Roman times, but nothing is definitely known of its possessors until the Norman Bishop of Bayeaux is found holding it in the Domesday Chronicle. Its lords seem to have been unfortunate in their relations with the Crown, for it reverted to the latter over and over again on the attainder of the occupant for treason. The village has a number of old timbered houses in its broad street, and is a picturesque little place.

Charing is a small but pleasant and very ancient town—it claims to be the Roman Durolenum—on the main road from London to Folkestone, and its sleepy ways of the last century have changed perforce to the alertness caused by petrol. It has a fine cruciform church, mainly of Decorated and Perpendicular date, with an ancient stone seat in the chancel. Interest, however, centres chiefly around the remains of the once splendid residence of the Archbishops, now fallen to humble uses, for the great hall has been converted into a barn, and the remaining habitable buildings are used as a farm-house.

From Charing, the Pilgrims' Way hugs the south-west slope of the hills, the modern high road and the Maidstone–Ashford railway running more or less closely together through the valley, and passing Lenham and Harrietsham. Both villages have fine churches—the Perpendicular tower of the last-named is one of the best in Kent—but are otherwise unremarkable. Their surroundings, however, are full of quiet and restful beauty, characteristic of the country, whether in Kent or Surrey, lying below the face of the North Downs.

The finest thing on this road is Leeds Castle, nearly five miles short of Maidstone. It is remarkable, both in its structure and in the unusual and picturesque position it occupies upon two islands in a small mere not far from the public highway. A Saxon fortified dwelling is said to have preceded the Norman building which was in turn superseded by the stately Edwardian pile we now see—though much of the structure was restored and rebuilt in the early part of the last century. It was Royal property for many years after the reign of the first Edward, and, for a time, became a prison for hostages of war during the seventeenth century

During this period, John Evelyn was Constable. Not everyone knows that this stronghold gives a title to the Duke of Leeds, who has no formal connexion with the great Yorkshire city. Leeds village is particularly rich in old houses and its church has a peal of bells rivalling in tunefulness those of most Kentish churches.

The pavements of Maidstone upon Saturdays and market-days are as crowded, and its roadways as dangerous for pedestrians, as any main thoroughfare in London, and despite the great numbers of visitors who add to the daily population of Canterbury, there is a vast difference between the two Kentish centres in the aspect of the pavements. Maidstone is not only the assize town but the chief mart of Kent, and, apart from the group of towns upon the north-east of Rochester where industry is specialized, it has the largest population of workers in the county.

MAIDSTONE.

For that matter, Maidstone may claim to be the headquarters of an important industry— the entirely pleasant and healthy one of hop raising.

Though lacking the attractions of Canterbury, the town is both interesting and to a certain extent picturesque, for it still retains many old houses. Chief of these is the fine sixteenth-century timbered Chillenden House, a one-time property of the Cobhams. It is now a museum of local natural history and archæology, admirably arranged and fairly complete. Here are also pictures and prints, and some relics of a famous son of Maidstone—William Hazlitt. At the back of the rambling building is a pleasaunce of some beauty, with well-planned flower-beds and fine old trees.

The handsome Perpendicular church of All Saints was once collegiate, and considerable remains of the medieval buildings of the college stand between church and river. The old Palace of the Archbishops is to the north of the church. The front is Elizabethan, but the interior of the structure is much older. A few fragments of the original Norman manor house are to be found on the west of the churchyard.

Among the places of historical interest in the environs of Maidstone, Pennenden Heath comes first. This was once a sort of folk-moot on a large scale, and here were enacted many dramas connected with the story of Kent and of England. Not least of these was the assemblage of the little army that set out in an endeavour to free the realm from its threatened bondage to Spain and Rome through the marriage of Mary Tudor.

At Boxley, two miles north of Maidstone, are the remains of a Cistercian Abbey, and on the wind-swept Burham Downs, two miles farther, is the celebrated cromlech—Kits Coty House. A short distance away to the south-west are the "Countless Stones," a circle of fallen boulders thought by some to have been a rude and miniature Stonehenge ; or the stones may perhaps denote burials subsequent to the important sepulture upon the hill.

A pleasant journey up-stream to Aylesford passes Allington, where there is a picturesque ruined castle, the foundations dating from Saxon times. In the last years of the fifteenth century it became the property of the Wyatts. To this family belonged the poet, Sir Thomas, whose unhappy connexion with the matrimonial troubles of Henry VIII is a matter of history. His father, Sir Henry, is the subject of a possibly true story that tells how the life of the knight was saved by a cat. Forgotten by his jailor, Sir Henry was languishing in a dungeon in imminent danger of starvation when the animal, to whom it is presumed he had previously shown some kindness, brought in through the window a freshly-killed pigeon, and continued to do this until the prisoner was liberated.

Not far from Allington, and quite close to the river, is Cobtree Hall, a Tudor building identified by some as the original of " Dingley Dell " in *Pickwick*.

Aylesford is on a bend of the Medway justly famed for its beauty, though we are not far from the reaches marred by the tall chimneys and dusty surroundings of the Portland cement works. Here at Aylesford was fought one of those battles between the original Men of Kent and the invading Jutes, which resulted in overwhelming defeat for the Romano-British, but cost that half-legendary leader, Horsa, his life in the moment of victory.

YALDING BRIDGE.

Aylesford Friary is said to be the earliest foundation of the Carmelites in England. Its few fragments lie close to the river bank. They have been partly incorporated in a house where was born in 1639 Sir Charles Sedley, poet and epigrammatist. An old almshouse in the village street was founded by the poet's father. The Decorated church of St. Peter has a series of memorials, chiefly of the Colpepers, Sedleys and Milners.

Another delightful excursion is to Yalding, nearly six miles south-east of Maidstone, where there is a fourteenth-century bridge. This way goes past East and West Farleigh, both unspoilt and beautiful villages. Here we are again overstepping the arbitrary bounds set by the printer, and a return must be made to the main London Road, hereabouts running through six miles of well-wooded country to West, or Town, Malling. This is a most attractive place, of importance in the eyes of the antiquary, and possessing a bright and picturesque village street with the charming surroundings of parklands, wood and watercourse. A Benedictine nunnery was founded here in 1090, and considerable remains of the noble Abbey Church are still in existence. The Late Norman tower is a very fine example of that period. Of even greater interest is the so-called St. Leonard's Tower on the Mereworth road. This was part of the fortified residence of Bishop Gundulf, and is an early specimen of Norman military work. For its great age, it is in a state of very fine preservation, and should not be missed by the traveller, who will be impressed by its stern and massive dignity. Another specimen of archaic Norman is found in the tower of Malling church, though the remainder of the building, through over-restoration, is of little interest.

South of Malling are several miles of uncultivated country, chiefly heath and forest. The largest tract is called Mereworth Woods, and delightful rambles can be taken by more than one path to Mereworth, to Wateringbury, and—past the curiously alien pile of Mereworth Castle—to Plaxtol. The latter is not far from the most celebrated of Kentish manor houses— Ightham Mote. This truly charming house, the earliest portions of which go back to the first half of the fourteenth century, is well seen from the public road. As its name denotes, it is surrounded by water, and few more characteristic English scenes can be imagined than the richly coloured old walls rising from the moat, the whole framed by a background of the dark foliage of ancient trees. Ightham village, some distance to the north, is itself a picturesque place, with a fine church and many ancient houses. It was in this neighbourhood that the late Mr. Harrison, who lived in the village, carried on his patient researches in the palæolithic flint implement "factory" upon the nearby Downs, where here is also a large prehistoric camp.

On the north side of the Maidstone branch of the Southern Railway, the Kentish North Downs stretch in

IGHTHAM MOTE.

a long wavy line from the break of the Medway Vale above Trottescliffe—"Trosley"—to the pass of the Darent at Otford. Just below the hills, and in the eye of the sun, lies Wrotham—"Rootham"—another pleasant village containing a handsome Decorated church, where may be seen several medieval brasses of the Peckhams of Yaldham. Here, close to the church, stood another of the several homes of the Archbishops of Canterbury. Between Wrotham and

Malling is Offham, a picturesque group of houses surrounding a charming green, upon which is to be found the last quintain in England. Most motor tourists speed here just to glance at the post and crosspiece, and hurry away again without exploring the pleasant surroundings. Although the quintain at Offham is " unique," it is but a copy of the original. Another that existed at Deddington in Oxfordshire was scrapped a few years ago for some unknown reason. The sport is usually described as that of a horseman tilting at the swinging bar while galloping past, but the point in the game was to escape the heavy sand-bag

hung at the other end. This would strike the unskilful player with such force as to unhorse or even disable, him. The usual prize was said to have been a peacock, but whether alive or trussed is not re corded, as far as the writer is aware.

QUINTAIN, OFFHAM.

From Wrotham, a road crosses the Downs through a series of little hamlets to Meopham, nearly six mile away. The village can be more easily reached from Cobham, for it is barely three miles from the " Leather Bottle," and was a favourite expedition with Dickens For those who wish to see a little-known district of Kent, it is well to make this an alternative route for the return journey to Dartford and London, and to make the exploration of the Darent Valley—of which more presently—a separate tour. Meopham has a fine Decorated church with a tower rather older than the rest of the structure, situated in surroundings that are quite delightful, although the village itself is common place. Some pleasurable time might be spent in rambling about the by-ways between the highlands traversed by the main road and the Darent. Here lie the sequestered villages of Ash and Fawkham Green. The district is crossed diagonally by the London–Maidstone road that passes through the north end of Wrotham village.

We now approach the head of the Darent Valley, a district quite as beautiful as those better known river-hollows that cut the chalk at Box Hill and elsewhere. To the left of our road is Seal and to the right, Kemsing; both pleasant places, though the latter gains by being close under the escarpment of the Downs where the Pilgrims' Way scars the hill-side. In the street of Kemsing is St. Edith's Well, once of more than local repute as a miracle-performing fountain for those matrons who were not blessed with offspring. The old church possesses a handsome screen, and an early brass commemorating a priest who is supposed to have died in the early years of the fourteenth century.

Otford stands near the opening of the valley, though the river rises some distance away in the highlands to the south-west. The village is the first of three that have lately become much in favour with artists and photographers. During recent years new buildings, passable enough in themselves, have greatly altered the aspect of this neighbourhood, and a little of the sylvan beauty which characterized the tiny Darent has departed. The threat to run an arterial road through the length of the valley has been received with so much indignant remonstrance that the scheme is likely to be abandoned. Otford has the scanty remains of yet another palace of the Archbishops, and an interesting old church near the green and pond

at the east end of the village street. This drops in a
picturesque curve to the stream at the foot. The
ford here was the scene of two important battles;
the first in 775, when Offa of the Mercians won a great
victory over the men of Kent, and again between
Canute and Edmund Ironside when the English king
was, for the moment, victorious. The church, mainly
Decorated in style, retains some pre-Conquest walling,
and has a number of monuments to the Polhill family.
One of these, on the south wall, has an interesting
reference to the family of Oliver Cromwell, and to
Ireton, with whom the Polhills
of that time were connected.
The oak reredos of the War
Memorial Chapel includes some
old linen-fold panelling rescued
from the ruined archiepiscopal
palace near by. In the chancel

ARCHBISHOPS' PALACE,
OTFORD.

window are some small but
beautiful fragments of Italian
glass. The seventeenth-century church registers are
in excellent condition and of much interest.

A short two miles down the valley is Shoreham, in
perhaps the most picturesque part of the valley.
Hereabouts, the hills rise in boldly-wooded bluffs above
the rich green of the meadows bordering the Darent.
The cottages, their gardens ablaze with flowers in the
summer, are in request among City folk desiring a rural
retreat within reach of a convenient daily train ; a
doubtful blessing which is responsible for the late
outbreak of red brick above Otford. Shoreham Church
has a remarkable amount of finely-carved woodwork
not only in the rood screen and loft, but also in the
exterior porch, reckoned to be one of the best in Kent.

The main road traverses the east side of the valley high above the winter floods. But there is a pleasanter way on the other side of the stream starting from the west end of Shoreham village. This presently skirts Lullingstone Park, close to the old gateway of the house of that name. Not far away is Lullingstone, or Shoreham, Castle, and much confusion arises through the former appellation being given to the residence of the Hart Dykes which stands on the site of an equally ancient building, for the place once belonged to the famed and feared Odo of Bayeaux. Close to the house is the church, which should be entered, if only for the sake of the fine series of monuments to the different families that have held the manor.

Eynesford is but a mile from the junction of our route with the main road, and is the best known of the Darent villages. Though the surroundings are hardly as fine as those of Shoreham, the village, with its wider stream and the open view of the old bridge, is the more picturesque of the two. It contains an interesting Norman and Early English church with a fine tower and shingled spire, and the remains of a castle that, as far as strength and spacious plan are concerned, once ranked with the more important fortresses of Kent. It is said to have been abandoned as long ago as the period immediately following the martyrdom of Becket, in consequence of the excommunication and disgrace of the owner—William de Eynesford—who was held responsible for the last misunderstanding between King and Prelate. Fragments of Roman tile in the masonry prove that on or near the site a Roman building—perhaps similar to that at Darenth—once stood.

The last village of the four in this beautiful upper

section of the valley is Farningham, where we are once more on the great artery from London to Maidstone and Folkestone. Despite this fact, there appears to be less new property here than on the side-track to Sevenoaks, although the motor-bus from far-off Wood Green, in the north of the Metropolis, comes half-way down the narrow street. The picture of the bridge, the pleasant grounds of the near-by hotel and the grey walls of the old church, is quite delightful, and the village is perhaps the least spoilt by modernities of any for several miles on this great highway. Westwards, towards London, the road has become a smooth motor track over most of its course, cutting through the orchards around Swanley in a very drastic fashion. The latter is a small railway town, and calls for no remark, though pleasant wooded country—much of it the profitable woodland of apple, plum and small fruit—surrounds the town, and extends for some distance in the direction of London.

The parallel valley of the Cray is reached at Foots Cray. This has lately become a suburb of Sidcup. To the right, in the direction of Bexley, is North Cray, a village consisting chiefly of two or three large eighteenth-century houses accompanied by a small church of little interest. That at Foot's Cray, however, is quaint and old-fashioned, and is in a delightful situation above the water-meadows. Paul's Cray, on the Orpington road is so named, but the unusual dedication of the old church is really to St. Paulinus. Though this building has some good points, the village is uninteresting, and the road southwards to St. Mary Cray is disfigured by mean shops and dwellings, occasionally relieved by glimpses of the water-meadows of the Cray and the uplands to the east. The last and highest of the Crays

has important paper mills which utterly dwarf the
little church of St. Mary. The valley here is spanned
by the lofty viaduct of the Southern Railway, once the
main line of the old London, Chatham and Dover.

From St. Mary Cray, a road turns uphill to the east,
and leads us through the pleasant glades of Paul's
Cray Common, a favourite place for picnickers. At
the farther extremity, this merges into Chislehurst
Common, and where the two open spaces meet stands
Chislehurst Church, in one of the best kept churchyards in a county remarkable for the beauty of these
hallowed places. The Perpendicular building has
some remains of its predecessor incorporated in the
fabric. It is spacious and handsome, with some
interesting memorials, chief of which is the altar tomb
of Thomas Walsingham, dated 1467.

Camden Place is on the west side of the Common,
and in the original building Camden, the famous
antiquary, once lived. To its successor came Napoleon
III with his wife and son after the *débâcle* of 1870.
The unimpressive memorial to the ill-fated Prince
Imperial stands upon the Common, and is now the
sole reminder of the melancholy episodes which caused
Chislehurst to become known to the world at large,
and, incidentally, to become a fashionable " outer
suburb " of the latter half of the nineteenth century.
Camden Place itself is now the headquarters of a
golf club. A remarkable series of " Caves," more
correctly described as underground galleries, exist in
the chalk beneath the western slopes of the hill. Their
origin is still an unsolved mystery, though several
plausible explanations are current, of which the most
likely is quite unromantic. During the European
War they were used for storing high explosives.

THE UPPER MEDWAY.

CHAPTER VIII

TO TUNBRIDGE WELLS

OF all the old towns surrounding London, Bromley seems to have changed most through that proximity. Within the last twenty-five years, it has suffered greatly in character by losing that air of self-sufficiency which still pervades some others scarcely as distant from the heart of the City. An almost unbroken line of villas, with an occasional " parade " of shops, links up Catford with Plaistow, the northern suburb of Bromley ; and the picturesque pond and old houses at Southend, only a few years ago surrounded by meadows, are now submerged in the urban tide.

A continual stream of vermilion buses pours through the narrow artery of the main street, bound for Westerham Hill, Keston and Farnborough, and the way to Sevenoaks appears to have replaced the more famous Ripley road in the affection of the Sunday morning cyclist. The neighbouring town of Beckenham, which became suburban long before Bromley, is now quiet and semi-rural by comparison and has, in Kelsey Park, one of the most beautiful places of recreation to be found near London. A former owner of the mansion still standing on the west of the park had the happy thought of building a dam across the Pool, a small stream flowing through the demesne, thus forming a fine sheet of water now much appreciated by the inhabitants. The old Beckenham church has disappeared, but the handsome modern building which replaces it has an exceedingly fine square panelled tower, worthy almost of Somerset, that land of splendid church towers, in its ornate decoration.

Bromley College, situated on the London road as we enter the town, was founded in 1666 for the widows of clergymen, by John Warner—one of the Bishops of Rochester who were intimately connected with the town. The old church, a notable landmark high on the ridge carrying the London road, is found just off the main street on the path leading downhill to Shortlands. It contains some brasses, the grave of Dr. Johnson's wife, and other interesting memorials. Despite several renovations, it retains a certain air of antiquity. Those who remember the old market hall which stood in the small square, now marred by a singularly ugly red brick erection, will regret that restoration rather than rebuilding could not have been effected here.

Bromley Palace, near the Chislehurst road, was the one-time residence of the Bishops of Rochester, and the present red brick building was erected by Bishop Thomas in 1775. In the park, a chalybeate spring known as St. Blaize's Well was once of local repute, though probably few of the present inhabitants of Bromley have ever heard of it. To the east of the Palace is Bickley, which has been an important residential suburb for many years. Of more recent growth is the smart new town at Orpington, over two miles to the south-east, where one may see prosperous shops with plate-glass windows dwarfing the picturesque low roofs of the pleasant old village street. This ancient place—it was in existence before the days of Canute the Conqueror—is surrounded by uplands much invaded by new villas, but still of some beauty. It contains a very interesting church situated in another of Kent's beautiful churchyards. The fabric shows some important remains of the original Saxon building in which Roman materials were used. An unusual feature is the canopied tomb of a rector, dating from 1370, in the western porch, where there is also an ancient holy-water stoup. Within the building is a fine thirteenth-century font with a cover of much later date, and several interesting medieval memorials and brasses.

The so-called Priory House—the picturesque old building near the church—was a one-time residence of the Prior of Canterbury. Part of the house appears to have been set aside for the use of the parish priest. It is now in private hands. It will not be forgotten that from Orpington came those first guides to right thinking in matters of art, intended for our Philistine Victorian fathers, who obediently swallowed the whole of their authoritative pronouncements. How many of us read Ruskin now?

Chelsfield is high upon the hill which divides the head-waters of the Cray at Orpington from the parallel valley we have lately traversed through Shoreham and Eynesford. Here is an Early English church with some indications of its Norman predecessor. From this village, it is only two miles to the Sevenoaks road at Green Street Green, and we have, therefore, overshot the terminus of one of the before-mentioned bus services at Farnborough, now a place of tea-houses and small shops that cater for the day visitor. It is an excellent starting-place for visiting the still unspoilt Keston, three miles to the west. The way passes the churchyard, where reposed for a short time the remains of John Lubbock, Lord Avebury, good friend of the thousands who come hither on bank holidays. He lived at High Elms, not far from the village, and the neighbourhood is remarkable for the famous folk who are connected with it, for our road, a very beautiful one in its surroundings, presently passes near Holwood Park, the property of Lord Derby, and once that of the young Pitt. The northern portion of the park has been cut up into building sites, but a pleasant public path runs through that part nearest to Keston, and passes a stone seat set up to commemorate a conversation between Pitt and Wilberforce which took place at this spot, and eventually resulted in the abolition of the slave trade in the British dominions. Hayes Place, near the village of that name, and not far from the south end of Bromley " Common," was Pitt's birthplace, and here his father, the Earl of Chatham, died after his seizure in the House of Lords. Hayes is unremarkable now, except for its open breezy common, but Keston has both a common, commanding wide if intermittent views, and a chain of quite delightful ponds from which the Ravensbourne runs to Deptford Creek. The church is in a charming position high above the southernmost of these miniature lakes, overlooking the gradual rise which eventually becomes the North Downs at Westerham Hill. South-east of Keston, and approached by a picturesque and hilly lane, is the out-of-the-way village of Downe, where Charles Darwin died in 1882 after a residence of several years.

From Green Street Green the main road continues, with little to remark except some occasional fine views, to Dunton Green near Sevenoaks, but an alternative road to the right about a mile from Green Street leads through wooded and sequestered ways to Knockholt and Chevening. Knockholt is almost on the ridge of the Downs, and its landmark " Beeches " are visible not only over the Weald of Kent and Sussex, but from most of the South London heights. The hill-top is but 770 feet above the sea, and would not be noticed apart from the remainder of the ridge were it not for the fine group of trees upon the sky-line.

Chevening lies to the east of the park of that name. The Place, the seat of Earl Stanhope, is a treasure-house of relics and curiosities. The building was the work of Inigo Jones, but has been much altered, and certainly not improved, since that architect's day. Chevening church has also suffered from injudicious restoration at various times, but it should be visited, if only to inspect the remarkable carving by Chantry of the figure of Lady Frederick Stanhope.

The most noteworthy event in the history of Chevening was the successful passage across the lake in the park of a model craft, the very first to be propelled by steam.

The branch railway to Westerham is now passed, and soon afterwards the important high road, traversed by the " East Surrey " motor-buses, connecting Maidstone with Guildford and, for the greater part of the way, running close to the foot of the Downs. Turning westwards, we should presently enter the scattered village of Sundridge, leading into picturesque half-timbered Brasted, but our way is to the east by Riverhead, situated on the main road to Sevenoaks. Here, turning southwards, we are soon in the outskirts of that town.

To say that Sevenoaks is one of the most attractive towns in Kent is an easy way out of a difficulty that faces every topographical writer. No Kentish town is entirely unattractive, and a round half-dozen or so can hold their own with any in England. Perhaps the only fault to be found with Sevenoaks is that it is too near London, and that the Southern Railway has for many years proved too kind in the matter of City trains. In other words, it has long since become "suburban," but no one can blame the discerning Londoner for making his home on the sandy slopes of this notable hill. A recent plan to build a huge "garden city" on the north side of the town—obliterating the pleasant meadows of the Darent—is to be viewed with regret; though it is possible that haphazard building will eventually do more harm than a cut-and-dried scheme presumably scrutinized by qualified persons.

It is in its immediate surroundings that Sevenoaks excels, and Knole, one of the most famous and beautiful of "stately homes," is on its very edge. We climb the hill to the spacious Perpendicular church of St. Nicholas, and find the entrance to Knole Park on the other side of the way. It is a most remarkably diversified expanse of open sward and woodland, and the greater portion is generally open to the public, a privilege apparently appreciated in a practical manner by those who visit it, for on no occasion has the writer noticed even a match-end disfiguring its velvet turf.

The magnificent timber includes an avenue of oaks called the Duchess Walk and several single trees of great size. Of these, the most imposing are the King Beech and an oak, called " old " in the seventeenth century. But this one-time forest monarch is now decrepit and in crutches.

The house was commenced by Archbishop Bourchier of Canterbury about 1460, though a manor had been in existence long before. It remained in the possession of the prelates until it was handed by Cranmer to Henry VIII. Elizabeth presented it to her relative —Thomas Sackville—in 1603, and the Sackville-West family now hold it. The principal treasures are pictures, but the sixteenth-century tapestry of the chapel is perhaps the most interesting relic in this grand old house.

The Wilderness, another fine demesne to the north of Knole, was once the property of Lord Hillingdon. It is in process of disintegration, but a delightful path passes through it by which we might ramble to Seal, a pleasant and picturesque place with a fine church high upon a sandy knoll, of which a glimpse was caught in the last chapter. But our way is now by the Hastings road, and as we proceed, several alluring panoramic views of the " far-flung Weald " are visible upon the eight-mile course through Hildenborough to the old Medway town of Tunbridge. There appears to be an agreement among map-makers and railway powers to spell the first syllable of this name with an " o," while the original " u " is reserved for " the Wells." But every native says Tunbridge, and we will adhere to the old spelling.

Among the ancient houses still remaining, the best are the timbered sixteenth-century " Chequers " inn and the "Portreeves House" in Bordyke. But the chief interest of the town is in its Norman Castle, to be found—like several others south of the Thames—in the centre of a public garden. The original builder was one FitzGilbert, who lived in the reign of Henry I. The stronghold was evidently placed at this point to guard the important river-crossing on the road from Hastings to London. The fortifications were dismantled during the Civil War, and it would appear that whatever masonry could easily be broken up was afterwards used to build a private residence near the gatehouse. The keep still remains in a state of fair preservation.

TUNBRIDGE CASTLE.

Tunbridge Grammar School is of more than local repute, and has had a history of nearly four hundred years, though the original buildings of Lord Mayor Judd have been swept away in modern improvements. The church, spacious and dignified, does not contain many details of interest, and has been much rebuilt and enlarged in modern times.

The best excursion from Tunbridge is westwards to Penshurst, a small village situated in a delightful and secluded part of the Medway valley, and having in its "Place" perhaps the finest of the ancient houses of southern England. Our way goes uphill to picturesque Bidborough, on rising ground commanding glorious views over the country we have lately traversed, and also south-westwards towards Ashdown Forest. Penshurst is nearly five miles from Tunbridge, and is little more than a hamlet, with church and inn—the

" Leicester Arms "—grouped upon the summit of a steep hill above the river. Some restored timber cottages mask the churchyard, and the entrance thereto is under one of them. St. John's Church is a mixture of three styles—Early English, Decorated and Perpendicular. It was " restored " with a heavy hand by Sir Gilbert Scott, and it is now difficult to identify the ancient work. The chief interest of the building naturally centres in the memorials of the famous family whose historic seat is just beyond the north wall of the churchyard.

Penshurst was once called Penchester, and this was the surname of the Norman lord who first possessed the property. After being connected with several names famous in the story of England—including that of Sir John de Pulteney who was four times Lord Mayor of London—it was given to Sir William Sidney by Edward VI. The present owner—Lord de Lisle and Dudley—is a descendant of that knight.

The principal gateway with its tower, and the north and west sides, were erected in the sixteenth century. That part called the Buckingham Building is over one hundred years older, and was built by the Duke of Bedford, son of Henry IV. Still more ancient is the fine hall of Sir John de Pulteney, said to be the best example of its kind in England. The perfect proportions and magnificent details are noteworthy, but, strangely enough, the first impression is that the hall is small. This, and the state apartments with their many family portraits, are open to the public on certain week-days, and the personal relics of the Sidney family usually come in for interested attention. A personal belonging of the most illustrious of the line—Sir Philip —brings perhaps most remark : it is his shaving-glass.

The gardens vie with the park in the beauty that comes after centuries of care and attention, and though the latter is not of great extent, it presents a series of aspects each quite different to the other : the finest is naturally that which commands the incomparable north front of the Place. A path running for some distance through the park, and parallel with the road, leads towards Penshurst station, two miles away.

Resuming the southward way, we may bear to the right after climbing the hill from Penshurst bridge and make for Speldhurst, where there is a rebuilt church containing ten windows by Burne-Jones. Here there is a choice of roads to Tunbridge Wells, either by way of Southborough on the London road, or southwards to the narrow ridge that ends in Rustall Common, where we shall find the famous Toad Rock, one of the sights of the Wells, and a good object-lesson—for amateur geologists —of the effects of denudation.

LYCH GATE, PENSHURST.

Like the older inland watering-places—Bath, Cheltenham and Leamington—Tunbridge Wells has settled down to be a residential town, though there seems to be a greater proportion of young people here than in the western spas, with a consequent greater liveliness and bustle in its streets. It is true, also, that many sensible folk spend their summer fortnight in exploring the delightful borderland of Kent and Sussex, returning each night to sleep at the Wells, as a pleasant relief from the yearly monotony of the seaside. Given fine weather, it is safe to say that the born explorer could easily find some entirely fresh beauty for each of twelve days within a few miles' radius from the Pantiles. This picturesque row of shops and dwellings, so called from the original pavement, was—apart from some temporary wooden buildings erected in a hurry for the rush of health-seekers—the first row of houses to spring up in the early part of the seventeenth century, soon after the waters had been " discovered " by Lord North. It has always been the centre of the town and, with the near-by common, is still the most attractive quarter. At one end is the Chalybeate spring, where a soberly-dressed custodian dispenses the nectar, elsewhere pronounced by Sam Weller to taste of warm flat-irons, at one penny per glass. At the other is the Pump Room, and the seventeenth-century church, with its rare dedication to King Charles the Martyr.

The breezy, sunbaked common introduces us to two of the nearer natural attractions of Tunbridge Wells—the Happy Valley and the High Rocks. Near the former are outcrops of greensand, much scarred by Cockney immortality-seekers, but with surroundings more or less innocuous. The High Rocks have been enclosed in a sixpenny show-case, to their obvious detriment.

The excursion to Eridge should be undertaken, if only for the sake of the views across a countryside which has nothing of Kent or Sussex in its composition but is distinctly Devonian in appearance, and especially reminiscent of the portion of that belauded county bordering upon Dorset. Eridge Castle is the seat of the Marquis of Abergavenny, and the magnificently wooded park may be seen by the visitor armed with an easily-obtained pass. At Eridge Green is another series of sandstone rocks weirdly shaped by rain and frost.

From Tunbridge Wells to Groombridge is a delightful walk of four miles from the Pantiles. Groombridge church is a strange, debased Gothic building of 1625, built of red brick and containing some very fine brass chandeliers. Here also is the moated Groombridge Place, once the prison of a Duke of Orleans captured by the then owner—Sir Richard Waller—at the Battle of Agincourt. From the village, a road bears north-westward to Ashurst near the Med-way, and thence, by way of remote and beautiful winding lanes, we eventually reach Hever, in the Eden Valley, some eight miles or more from Groombridge.

THE PANTILES.

Hever Castle shares with Penshurst and Knole the fame of being one of the three best fortified mansions in Kent. It is, unfortunately, impracticable for us to compare it with the others, access to the grounds and castle being difficult, though the stringency of the regulations have been relaxed during recent years. The building, surrounded by its moat, is extremely picturesque, and the modern buildings across the moat are highly successful adaptations of old work. The ancient portions date chiefly from about the year 1450. The owner at that time was another Lord Mayor of London—Sir Geoffrey Boleyn—whose great-grand-daughter Anne had the misfortune to attract the notice of Henry VIII. The burly image of that monarch swings to and fro—with a separate front and back view—outside the village inn.

Hever church is partly Early English, but with much Perpendicular additions. It contains the tomb of Sir Thomas Boleyn, Queen Elizabeth's maternal grandfather, surmounted by a very fine brass of the knight—he died Earl of Wiltshire—in the insignia of the Garter. Another ancient and remarkable brass is that of Margaret Cheyn, dated 1419. Among other noteworthy details of this church is the rare feature of a fireplace that has been in existence far beyond the times when such comforts were a not unusual feature of the great man's pew. The wrought-iron lectern is of local manufacture, as are some other examples of iron-work within the building.

CHIDDINGSTONE.

About two miles east of Hever, on the way to Penshurst, is Chiddingstone, a village possessing several very beautiful old half-timbered houses and an interesting Perpendicular church. Our path, however, is northwards to Westerham, and we cannot do better than join the main road at Edenbridge, which, as its name denotes, is built around the crossing of a tributary of the Medway. The bridge itself is said to incorporate much of the ruined masonry of Sterborough Castle, near Lingfield. As a consequence of its railway station Edenbridge has lately grown some suburbs—quite inoffensive but in great contrast to the old village street, where are still left a few good ancient houses

One in particular, on the right hand as we proceed in the direction of Westerham, was once occupied by Sir William Taylor, Lord Mayor of London in 1469. It still bears his own arms, and those of his Company, upon the doorway. The church, a mixture of styles from Norman to Perpendicular, has part of its roof covered with slabs of Horsham stone, a material very commonly used for this purpose in past days throughout the Weald.

The Westerham road climbs steadily to Crockham Hill with fine retrospective views. It then descends to the narrow vale in which lies Westerham, the bold line of the Downs flung east and west in front. The town itself is quite unspoilt and rural in its immediate surroundings, despite the fact that the great east and west road between Maidstone and Guildford is here crossed by a much used motor-road to the coast. Happily, the railway station forms the terminus of a branch line from Dunton Green, and the service cannot be called suburban.

The hero of Westerham is Wolfe, and a spirited statue of the victor of Quebec stands upon the green, while the church has a tablet to his memory over the south door. This over-restored building contains many interesting brasses, but little besides to detain the visitor. Quebec House, much altered since the days of Wolfe's boyhood—he was unexpectedly born at the vicarage, where his mother was staying for a short holiday, but afterwards lived here—is still in the possession of a member of the family. Another fine house called Squerries, referred to by Evelyn the Diarist, contains some relics of the soldier. It stands to the south-west of the town, near the trickling rivulet which eventually becomes the Darent.

The London road makes for the steep face of the Down forming the highest land in Kent, and by a sharp bend—the scene of hill-climbing contests in the earlier days of motoring—we reach the crossing of the Pilgrim's Way, and presently the scarlet coat of a " General " shows that Westerham Hill is within easy reach of London Bridge. To the right, on a windy hill, is the isolated church at Cudham, famous for its monster yews. To the left is the lighthouse for airmen, and presently, on the same side of the way, a long narrow combe, chequered in an extraordinary fashion by small fenced plots with every imaginable type of bungalow accompanying them. This locality is called Biggin Hill, a name well known to early " wireless " enthusiasts, for here transmissions from America were first caught for the benefit of Londoners " listening in." Here is also a depot of the Royal Air Force, whose hutments do not add materially to the beauty of the scenery.

High on a spur of the Downs to the west of Westerham Hill is Tatsfield, just across the border-line in Surrey. From this point, we may go on to Warlingham and Chelsham—the former much in favour at one time with " beanfeasters," the latter a pretty little village rather off the beaten track. Holiday parties in wagonettes are almost extinct, for the long-distance motor " charrybang " thunders farther afield—usually until its course is arrested by the sea. So nowadays Warlingham is in more request as a residential place and is as quiet as Chelsham. At Farley, a long mile to the north, there is a small church with a Norman doorway, but the enormous asylum close by has spoilt the rurality of the hamlet, just as the creeping lines of the Croydon suburbs have changed Sanderstead, a short distance to the west. The same fate is overtaking Addington, which, until lately, seemed to have been ignored by the builder. Addington Park was, for the greater part of the last century, the residence of the Archbishops of Canterbury in succession to the old palace at Croydon. It was originally a hunting seat of that baiter of prelates, Henry VIII, and a memorial brass to one of his servants will be found in the church, besides those of some of the Archbishops who resided here, and whose graves are in the churchyard.

Two miles north-east of Addington is West Wickham, where we shall be again in Kent. The church, a short distance from the uninteresting village, is notable for its picturesque situation, and for some ancient stained glass. Close by is the fine mansion called Wickham Court, the oldest portions dating from the late fifteenth century. From the west end of the village, we enter the new and smart suburb called Langley Park and, passing through this district, reach Shirley, a district of miniature pebbley hills much frequented by picnic parties from Croydon.

CHAPTER IX

CROYDON TO THE NORTH DOWNS

THOSE Londoners who are in what they very rightly term the prime of life will readily remember seeing haymakers at work between the old tram terminus at Streatham and the northern edge of Croydon, but one must now travel several wearisome miles south of the great County Borough before country sights and sounds are in evidence. Croydon would be properly recognized as one of the large towns of England if it were farther removed from the Metropolis. It is, of course, quite separate and shares with Guildford the honour of being the chief seat of administration in Surrey. In its retail trafficking and trading, it yields first place to no town south of the Thames. It is exceptionally fortunate in its beautiful surroundings on the east, west, and south ; and, despite its crowded bustle, is a pleasant and healthy town. Its history, on the evidence of the spade, goes back to Celtic days, and on the evidence of parchment, to 962, where it is called Crogdene—the Crooked Valley— and this same document—a will—also proves the existence of a church at that date. The main street has long been the despair of the Town Council, who threaten periodically to remove the old Whitgift Hospital in the interest of motorists bound for Brighton. " The Hospital of the Holy Trinity " is a late Tudor erection of red brick enclosing a picturesque grassy quadrangle, and was founded by Archbishop Whitgift for the use of thirty-six approved poor folk, eighteen from Lambeth and eighteen from Croydon. These were the two districts in which the founder was interested, for the country seat of the Archbishops was for a great length of time at Croydon Palace. This ancient pile, restored and much altered, stands on the east of the parish church and now—after extraordinary vicissitudes—is a school for girls. The handsome church is said to be a fair copy of that destroyed by fire in 1867. It still retains certain fragments of old work, and some restored tombs of the Archbishops.

Croydon possesses in Crohamhurst one of the finest recreation grounds of any town in the kingdom. This is a considerable wooded hill to the south-west, close to the Selsdon road. Another, farther off to the south-east, is the well-known Riddlesdown, much favoured by " treats " and " outings." It is possible to escape the monotony of the Brighton road through Purley by striking southwards from Crohamhurst by way of Sanderstead. New villas are, of course, everywhere in evidence, but the way is still pleasant and the gardens are bright with flowers in spring and summer. Following this by-way and bearing to the right, we arrive at Kenley, situated in the lower part of the picturesque Caterham Valley. This narrow combe retains a certain charm, though its sides are dotted with the substantial houses of the well-to-do, and Caterham itself is quite an elderly rural suburb.

Fortunately, the long narrow ridge of Farthing Downs has been saved from the builder, and the pedestrian should walk along its breezy length, and then take the lane which continues from the southern extremity of the open hill-top to lonely little Chaldon, where there is a church famous for its medieval wall painting, usually known as the " Ladder of Salvation." This was discovered beneath layers of whitewash during a nineteenth-century restoration and is one of the most elaborate and remarkable of its kind in existence.

THE WHITGIFT HOSPITAL, CROYDON.

The division across the middle of the design is reminiscent of the section plan of a floor and ceiling ; the ladder apparently passes through a small trap-door in the centre, and souls are seen passing up and down. Angels are receiving the good souls in Paradise, while on the lower floor some remarkably quaint fiends are dealing with the wicked in approved fashion. A reputed " Tree of Life " is thriving in this dungeon, but possibly because the artist had nowhere else to put it. His masterpiece covers the whole of the west wall. The earliest portion of the building is archaic

Norman, and it possesses a bell said to date from the middle of the thirteenth century.

To the east of Caterham is Woldingham, until recently an isolated church-hamlet just below the north side of the Downs. It is now a considerable though scattered suburb, but with many by-ways from which new red-tiled roofs are still out of sight. Unfortunately, the very top of the ridge itself has been invaded by the largest of these residences, and it is impossible to obtain an extensive view until we have walked eastwards to a point on the Downs, well over 800 feet above the sea, where the road leaves the edge of the escarpment and drops to Oxted. Several well-known summits of the Sussex Downs may be identified from this part of the height, which cannot now be encroached upon, and the prospect over the Weald is truly superb.

Instead of going directly into Oxted, we bear to the left past Titsey Church and soon reach Limpsfield, a pleasant place of gardens and odd pieces of common-land. The old cottages near the church are very picturesque. One house in particular, called " Detilens," is noteworthy for the old panelling in the interior. The parish church, though restored, still possesses some ancient features. The recess behind the altar is thought to have been a receptacle for sacred relics. On the far side of the village is a wild common of considerable extent, with the rather overpowering buildings of a large school upon its western side.

The route now lies along the much-travelled Reigate road, past the railway and the houses of New Oxted. Here an effort to deal with the architecture of the principal row of shops and banks has met with great success. The new is as picturesque and pleasing as is the old at the bottom of the hill. The church is a massive building of all dates from early Norman in the chancel-arch to mid-Victorian " restoration " work here, there and everywhere. Among the details are an Easter sepulchre ; an ancient iron chest ; a Jacobean Holy Table, unused ; and a queer brass, dated 1613, to a child of five, John Hoskins, who is represented as a dashing gallant of the period. His brother, who died at the same age, was also a precocious young-

LIMPSFIELD.

ster, if we may be-lieve the proofs so carefully set forth on his memorial.

We now pass through the old vil-lage, with its several timbered cottages and the ancient " Bell " inn, on our way to Godstone. At about one mile from Oxted is a lane on the left to Tan-dridge, where there was once a priory

of Augustinians. A coffin slab in the north porch of the church was brought from the site, but apparently no other relics of this religious house remain. Two noteworthy features of the church, which has been practically rebuilt, are the enormous timbers of the belfry and a magnificent yew in the churchyard. Three miles farther is Crowhurst, a charming little place on a small hill above the Weald. Here is another great yew and a picturesque farmhouse, once the mansion of an old Surrey family whose surname was Angel. Within the altar-rails of the church is a Sussex iron grave-slab to Anne Forster, dated 1591.

Resuming the main route, Marden Park and " Castle " are noticed upon the hill-slope away to the right, and soon the so-called Church Town of Godstone is reached, just off the highway and to the south. Here is a church restored to such an extent by Sir Gilbert Scott that he may be said to have rebuilt it. Within are two fine seventeenth-century marble effigies of Sir John Evelyn and his wife, and other memorials of the same family. The surroundings of the church are rendered delightful by the picturesque group of almshouses—built by Scott and far more worthy of praise than the work he expended upon the church—and the surrounding groups of fine trees and shady hedgerows.

Half a mile to the west are Godstone Green and signs of civilization ; for this is another terminus of the London bus services. But the green, pond and old tress, and still older inns, are much the same as they were a century ago. The old " White Hart," now called " The Clayton Arms," sets out that it was established in the reign of Richard III, and that it has been patronized by England's two greatest Queens. A more lasting title to renown comes from the pages of *Rural Rides*, for it was a house of call for Cobbett on his frequent journeys through central Surrey.

From the Green, the main Eastbourne road goes past Godstone station to Lingfield, some six miles or more to the south. A delightful place of old houses and quaint corners is Lingfield, with a village cage and a noble cruciform Perpendicular church, once collegiate, containing a series of interesting monuments of the Cobhams of Sterborough and also of the Effing-

ham Howards. Sterborough Castle, some distance to
the east in the direction of Edenbridge, is now merely
a site marked by a moat. It was the prison of Louis
Bourbon for some years after the battle of Agincourt,
where he was taken captive.

Bletchingley is the next village east of Godstone. This
was once a place of some importance with a weekly
market and two members of Parliament, of whom one
of the last was Lord Palmerston. As we enter from
the west, we pass the site of the ancient castle founded
in the Conqueror's reign by Richard of Tunbridge. It
was possessed by the Clares and Staffords until the last

THE " CLAYTON ARMS," GODSTONE.

of that line—the third
Duke of Buckingham
— fell into disgrace
with Henry VIII. The
manor eventually came
by purchase to Sir
Robert Clayton, a Lord
Mayor of London,
whose extraordinary
monument, erected before his death, is one of the
" sights " of Bletchingley church. This is an interesting building with much late Norman and Early
English detail in the fabric Its fine spire, which rose
forty feet above the battlements, was burnt, and the
ancient bells " destroyed in a great conflagration which
sorely dismayed the country around " in 1606. At
Brewer Street, an offshoot of the little town over half
a mile on the road to White Hill, is the old Gatehouse
of the Manor, and a little farther are two fine houses
—the Jacobean Pendhill Court, and another, of which
the reputed architect was Inigo Jones.

It is now a long mile to Nutfield, with its old posting

inn—the " Queen's Head "—and high-placed church, wherein we may see a Burne-Jones window and ancient carved stalls in the chancel. Here, if we desire to escape the red brick of Redhill lying straight before us, we may bear off to the right towards the hills, and make for Merstham on the London–Brighton road just south of the crossing of the Pilgrim's Way. On the way, we shall notice some strange greyish-blue scars on the hill-side. These are evidences of Nutfield's one industry, the excavation of fuller's earth—a rare commodity which still commands good prices.

Merstham church is a very much restored thirteenth-century building containing a few interesting brasses, a fine twelfth-century font, and a relic of old London Bridge consisting of a broken piece of carving. How it found its resting-place here is not told. The principal charm of the church is its pleasant situation on a mound just in front of the Downs, though the spot cannot in these days be called quiet ; the shriek of the London express as it enters the near-by tunnel, and an unending diapason of hoots, indicating the proximity of the Brighton road, have destroyed its ancient peace.

The Pilgrim's Way rises steeply to the north and west of Gatton Park, the seat of the Colmans of Norwich. The history of Gatton throws a queer sidelight on the former political history of this realm. In 1451 the manor was granted the privilege of returning two members to Parliament, and continued to do so until the Reform Act of 1832. Only two years previously, Lord Mondon had bought the estate for £100,000 solely with the idea of keeping the members in his pocket. However, he made the best of a bad bargain, and commenced to build a princely palace. He also embellished the small church with all sorts of exotic fittings which, though interesting in themselves, are out of place in their simple surroundings. A relic of the " rotten borough " days will be pointed out in the park ; this is a small formal erection on a mound. It served as the " town hall " for the election of members.

From Gatton, we descend to the northern suburbs of Reigate and, passing the railway station, enter the town by the unusual approach of a tunnel, which penetrates Castle Hill. The stronghold of the powerful de Warennes is no more, and the picturesque gate-

LINGFIELD.

way to the public gardens is in eighteenth-century " Gothic." The mysterious caverns beneath have given rise to all sorts of romantic tales as to their origin, but experts decide that they are merely sandpits, and we must leave it at that.

Very little of bygone days remains in Reigate. Some side turnings reveal here and there a steep tiled roof and timbered front, and a few years ago a thirteenth-century crypt was discovered at the back of Slip Shoe Lane. The market house, built on the sideways slope of the main street, dates from 1708, and is said to be on the actual site of a " Pilgrim Chapel " dedicated to St. Thomas, and used as a halting-place for prayer by devotees on their way to Canterbury. The earliest part of the spacious parish church is Transitional, the eastern end being Early English. The most notable memorial is to that Lord Howard of Effingham who was Lord Admiral of England at the time of the Armada. His body lies in a vault beneath the chancel, and the inscription on the brass is a copy of that upon the coffin. A monument of Richard Ladbroke, who died in 1730, so worried the congregation that it was removed some years ago to the vestry. The visitor who penetrates to this retreat will sympathize with the poor folk when he sees the strange conception. It is difficult to realize how devotions were possible in the presence of this nightmare. In complete contrast is the kneeling figure of Katherine Elyot, who died less than sixty years before, but quite evidently in a different age. Reigate Priory stands on the site of a home of Augustinians founded in the thirteenth century. It was once the home of Admiral Lord Howard, and is now that of Admiral Earl Beatty.

Three miles to the south-west of Reigate is Leigh, locally called " Li." We reach this village by traversing Reigate Heath with its derelict windmill, and then by wooded lanes we pass Leigh Place, an ancient moated house, much rebuilt, that is said to be on the site of a dwelling of the de Braose. The village is small and quite off the way to any important place, unless the winding lanes thither can be said to form an alternative to the crowded main roads to the south. The Perpendicular church contains brasses, dated 1449, of the Ardernes who once held Leigh Place.

A pleasant walk over Snower Hill now brings us to Betchworth, three miles away to the north. We come first to Betchworth Church End, a place quite separate from the straggling village on the high road. Here is a small church with a central tower incorporating some Norman work ; the remainder of the building is mainly Early English. The chief interest of the

R

interior is an archaic oak chest made from one piece of timber, and said to be eight hundred years old. There is also a brass to a vicar named William Wordsworth, dated 1533. Betchworth Castle is some distance to the west, and belongs to the Dorking district.

We now pass first over the Reigate–Dorking road and then the railway, and make for the landmark trees on the summit of the Downs called Betchworth Clump. Here is another wonderful view over the Weald, bounded by the distant South Downs. Below us to the east, the range is broken by Pebblecombe, through which passes the Banstead road. To the right, in the direction of Box Hill, the escarpment is defaced by chalk quarries, but the disfigurement is not so apparent from above as from Betchworth in the valley. Eastwards, Buckland Hill rises above the village of that name, and beyond is Colley Hill, above Reigate, forming the magnificent public park for that town.

The scattered villages of Headley and Walton on the Hill are a short distance north of Pebblecombe. The latter has a church containing a fine leaden font, a rare feature in this part of England. The Tudor farm-house called Walton Place was one of the homes of Anne of Cleves. To the right of the road stretches Walton Heath, where Roman remains have been found on more than one occasion. The spire of the modern Kingswood church appears among the trees ahead, and presently we arrive at the cross-roads on Banstead Heath. To the left is Tadworth, on the road to Epsom Downs, and some two miles or more to the right is the still secluded village of Chipstead and a fine cruciform church. Certain details here are of Norman date, but the greater portion of the building is Early English, and to this period belong the curious lancet windows of the chancel.

Banstead would be pleasanter if we could forget the Asylum. The great range of buildings on the sky-line —and it would be a very cold-hearted mortal who would grudge the patients the sunshine and fresh air of these heights—might be bearable if they had been erected at any other than that dreadful era for architecture in England—the " eighteen-seventies." Occasionally, however, we have a merciful hedge of trees, or a rise of Banstead Downs, to screen this brick enormity. These windswept hills were used for horse-racing before the Downs of Epsom, for that purpose, had been heard of. They are gradually disappearing under the urban tide, but rural amenities still linger around Banstead church, and the rustic lane leading to Woodmansterne is as yet unspoilt. The latter hamlet used to have a tiny church of the utmost simplicity, but a combined " restorer and enlarger " came along, and it is now featureless. Less than a mile to the north is a fine mansion called The Oaks, an improvement by a former Earl of Derby on a Tudor house which he thus renamed. From this house the famous " ladies' race " at Epsom obtained its title.

Beyond the Brighton road and railway, and at the foot of Farthing Downs, is Coulsdon, another little church-hamlet lately discovered and developed by the builder. Here again the hand of the restorer has been heavy, though the worst offender was perhaps a grandfather of him who maltreated Woodmansterne. Coulsdon church has not much to show, and we may turn northwards again through busy Purley with its clanging trams and thronging motor-buses—and every important inn on the road appears to keep its own waiting fleet— to the tower and chimes of municipal Croydon.

THE DOWNS FROM THE GUILDFORD ROAD.

CHAPTER X

TO GUILDFORD

THE western road from Croydon runs for some
miles through a string of villages and small
towns that have almost entirely lost their rural aspect
and are now frankly suburban, and growing at a rate
which threatens soon to achieve unbroken bricks and
mortar all the way to Epsom. The first two—Beddington and Wallington—call for little remark. The
former has an ornately decorated church, with several
memorials of the Carews who once lived at Beddington
Hall, now a school. Beyond Wallington is Carshalton
on the Wandle—a stream that still retains some pretty
rustic reaches on its short course to the Thames at
Wandsworth. As it flows through Carshalton, it
widens into a clear and picturesque sheet of water
which adds greatly to the attractiveness of a town
that is gradually exchanging its older landmarks for
things new and smart. The church has been so much
altered, doubtless to seat larger congregations, that it
is difficult to trace the indications of an older fabric.
Here are a number of memorials to Ellenbrygges and
Gaynesfords, once notable local families.

The west end of Carshalton becomes the east end of Sutton, a bright and busy suburban town on the way to Reigate—and the alternative road to Brighton. On its western side Sutton is, in turn, getting into touch with Cheam, until quite recently a place of small old cottages set among the trees at the south-east corner of Nonsuch Park. The present great house of Cheam stands near the site of the splendid palace built by Henry VIII on so magnificent a scale as to warrant its boastful name. It was handed over to Barbara Villiers by Charles II, and soon afterwards fell to the housebreaker. Much of the material is said to have been used in building some of the eighteenth-century mansions on the south of Epsom.

Cheam church is new and uninteresting, but the chancel of the old building stands apart and still retains a number of brasses, and also several memorials of the Lumley family. The best relic of old time here, however, is White Hall, an Elizabethan house of picturesque gables and chimneys set in a small but very charming garden.

It is less than two miles now to Ewell, where we are fairly on the way to the Downs—this time of West Surrey—and on Sundays and Bank Holidays the main street of the little town is thronged with cits bound for Box Hill and beyond. Most of the wheelers, glancing at the hoary old tower rising through the trees, think they have caught a glimpse of Ewell church, but the object is merely a shell, and was left " to beautify the landscape " by the church-breakers of last century. They gave the new building its own peculiar steeple—possibly not with the same intention.

Ewell is said to mean At-the-well, and the spring still gushes forth to form a limpid stream that, under the name of the Hogsmill River, finds its way to the Thames at Kingston. A more famous well—now quite forgotten, though the name lingers to indicate an outlying district—was at Epsom. This was a saline spring " discovered " about ten years after the chalybeate at Tunbridge became fashionable. In a very short time, booths and huts—in the Kentish fashion—had to be hastily run up for the use of visitors. Substantial building followed in due course, and by the commencement of the eighteenth century Epsom was well on the way to becoming a second Cheltenham. But before the spa had attained its centenary, a decline had set in, and all that remains to remind us of its vanished fame is a peculiarly disagreeable " salts " which was the bane of childhood and which, needless to say, has no particular connexion with Epsom.

It is through the famous Spring Meeting that Epsom has a world-wide notoriety, and on Derby Wednesday the otherwise quiet roads leading to the Downs are packed with slowly-moving crowds marshalled by a special force of Metropolitan Police. Apart from that exciting week, the town is almost demurely staid, and so wide is its High Street that we hardly notice the ordinary traffic bound for Dorking and the south-west. Where this main artery bears to the left for Ashtead are some elderly houses that introduce us to a pleasant break in the ever-growing villadom of the Dorking road. This is at Epsom Common, a breezy expanse crossed by the Portsmouth railway, and continued on the west by Ashtead Woods, beloved of school treat picnickers and blackberry gatherers in their season. A short distance to the west of the highway is The Durdans, Lord Rosebery's fine seat, the grounds of which extend nearly to the course of the Ermyn or Stane Street, a Roman road that traverses the Race-course Downs.

Roman brickwork has been used in Ashtead church, which retains fragments of a pre-Conquest building. It was erected within the walls of a prehistoric earthwork, and the course of the ancient road ran close by. The old village was always a small place, but railway Ashtead is extensive, and would be larger still but for the bar of the woods, and also that of the Park, within which the church is situated. The last of the new villas brings us within hailing distance of Leatherhead, an ancient town that boasts several Tudor, or perhaps Elizabethan, houses and an inn that was of note in the days of Henry VIII. This is the building known as the " Old Running Horse." Its landlady was the subject of a doggerel rhyme composed by Poet Laureate Skelton, entitled *The Tunning of Elinour Rumming*. A larger house, the " Swan," was a notable posting inn in the seventeenth and eighteenth centuries.

THE " RUNNING HORSE," LEATHERHEAD.

Leatherhead church, chiefly of Early English and Perpendicular date, is a cruciform building of some interest. The remains of a small cell, supposed to have been used by an anchorite, are pointed out on the north of the chancel, and the north transept has a curious double squint. Among some of the treasures is a chained Book of Homilies dated 1708, and among the memorials will be noticed the gravestone of Lady Diana Turner in the porch. She was paralysed and unable to leave her sedan-chair, and it is said that she expressed a desire to be buried where she had followed the service from the doorway. The town has done well in its useful—if not original—War Memorial. The brick and stone arcaded shelter blends admirably with the mellow tones of the old houses surrounding it.

The southern road drops to the Mole, but without crossing the river, and continues by or near the east bank to Burford Bridge—a three-mile course which introduces the traveller to some of the best scenery in mid-Surrey. There are better ways of approach, however, than by the high road, and the best is undoubtedly that ancient trackway running along the Leatherhead and Mickleham Downs, and called hereabouts both Ermyn and Stane Street—though the latter appellation is correct. Mickleham is about half-way to the Mole bridge, and if the high road is taken, a pleasant short cut can be made through Norbury Park, emerging in the village of Mickleham. On the west slope above the river stands Norbury House, and farther on to the south is the site of Camilla Lacy, perhaps the most romantic name for any house in Surrey, and so called because it was built with the money obtained for *Camilla*. It was destroyed by fire in 1919. The whole locality has a literary fame through its association with Fanny Burney, who was married to d'Arblay at Mickleham church. It will be remembered that he was one of several French exiles—with Madame de Staël and Talleyrand—who lived at Juniper Hall, half a mile south of the village.

The lower part of Mickleham church tower is Norman ; so is the west doorway ; but there is little original work left in the interior. The situation of the building is most delightful, though the Mole, true to its name, is not a principal feature of the scene. Hereabouts in dry summers the river occasionally disappears in the porous chalky bed, locally called the "Swallows." The charm of this part of the valley consists in the graceful sweep of the hills upon each side, with the huge banks of dark foliage accentuating the vivid green of the sward between them. At Burford Bridge the beauty of the vale is enhanced by the river, here fairly wide, and the famous inn does not strike a jarring note. It was in this hostelry that Keats finished *Endymion*; and the northern slopes of Box Hill will always be associated with a novelist whose name has suffered a partial decline in these latter days, for George Meredith lived for many years at Flint Cottage. His "Happy Valley" is Juniper Bottom, the combe which descends towards Juniper Hall. Before reaching the bridge and hotel, the ascent of Box Hill should be made by a track mounting steeply and commanding charming, though restricted, retrospects of the valley just traversed. After plunging behind the enormous box trees that cluster around the summit, the path suddenly emerges upon an open space, and we are confronted with a magnificent prospect of the Weald. Though equalled in extent, and surpassed in the beauty of the foreground, by several notable view-points on the North Downs, Box Hill is alone in the ease by which it is approached, by the cliff-like character of its transverse ridge, and also by the fine rearward prospect from this edge. Towards the sun are those well-defined summits of the South Downs, from Chanctonbury Ring to Ditchling Beacon, that we have seen from the more eastward heights. The landmark tower on Leith Hill is now much nearer, and a glimpse of Hindhead is obtainable, far beyond the opposing bluff of Ranmore.

An alternative route to Dorking is to continue for a short distance eastwards from the crest, and then downhill to Box Hill Farm and Betchworth Park, but for the moment we return to the Mole crossing and take a path on the right of the high road. After passing the railway station, this leads us towards the slender spire of Dorking church, a memorial of Bishop Wilberforce. Within this fine modern building is another beautiful memorial—the Chichester Chapel, erected in memory of the Canon of that name who was for twenty-five years a vicar of Dorking.

DORKING.

The path through the churchyard is said to follow closely the line of the Roman road to Porchester ; it emerges into the picturesque main street of the town, which, if it retains few old houses, still wears an old-world air. Its foremost interest, to Dickensians at least, centres in an old house in North Street, once the " King's Head," and accepted as the original of the " Markiss o' Granby," the scene of Mr. Tony Weller's chastisement of Stiggins. The " White Horse " is a good example of the old-fashioned English inn, and the " Red Lion " and " Wheatsheaf " are other ancient houses of call.

It is for its fine situation that Dorking is chiefly remarkable, and the town is perhaps the best centre in Surrey for the exploration of the beautiful country between Leith Hill and Leatherhead, Reigate and Guildford. Part of its surroundings on the north, or Downs, side has already been described. On the south-east is the once splendid estate of Deepdene, which includes Betchworth Castle and Park. The mansion has been converted into an up-to-date hotel. Here Disraeli wrote part of *Coningsby*, while the property was in the possession of the Hope family. The grounds are the most remarkable part of the estate, though they lack the more imposing natural features of Denbies, on the north-east of the town. A great part of the beautiful park has latterly been cut up for building.

Over the lower green slopes of Denbies a delightful path may be taken to West Humble, near Box Hill station ; or to Ranmore church, high on its breezy ridge, and then through Ashcombe, which gives a title to the present owner of Denbies. The church at Ranmore is, like Leith Hill Tower, a landmark for many miles. This work of Sir Gilbert Scott's is said to be one of his most successful, and the eight-sided steeple and admirable proportions of the building beneath— set in the green and tree-shaded expanse of Ranmore Common—possess an unusual beauty.

The popular excursion from Dorking is to Leith Hill, five miles to the south-west. The routes are several, and the most roundabout is perhaps the finest. This is through Friday Street, a small hamlet set in a scene usually described as " Swiss " in character. It would be nearer the truth if one likened the fir-fringed pool that forms its chief feature to similar localities in the Scottish Lowlands. But we are anticipating, and our way for the present goes by the " Nower," a small hill very popular with Dorking couples, direct to the village of Coldharbour, through woodlands once of sombre beauty, but shorn of much of their former glory by the Forestry Corps during the Great War. The road ascends steadily through Redlands Wood, making direct for Anstiebury Camp, an ancient entrenchment covering ten acres, under which are the scattered houses of Coldharbour, a name recalling a former refuge for travellers, but without food or fire. It is a fairly common place-name in the south country. Anstiebury is the Hean Stige Byrig, or highway-bury, and indicates a station on the ancient road already noticed north of Dorking.

To the west of Coldharbour is the steep ascent

leading to the highest summit between London and the sea—965 feet above the latter. The Lower Greensand thus tops the loftiest of the chalk downs, and although the approach to this summit is not particularly imposing, the adventurer is rewarded by a superb view in almost every direction, though naturally that to the south and west is the most interesting—as

LEITH HILL.

it is the most varied. On clear days Chanctonbury Ring is conspicuous nearly due south, but it has never been the writer's fortune to distinguish the " grey glimpse of sea " referred to by most guide-books as visible through Shoreham Gap, to the left of the Ring. It is said to be possible under certain conditions—of weather, and with a glass—to see St. Paul's dome and the Channel with one complete right-about. However that may be, on one fine Sunday evening near Midsummer Day—Sundays are the only days on which it is possible to get a fair view *across* the Metropolis—

Leith Hill Tower was distinctly visible from the high ground near Harefield in Middlesex.

The shelving ridge of Blackdown is about south-west from where we stand, and just to the right of it is Hindhead. Then due west comes Hascombe Hill, followed by Pitch Hill and—nearer to the observer—Holmbury. St. " Martha's " Hill, crowned by the Chapel of the Holy Martyr, is nearly north-west ; then comes the long ridge of the North Downs, split by the Mickleham defile. To the east are the broken uplands, formed by the Greensand of East Surrey and Kent.

The tower on the summit was built by Richard Hall of Leith Hill Place in 1766 to enable the traveller to stand 1,000 feet above the Channel. By his own wish, he was buried beneath the floor six years later. From the top of the tower the limits of the horizon are amazingly extended, and the far-away blue line to the north-west can only be that other chalk ridge that ends at Streatley-on-Thames.

To descend the hill to the north-west and then bear to the right is the best way to Wootton Common. The sandy road passes on through pleasant pine woods, with—in the open patches—an undergrowth of whortleberries, to Abinger Bottom. It then rises for a short spell, and drops to Friday Street, the goal of countless ramblers brought by motor-bus to Dorking. A quarter of a century since, the average townsman had never heard of the quaintly named hamlet, but walking-clubs have a way of talking of their discoveries, and although the neighbourhood is still unspoilt, it is certainly not lonely on the fine Saturdays and Sundays of summer.

The picturesque red-roofed cottages, the still sheet of water—always sombre, even on the brightest day,

from the shadow of the dark firs on the ridge above—
and the accompanying music of the wind for ever
singing through their branches, make this little hamlet
the most romantic spot in Surrey. And we do not
quickly overtake the commonplace. All around, the
broken landscape—thickly wooded for the most part—
has a distinct individuality. On the west, about a
mile away, is Abinger, with its Early Norman church
set high above the surging woods. Here are a village
stocks and a manor house retaining a fine old Jacobean
porch. Southward, by a path opposite the " Abinger
Hatch," we may reach Felday and Holmbury St. Mary,
both in an equally beautiful setting.

From near the " Stephen Langton " at Friday Street,
a delightful path runs down the Tillingbourne valley
in the direction of Wootton House, the home of the
Evelyns, of whom the most famous was John the
Diarist. Here is kept, as a priceless treasure, the
Prayer-book used by Charles on the scaffold, and
stained with the blood of the King. Wootton Church
stands in as fine a situation as could be conceived,
and is approached by a stately avenue of chestnuts.
It is a very ancient building, sadly marred by would-
be-clever restorers, who left, perhaps unwillingly, some
old work said to date from Saxon days. The north
chapel and its eighteenth-century extension are not
open, but a glimpse of the Evelyn tombs may be had
through the dividing screen. Two coffin-shaped tombs
on the floor are those of John Evelyn and his wife
Mary.

On the road back to Dorking, near Westcott, with
its water-mill and church built by Gilbert Scott, is
The Rookery, in the grounds of which a beautiful
lake has been formed out of the waters of the Pipps

Brook. This was the birthplace of David Malthus, economist. Our way, however, is westwards, and from the church we may take a path that eventually passes along the north edge of Deerleap Wood and emerges on to a wild strip of common called Eversheds Rough. Here will be seen a Celtic cross marking the spot where Bishop Samuel Wilberforce lost his life in 1873 through his horse stumbling over a rabbit-burrow. The stone is simply inscribed S.W., with the date. A pastoral staff runs through the initials, which signify Samuel Winton.

Abinger Hammer may be reached by a continuation of the path across the common. This village is on the Dorking–Guildford road, and is named from the foundry that stood here in the days of south country iron. A curious effigy of a smith decorates a large clock commemorating this industry, said to have been started here by John Evelyn.

ABINGER HAMMER.

The village is pleasantly scattered along one side of a large green, made more pleasing still by the waters of the Tillingbourne. To the right as we go forward are the rounded uplands, here called the Hackhurst Downs. Beyond the hills is the wide expanse of Netley Heath, a lonely and unfrequented downland, except perhaps in the blackberry season when parties of townsfolk vie with rustic youngsters in " getting the black ones " first.

Gomshall is but a short walk from the last house in Abinger Hammer, and here is a convenient railway station on the line from Reigate to Reading. The village, though beautifully situated, has nothing of interest beyond a good inn—" The Compasses "—and we press on to Shere, haunt of artists, and said—with some degree of probability—to be the prettiest village in Surrey. The picture of the many-gabled village street with the tower and spire of the church and the graceful masses of foliage in the background is in every way delightful. Some of the houses are good

SHERE.

specimens of ancient village architecture and the " White Horse " boasts of a room over four hundred years old. The only drawback to Shere as a perfect specimen of the English village is its unfortunate situation upon a road which becomes more crowded with motor traffic every year. However, the most charming quarter is on the Ewhurst road, a less frequented highway than that leading to the Surrey capital. We pass up this by-street to the church, an object-lesson in successful restoration, where nothing has been altered or taken away. The building is cruciform, and mainly of Norman date with Early English additions. A noteworthy feature is the western gallery, reached by an outside stairway. Among the memorials, that to Robert Scarlyf, Rector of Shere—who died in 1412—showing the priest attired in mass vestments, is of much interest ; other features include a squint and some indications of an anchorite's cell. An ancient chest in the south porch is said to date from the fifteenth century.

A delightful walk southwards would take us to Pitch Hill and another almost perfect village—that of Ewhurst, with its old church and cottages set among tumbled hills. Or a road branching off to the left of this, just outside Shere, leads by Burrows Cross to Peaslake, a lonely hamlet surrounded on the south by wooded hills. At the former dwelt for many years before his death the landscape artist, Leader.

An alternative route to the west—by which we may escape the fast traffic on the Guildford road—goes through the finely timbered Albury Park, a seat of the Duke of Northumberland, and passes a partly ruined church that may possibly have Saxon work in the tower and lower part of the nave walls. The original Albury village once surrounded the building, but the estate was bought by an individual with more money than good taste, who was also the leading light in an almost forgotten sect—the Irvingites. On the north-west corner of the park he erected a so-called " Catholic Apostolic Cathedral," allowed the parish church to fall into disrepair, caused the cottages to be pulled down, and so ensured a vulgar privacy for himself. Albury village is now a mile to the west and, though picturesque, is of little interest.

On emerging into the cross-road, we turn right, and crossing the Tillingbourne, which flows through the park, we pass the " Cathedral " and arrive at the Guildford road and the much vaunted " Silent Pool," reached by a short footpath on the north side of the way. This picturesque pond, for it is little more, first became known to the outside world by that long-forgotten book of Martin Tupper's—" Stephen Lang-

ton." From the Pool, we may ascend the Downs to
Newlands Corner, a famous open view-point, now
almost as popular and well known as Box Hill itself,
and commanding quite as delightful a view to the
south and west, especially in the direction of Hindhead
and Haslemere. The buildings of Charterhouse School
are prominent in the direction of Godalming, and St.
Martha's Chapel upon its picturesque hill is a feature
to the near west, while to the south-east, Leith Hill
Tower still tops the long, sombre tree-crowned heights
rising beyond the Tillingbourne valley.

ST. MARTHA'S CHAPEL.

Just below the summit
of the Downs runs the Old
Road, while the Pilgrim's
Way, hereabouts distinct
from the former, is seen
scarring the east side of St.
Martha's Hill. The Chapel
of the Holy Martyr—for
that was undoubtedly its
original name—took relig-
ious wayfarers from the old track to make their orisons
before its altar, and afterwards—for some miles in all
probability—the newer way of the Canterbury Pilgrims
kept to the valley and its creature comforts.

Below St. Martha's Hill is Chilworth, and the
inhabitants have to climb up to the lonely building
on the hill-top when they go to church. This village
is on the valley route to the capital of Surrey via
Wonersh, and it is proposed to adopt this route instead
of cutting across the hills by the nearer road, so that
it may be possible to glance first at the delectable
country lying to the south of the valley of the Wey.
It will be difficult to know where to stop when we are

fairly on the Hindhead road, but by bearing southwards to Wonersh may be commenced the exploration of a circle of villages and towns which will eventually bring the traveller to Guildford.

To reach Wonersh, we pass near the beautiful Great Tangley Hall, a moated manor house dating from the sixteenth century. Wonersh has some wonderful old half-timbered houses belonging to the days when this was a manufacturing town devoted to the making of clothes. The fine church is to a large extent Norman and the font, of this date, is of an unusual pattern. Another rare feature is the combination of squint and piscina. The brass of Henry Elyot and his wife, dated 1513, is noteworthy, for it records the number of their offspring—twenty-three in all.

Close to the church is Wonersh Park and a fine Georgian mansion, once the seat of Lord Grantley. The house retains part of an earlier Elizabethan dwelling. The district we are entering has a great number of ornamental timbered dwellings, of which there are more in the region between Guildford and Haslemere than in perhaps any other part of England outside the Severn-lands.

Barely a mile west of Wonersh is Bramley, with more old houses, an ancient inn, "The Jolly Farmer," and another Norman and Early English church, much altered and restored. From this village, a delightful by-way leads southwards to the Hascombe district, which, being some miles from a railway and on the way to no particular place, is perhaps the most unspoilt locality in Surrey. Hascombe itself lies in a lofty valley between hills crowned with noble beech woods. One of the heights to the south is called Castle Hill, crowned by a small prehistoric encampment. Lonely but beautiful lanes wander among the sandy upland commons westwards to Hambledon, a village about one and a half miles from Witley station, and therefore better known than the last. It is also an alternative road to the south from Godalming. The church is some distance from the village, but it is of little interest, having been rebuilt in the early days of the Gothic revival. The magnificent yews in the churchyard are noteworthy, and the surroundings are very delightful. The charming examples of cottage architecture hereabouts make these by-ways among the most fascinating in England.

WITLEY.

From Hascombe the sandy lanes may be traversed northwards to Godalming, or the main road can be joined at Witley. As this village contains an interesting cruciform church, and is itself a picturesque and charming place with many old houses, the longer route will be the best. The south doorway of the church is very early Norman, but the remainder of the fabric is mainly Early English. Within will be found several brasses, of which one, dated 1468, is to George, Duke of Clarence, " ac fratris Edouardi quarti, regis Anglie et Franc." Near the church is the old " White Hart," a typical old-time Surrey inn, and the several half-timbered houses and cottages in the village street have attracted the notice of artistic and literary people in the past. Birket Foster, who did much to immortalize rural Surrey, lived in the village, as did George Eliot, who here wrote *Daniel Deronda.*

At Milford, a mile to the north, the Portsmouth road is reached. Here a number of new houses have been erected between several ancient ones, the chief of them being a sixteenth-century manor house called Mousehill. To the north-west, the Farnham road traverses a comparatively flat country, and passes through Elstead, another charming village surrounding a large green, with a church containing much fine medieval timber-work, and an ancient bridge over the river Wey. The name of the village is said to be derived from a one-time home of Ella, the great Saxon chieftain who became ruler of the South Saxons. At Peperharow, on the Godalming side of Elstead, is the fine park and seat of Lord Midleton, containing several magnificent trees of great age. An enormous yew is in the churchyard, close to the mansion, together with masses of cypress, juniper and other " funereal trees." The church is a stately building, restored by Pugin. It contains several interesting memorials of the great families of Peperharow.

Like Guildford and Haslemere, Godalming has developed a growth extraneous to the natural expansion of the town. In other words, it has become known to the City man ; though the thirty-five miles that separate it from Waterloo render it an impracticable home for the humbler rank of worker. The new red-brick dwellings in the vicinity are mostly of the villa-mansion type, and while not exactly offensive have destroyed much of Godalming's old-world character. The centre is still a place of narrow streets and quaint gables, and the " White Hart " retains much of its ancient amenities. Some of the mellow brick houses in High Street are as delightful as anything to be found in Surrey. The Market House, sometimes called the Town Hall, is another pleasant feature, of a type more common north of the Thames than in Surrey or Kent. The Wyatt Almshouses, founded in 1632, on the other side of the town, are another quaint range of buildings. All these older aspects of Godalming now give place in importance to the splendid pile of the Charterhouse School, erected in 1872, which stands upon the hill-side to the north. The tower is in memory of Thomas Sutton, who founded the school in London in 1611. It rises to a height of 130 feet and commands a great view. A War Memorial chapel has recently been added to the extensive group of buildings.

GODALMING.

Godalming church is spacious, and interesting by reason of the many different styles and dates shown in the structure, but it has been over-restored and otherwise maltreated. A great deal of Norman work remains, especially in the lower part of the tower, also said to retain traces of earlier Saxon masonry. A memorial to the north of the church is to J. G. Phillips, the wireless operator on the ill-fated *Titanic*.

From Godalming to Guildford by the high road is a short four miles of incessant traffic. Apart from this, the way would be a pleasant one, though the only object of interest is the ruined Chapel of St. Catherine on its steep sandstone hill close to the river. An alternative route on the east of the river Wey goes through Shalford, a large village built round the edges of an extensive common, once the scene of a notable fair which is said to have provided Bunyan with the idea of " Vanity Fair." The inspired dreamer lived for a short time in the village, but the cottage he inhabited has long since been pulled down.

Though Guildford has for many years thrown out ever-extending suburbs, and is likely to carry a still larger population now that electric trains connect it with central London, the picturesque aspect of the town, clinging to the hill on the east bank of the Wey, is still retained. So much has the famous High Street been praised, not only in the pages of local guide-books, but by writers without any axes to grind, that we are prepared for something quite superlative. If any disappointment is felt, it will not be due to lack of charm in the ancient buildings lining the steep street, or to lack of taste in the fashion of their restoration and care, but rather to the spirit of modern bustle and rush and the smartness of the human throng on the pavements and roadway. The soul of old Guildford has gone, but its new dignity as titular city of the see of Guildford is likely to result in developments that will do much to restore the amenities of the place.

There is no doubt about the age of Guildford, for its records go back to Alfred's reign, and in the tower of St. Mary's Church are unmistakable Saxon details, though the greater part of the fabric is late Norman— much restored during the Victorian " furbishing " era. A remarkable feature is the three distinct floor levels, and it should be noted that the reredos dates from the fifteenth century. Two other old churches—St. Nicholas or " Low Church," close to the bridge, and Holy Trinity or " High Church," near the Castle— have been superseded by singularly uninteresting structures which retain a few monuments from the medieval buildings. The former church has also the Perpendicular Losely Chapel with memorials of the Mores. In Holy Trinity—the Cathedral of the new diocese—may be seen the tomb of Archbishop Abbot, who built the picturesque Abbot's Hospital in 1619. This stands at the top of High Street, and is undoubtedly the best thing in Guildford; in fact, it is one of the

HIGH STREET, GUILDFORD.

finest examples of Jacobean brickwork in England— perfect in its proportions and detail, with characteristic chimneys and turrets. The interior is remarkable for its carved oak and the contemporary stained glass in the chapel. The foundation is similar to that of the Whitgift Hospital in Croydon, founded by Abbot's predecessor on the throne of Canterbury.

A pleasant public garden now surrounds the grim Norman keep of Guildford Castle, which was erected in the years of Henry II on an artificial mound that may have been the work of the West Saxon monarchs. For many years the Castle was used as a gaol, but its ruin had commenced before Cromwell's inspectors had a chance to "slight" it. Since 1885, the old walls and slopes of the mound have been the property of the citizens, and Guildford owns, too, a picturesque old building within the precincts that houses an interesting museum of local antiquities and, latterly, certain relics of the Great War.

Like that of Rochester, the main street of the town is dominated by a clock. This belongs to the seventeenth-century Town Hall. In the Council Chamber here, above the open ground floor, are a series of interesting portraits, including two by Sir Peter Lely of Charles II and James II.

Another fine old stone house of three gables is the Grammar School, dating from 1550 and, according to an inscription upon the front, ascribed to Edward VI; but the actual founder was a citizen of Guildford named Robert Beckingham, who died forty years earlier.

The electric trains from Waterloo will not only cause the rapid extension of Guildford itself, but also of those districts to the north of the Downs served by the line, and from the heights east and west of the town ever-widening splashes of vermilion amongst the greenery of the Wey Valley show that villadom has captured this old centre of country life. Even the Hog's Back, a long narrow continuation of the chalk hills westwards in the direction of Farnham, has been caught in the tentacles of the estate agent, and the northern slopes of the uplands which sink to the Leatherhead road have been made hideous by hundreds of flimsy week-end bungalows that appear to have been sprinkled anyhow out of a giant castor on to the bare sward. This outrage is not apparent for the first few miles out of Guildford, and Merrow is much the same village one saw forty years ago, when the old " Horse and Groom," an early seventeenth-century inn, had no knowledge of motor-buses drawing up to its door. A road turns right-hand near the church—where has

been left, in spite of rebuilding, a fine Norman door—
and in a little over a mile brings the wayfarer to Newlands Corner.   Just beyond Merrow village are the
gates of Clandon Park, through which there is a right
of way to West Clandon village, and the pedestrian
is well advised to make the detour.   After passing
some fine isolated trees, the path crosses the outflow
of a picturesque sheet of water.   Above rises the

ABBOT'S HOSPITAL, GUILDFORD.

imposing home of
the Earl of Onslow,
a red-brick man-
sion built in 1731.
A short distance
farther the path
emerges in the
village, with its
interesting church,
mainly of the
thirteenth and
fourteenth cen-
turies, though both
doorways are of
Norman date.
Among its remark-
able features are a sundial on the chancel wall,
as old as the doorways, and some oak panelling
with medieval paintings thereon of SS. Peter and
Paul and Thomas of Canterbury.   Of other ancient
things may be noticed a twelfth-century font of Petworth marble, a piscina of the same era, and a holy-
water stoup by the south door.

A footpath leaves the village street, about half-way
between church and railway station, for East Clandon,
where there are a number of half-timbered houses with

pretty gardens, and a much-restored Early English church. The belfry rests on an original timber frame rising from the church floor, and the chancel is lit in an unusual way by two narrow lancets. Apart from these features, there is little of interest left, but it should be noticed that the original walls are constructed of chalk.

The Leatherhead road now skirts Hatchlands Park and on the farther side is West Horsley. Here is an interesting church said to have Saxon work in the lower portions of the nave walls. The first noticeable thing is the curious shape of the spire, and the massive tower beneath. Its timber porch is dated 1450. The lancet windows of the chancel are distinctive, and a noteworthy fourteenth-century effigy is said to represent Ralph Berners, Rector in 1348. The monkeys' heads on the canopy are the cognisance of the Berners family, and Sir James, a patron of the living, is shown in the stained glass above. One should notice also a thirteenth-century chest, and a bas-relief of the Nativity found during restoration. The Nicholas Chapel contains memorials to that family, who lived at West Horsley Place, seen across the park as the church is left. Their predecessors at the Place were the Raleighs, and it would seem to be a well-attested fact that the head of Sir Walter Raleigh was buried at the side of his son Carew, after being kept by the widow for over twenty-five years in a leather bag.

The Place is a fine brick pile of varying dates. Those portions to the rear are said to have been erected by Sir Anthony Browne, a master of horse to Henry VIII. Another great house called Horsley Towers is not far away at East Horsley. The park here is surrounded by a remarkably ornate brick wall which has run its pattern over the village generally, but has, fortunately, not touched the church. Here again we find Saxon work, this time in the tower. Within will be seen the brass of a Bishop of Exeter, John Bowthe, who died near by in 1478, and in the north aisle are the effigies of Thomas Cornwallis, Queen Elizabeth's groom-porter, and of his wife.

The high road is now rendered hideous by the afore-mentioned bungalows, and at Effingham, the next village, we may well take a parallel road to the north threading the Bookhams—Great and Little—and Fetcham. Effingham gave a title to that Lord Howard whose son's patriotism came before his Catholicism. The church, after close inspection, is disappointing, for most of its original features have been restored away. The village is most picturesque and pleasant, however, and signs of the suburban builder are absent in its immediate neighbourhood. An innkeeper here, during the middle period of the Great War, had the original idea of renaming his house after a latter-day hero. This gives rise to the thought that modern celebrities are not in demand for hotel nomenclature. Countless Lord Nelsons, Duke of Wellingtons, and even Bluchers, are scattered over the roads of England, and the honours were doubtless conferred while the other rewards of success were being showered upon those persons or their memories. On one solitary ramble we seem to remember having bread and cheese under the pleasant smile of " Sir Garnet," but rustic inn-keepers must be even more conservative than their great-grandfathers.

Little Bookham, with its small church and near by manor house, is also an unspoiled place, though perilously near to Bungalow-land In the churchyard

is a great spreading yew of unguessable age, and in
the church restoration has left a Norman arcade
belonging to an aisle that has disappeared. Great
Bookham church has remains of this period in the
nave, with much of later date in the chancel and aisle
windows. The east end, as set forth in an inscription
upon the wall, was built by an abbot of Chertsey—
John Rutherwyke—in 1341. Of the monuments in
the church, that to Colonel Thomas Moore, dated 1735,
is the most curious, and those to some of the Howards
of Effingham the most interesting. The latter are in
the Slyfield Chapel, which contains a brass to Edmund
Slyfield, dated 1598, and a window in memory of Lord
Raglan. Slyfield Manor House, much denuded of its
former glory, stands some distance away on the banks
of the Mole.

Of the picturesque in Great Bookham village, the
best thing after the church—a delightful picture with
its Horsham stone and shingled spire—is the Old Barn
Hall. This fifteenth-century structure has been converted into a place of recreation for the villagers.
Another resort for fine days, and open to all, is the
glorious expanse of Great Bookham Common. This
stretches away to the north towards Effingham
Junction and—where its timber does not obstruct the
prospect—commands fine views of the Leatherhead
Downs and the defile of the Mole.

Fetcham was, until recently, quite unchanged from
its eighteenth-century character of a small church-
hamlet depending on the " great house " near by.
But the cutting up of Fetcham Park has altered all
this, and superior modern residences cover the bosky
slopes admired by Fanny Burney and her coterie.
The church here retains Saxon masonry in the south

and west walls, with Roman bricks and tiles built in. In the chancel are ancient sedilia and piscina, dating from the end of the twelfth century.

If we ignore the haphazard sprinkling of the temporary dwellings already alluded to, there are delightful walks across the Fetcham Downs towards Dorking, either by Polsden Lacy and Ranmore, or by the scanty ruins of the Pilgrim's Chapel under Ashcombe Wood; but our way lies northwards by the rather frowsy " back end " of Leatherhead Common—actually the Kingston Road.   After passing the fork to Oxshott, the route becomes pleasant, with delightful fir plantations on each side ; those on the east presently merging into Ashtead Woods.   After crossing the rise of Telegraph Hill, the straight highway descends to Chessington, uninteresting so far as that portion situated on our present road is concerned, but by making a short detour to the right, we pass the Hall with its memories of the Burneys, and the mulberry tree around which Fanny danced on hearing of the success of *Evelina*. Within the much altered church is an epitaph written by Dr. Burney to the memory of Samuel Crisp of the Hall, " whose wisdom and wit chear'd and enlighten'd all this hamlet."

Hook, farther on, is merely a suburban appanage of Surbiton, so we will turn left, and westwards, to Claygate, growing rapidly since the advent of the electric trains, but retaining some of the amenities that linger about the Oxshott country.   Just as the famed Ripley Road is undoubtedly the most beautiful of the great highways converging upon the Metropolis, so also the railway from Surbiton to Guildford, running closely parallel to this road, traverses a remarkable succession of lovely woodland, interspersed with glimpses of flowery meads, distant hills, and one glimpse of limpid waters. Yet we have confessed to Guildford having fallen, and the residences of the wealthy cit at Oxshott and elsewhere upon the railway thither prove that we are well within the influence of the Wen.

Esher is but a short distance west of Claygate. The older part is grouped around a village green just half a mile less than half-way between Hyde Park Corner and Guildford High Street, according to the old road-stone, dated 1767, at the fork of the roads to the Thames Valley and Portsmouth. The old " Bear " coaching inn is the chief relic of past days in Esher, for about the middle of the last century the local bigwigs decided to abandon the old parish church and erect in its place the ornate Christ Church. This contains a fine monument of King Leopold, who lived at Claremont, a stately mansion with many memories of royal and other famous tenants. The first building, by Sir John Vanburgh, was erected for the Duke of Newcastle, who was also Marquis of Clare—hence the name. The Princess Charlotte, wife of Leopold, died in the present house, built by the first Lord Clive. Here died also the exiled Louis Philippe and his consort. Another relic of past greatness is a brick gateway at Esher Place, all that remains of a mansion built by Bishop Waynflete of Winchester in the fifteenth century. The house was used by Wolsey after his fall from power.

Passing the broad expanse of Esher Common, we reach renowned Fairmile with its pines and sand. It is a delightful and secluded walk through these woods to Oxshott station, passing under the steep sandy knoll now crowned by a great stone cross to remind us of the sacrifice of Surrey men in the War. From this point, we may proceed by a by-road to Church Cobham, a picturesque village on the banks of the Mole, here, near the Mill, at its widest, and flowing right up to the highway leading towards the Portsmouth road. A picturesque old brick bridge spans the stream beyond the church and leads to the Effingham road, a way of some beauty in the autumn when the woods that line its sides are changing colour. The church at Cobham, though much altered, retains a fine Norman doorway, and the tower is also of this period. Two remarkable brasses call for notice. One is a

COBHAM MILL.

palimpsest, with a knight on one side and a priest on the reverse. The other depicts the Adoration of the Shepherds, and is said to be unique of its kind. The north chapel is Early English, with windows of a later date. The modern War Memorial Chantry has a floor made of waste pieces from the manufacture of rifle stocks. The best bit of ancient domestic architecture hereabouts is " Church Stile House," just without the churchyard. It is now a Home of Rest for indigent women.

Stoke D'Abernon is barely two miles south-east of Cobham, and contains a noteworthy church, badly maltreated in 1866 when large portions of the original Saxon fabric were ruthlessly destroyed, though the present south wall with its sundial is largely pre-Conquest. The building contains several items of unusual interest. On the right hand of the finely-

vaulted thirteenth-century chancel is a wall painting
—part of a subject representing the Adoration of the
Lamb. On the opposite side is an attempted restoration. Here also is the fifteenth-century Norbury
Chapel, containing an ancient fireplace, a very rare
feature for the period. The brasses in this chantry
chapel are of much interest, but the great attraction
to antiquaries is the memorial of Sir John D'Abernon,
dated 1277, on the chancel floor. This is the earliest
known brass in England, and is marvellously well
preserved. Another knightly member of this family
is also commemorated by a brass. The funeral helm
and surcoat upon the wall of the chapel are those of
Sir Thomas Vincent, who died in 1623. The knight
and his lady recline beneath a canopy below.

The church treasure-chest is a fine example of its
kind and dates from the thirteenth century. The
elaborate Early Jacobean pulpit with its hour-glass
stand in iron scrollwork is remarkable in design and
execution, and if the hand of the restorer had been
kept from the fabric sixty years ago, Stoke D'Abernon
would probably have possessed the most interesting
village church in Surrey.

From Fairmile, the " Ripley Road " goes on to
Street Cobham, where is the famous " White Lion,"
a noted house of call in the palmy days of the " push-
bike." Here is a small museum, of which the most
interesting exhibits are naturally some archaic specimens of early machines. The present building, though
dating from the seventeenth century, is not the first,
for an inn has stood upon this spot for over four hundred
years. Beyond the hostelry is Painshill Cottage, once
the home of Matthew Arnold. Then we cross the
Mole and enter the finest stretch of the road between

T

London and Hindhead. Pine woods and parklands border the way until we reach a romantic pool on the left called Boldermere. Here is another well-known hotel—the Wisley " Hut "—and then the pines and heather of Wisley and Ockham Commons accompany us to Stratford Bridge. To the left is one of the ways to Ockham, a small village of delightful gardens and cottages of unusual charm. Hidden away among the trees of Ockham Park is a church of several styles and dates, remarkable for its fine Early English east window of seven lancets, ancient choir stalls, and carved piscina.

The main road now rises to Ripley, a much too busy place on Saturdays for the humble pedestrian, who must find sanctuary in the beautiful old gabled " Anchor " inn. Another ancient house called Hole's Cottage will be remarked. This was once the local manor house, and shows some notable Jacobean brickwork. At the far end of the village is the church, rebuilt with the exception of a Norman chancel. From this point to Guildford the road becomes ordinary in character, with occasional charming views of distant wooded hills and the mauve of heather-flushed commons.

CHAPTER XI

THROUGH THE PINES TO FARNHAM

THE road-stone at Esher directs the wayfarer westwards to Weybridge. Along this road, upon certain days, passes a continuous stream of waspish cars bound for the great Brooklands racing track. Indeed, it appears at all times to be more popular with the speed-demon than the wider and safer highways to the south-west and south. At Hersham, however, we may leave this road at a point close to the fine modern church, and bearing left we are soon among the woods that still clothe the slopes of St. George's Hill. On the summit of this eminence is the largest earthwork near London, and from near the walls of the camp extensive views are still to be had—despite the builder and the restrictions of the golf course—of south-western Surrey and towards the towers of Windsor, to be distinguished rising proudly above the long blue line of the Forest.

To the south of the hill, sandy ways lead to Byfleet, a large village with rapidly growing suburbs, soon to be left by making for the church, nearly half a mile away to the south. The wooden belfry belongs to the

fifteenth century, but the greater part of the main
fabric is over one hundred years older. Within is a
brass to a rector named Teylar, dated 1480, an ancient
fresco, and some battlefield crosses brought here from
France. Continuing southwards, a footpath presently
leads to Wisley church, on the banks of the Wey.
This is a small Norman building without aisles and
practically unrestored. The pleasant old-world farm
buildings near by, and the remote and secluded character of the country around, make this quite a delightful
spot, though it is not two miles to Byfleet station.

From Wisley, it is but a short walk to the " Anchor "
inn on the Wey Navigation Canal, a derelict but

NEWARK PRIORY.

picturesque waterway. From
the bridge, sandy and devious
lanes lead south-westwards to
Pyrford, still a remote and
picturesque retreat despite its
nearness to the growing rail-
way town of Woking. Here will be found another
small Norman church, much restored, but retaining some old seats and remains of ancient wall
paintings. Beyond the several streams of the Wey
are the ruins of the Augustinian Newark Priory,
founded by Ronald de Calva about 1190, probably
on the site of an old Saxon religious house. The
fragments of Early English architecture are readily
identified as part of the south transept and choir.
Near the abbey, a footpath goes on to Old Woking—
it is a long way round by road—and passes the scanty
remnants of Old Hall on the bank of the river. The
village is a revelation to those who only know the
utterly uninteresting northern extension around the
junction. Here is a picturesque street of old houses

with an Early English church containing ancient seating and a very early Norman west doorway belonging to the former building, and concealed beneath the tower. To the south, a pleasant road leads to Send, which has several centres—" Marsh," " Holm," " Grove " and so on. The church stands some distance away on the banks of the Wey. It has a remarkably broad nave of the Perpendicular period, and an older Early English chancel. The ancient rood screen and seating are worth noting. The balustraded west gallery dates from 1660.

In a loop of the Wey, to the south of Send, stands the fine Tudor mansion called Sutton Place. It was built by Sir Richard Weston in 1524. The removal of one wing in the eighteenth century spoilt the original quadrangular plan, but it is still a remarkable example of the sudden change from the medieval domestic building of moat and defensive battlements to the comfort and spaciousness of the sixteenth century. No stone can be seen in the exterior, which is entirely of brick and terra-cotta, and the ornamental work in this material is both beautiful and interesting.

We are now nearing the northern suburbs of Guildford, which extend towards Slyfield Green and the barracks at Stoughton. Beyond the latter are several commons—Littlefield, Wood Street and Broad Street. Across the latter, by a series of by-ways, we may circle south to the Hog's Back—that rather featureless section of the North Downs over which runs the Guildford–Farnham high road—at a point above Monkshatch. Here a path drops to the Watts Picture Gallery. The great artist lived at " Limnerlease," close by. Another memorial of the painter consists of a well-head on the road to Compton, and a cloister in Compton designed by Mrs. Watts, and executed by the villagers, together with the grave of the artist. The circular terra-cotta cemetery chapel was built from designs by Watts, and is an interesting relic of a style that is as defunct as that which had the Albert Memorial at Kensington as its apotheosis.

Compton church is one of the most interesting in England. It is unique in having the sole remaining two-storied chancel in this country. It is supposed that the upper floor was used as a shrine for the relics of a saint, with their attendant priest and special devotions. One or two other examples of this unusual feature once existed in this country, but have long since been swept away, either during the Reformation period or in later Puritan days. The west front of the upper chamber is guarded by a Norman balustrade of wood, said to be the oldest of this date now remaining *in situ*. The so-called anchorite's cell may be the remains of a watching-place for the priest guarding the relics. Older than the double sanctuaries —said to be late Norman—is the western tower, which may even be of Saxon workmanship. Among other interesting details of this church, the early and curious font, and the magnificent Jacobean pulpit and sounding-board, are notable.

On the east of Compton is the splendid Elizabethan manor house of Losely. It was built about 1564 by Sir George More and is unlike other similar erections of this date in the picturesque irregularity of its many gables and its ground plan. It stands in a beautifully wooded park, across which the pedestrian may ramble in the direction of Littleton and Guildford. To the south of Compton, other delightful paths take the rambler towards Charterhouse and Godalming.

Our way is now westwards to Puttenham, a village lying snugly embowered in wooded slopes below the Hog's Back. It is a place of ancient houses and cottages with nothing new or blatant to offend. Hidden behind thick foliage is a badly restored Norman church with Early English additions. It contains a brass commemorating a rector named Edward Cranford, dated 1431, but little else of interest. The village is upon the Pilgrim's Way, and the road, though unable to command the wide views from the highway upon the hill above, runs through delightful woodlands to Seale, with occasional peeps at the western heights, dominated by the conical Crooksbury Hill. At Seale, a place of delectable cottages, is a cruciform church, almost entirely rebuilt seventy years ago, but retaining a medieval timber porch and a few remnants of the original building.

FRENSHAM GREAT POND.

Instead of proceeding directly to Farnham, a detour by Crooksby Common will repay the traveller in search of the picturesque, and this journey may well be extended to include Surrey's lake district at Frensham. The tracks across these thickly wooded commons are occasionally bewildering and are mostly ankle-deep in loose sand, but they have the great virtue of being clean, and without the devastating bogs of the clay lands. At Tilford, where for a short space we leave this loose sand and drop to the river, there is a picturesque group of bridge and inn. We then rise again to Tilford Common and the Abbot's and Little Ponds—

serving as an introduction to the Great Pond of Frensham. Here a broad and delightful prospect greets the traveller of a fine sheet of water backed by the romantic outline of Hindhead and the " Devil's Jumps," those curious flat-topped conical hills which form the subject of several local folk-tales. This way of approaching Hindhead and the Devil's Punch Bowl, though far more strenuous, is much to be preferred to that by way of the villas of Haslemere. Though of late years new houses and bungalows have sprung up here and there near the Great Pond, they are not yet sufficiently numerous to entirely spoil the prospect.

The most direct road to Farnham crosses Farnham Common, and has little to recommend it. A pleasant by-road from Tilford passes through delightful woods, and near the ruins of Waverley Abbey, first of the Cistercian houses to be established in England. It was founded by a Bishop of Winchester in 1128, though the remains of the transepts and conventual buildings date from about one hundred and fifty years later. The ruins are beautifully situated on the banks of the Wey and within the parklands of a modern mansion.

Farnham, though less picturesque than Guildford, keeps more of its old character as a rural centre and is perhaps less altered than any town of its size in Surrey. The extensive northern suburbs have really nothing to do with Farnham and are actually outliers of Aldershot. Evidences of the proximity of this great military camp are to be met with in the streets of the town, and upon the pleasant paths of the park, wherein rises the great fortress-palace of the Bishops of Winchester. Here we may see some of the actual masonry of the time of Bishop Blois, who built the keep about the middle of the twelfth century. The residential portion of the castle is due largely to the Restoration Bishop Morley, but the entrance tower of brick was erected in the early days of Henry VIII by Bishop Fox. The whole of this great pile was left in a ruinous state by Waller, who treated it with rigorous doses of powder when, after a long defence for the King by Sir John Denham, it fell into his hands. Centuries before this, it was partly dismantled by Henry III, who considered that the castle was a menace to his sovereignty.

Farnham church, a cruciform building dedicated to St. Andrew, has been so much restored that little ancient work can now be identified, but the churchyard contains a tomb of much interest to those who love the fields and by-ways of Eng-land, for here lies Cobbett, not far from the house where he was born, now the " Jolly Far-mers " inn.

HINDHEAD.

Old houses are few. The town hall has been modernized on its street front, but the ancient character of the building is preserved in the side walls. The Windsor Almshouses in Castle Street date from 1619, but they are not particularly picturesque. It can be said, however, that the streets of Farnham have that pleasant air, so usual in the south country, of " con-tented dependence upon the great lord in his castle." As in this case the lord is a prince of the Church, the tone is perhaps more sedate and suave than usual, despite the proximity of that antithesis of calm and quiet—Aldershot.

Through this modern military settlement—it was

but a small village prior to 1854—we must now take our way. The camp itself covers over ten square miles, and many new and permanent buildings have sprung up since the commencement of the European War. Although Aldershot is of course an interesting place in many ways—there is a wonderful museum for those interested in military relics—it is simply detestable on a windy day. All the sands of the high plateau upon which it is placed seem to rise and rotate up and down its arid highways, and one can understand —and forgive—the thirst of its major population. The original village is marked by St. Michael's, the old parish church. A new and ornate structure in the best Gothic style of the eighteen-seventies was erected for the increasing civil population, but the soldiers have several churches of their own. North and South Camps are divided by the old Basingstoke Canal and each of these districts has its own railway station. On the west of the town is the enormous effigy of the Duke of Wellington, surely the most "wooden" of all our British statues. It once disfigured Hyde Park Corner, for it was made to surmount the arch now graced by the quadriga of victorious Peace.

Still within the region of pines and heaths that follow the outcrop of the Bagshot sands, we traverse a region largely given over to manœuvring, camps and other military purposes, and, leaving Farnborough and the Hampshire heathlands away to the left flank, arrive at Pirbright. The woods of this district are among the best in north-west Surrey—though the sombre tones give a bleak and dour turn to the scenery, and perhaps the most colourful place in these parts is the London Necropolis, the large and beautiful cemetery at Brookwood, laid out and planted about the middle of the last century on what was then Woking Common.

Old Woking has already been noticed, lost among the lanes to the south, and Woking, the railway town, will not tempt the traveller, except for the fact that it is the obvious way to London. Far to the west of its vermilion suburbs, a way leads across the heather-clad uplands known as Chobham Ridges, one of the healthiest districts in the South of England ; in fact, the whole of this borderland between Surrey, Hants and Berks has a well-deserved reputation. S a n d s, pines, and a bracing air contribute to this salubrity, and the choice, during a period unremarkable for hygienic wisdom, of this region as a great military training-ground is a matter for congratulation.

BISHOP FOX'S TOWER, FARNHAM.

A small stream called the Hale Bourne runs through Chobham village. Here is a church still retaining some vestiges of Norman work of the twelfth century, despite the efforts of Victorian restorers, who expended great efforts and large sums to " improve " the fabric. In the rebuilt chancel lies the body of an Archbishop of York—Nicholas Heath—who was also Lord Chancellor for Mary I, and so much respected by her Protestant sister that, during the reign of the latter, he was allowed to celebrate Mass during his retirement at Chobham Park. Another interesting tomb is that of Sir Edward Banks, " builder of the three noblest bridges in the world." The font is curious : it has a leaden bowl surrounded by oak panels, and the old parish money-box for offertories is of an unusual and quaint design.

Ottershaw, the next village to the east, is set among woods to which its delightful name is a fitting introduction. Springtime here makes a wonderland of bluebells and primroses. Wide-spreading views in every direction repay the traveller who makes his way to the mount upon which is built a little modern church. This part of London's country is probably less known to the townsman than any other locality in the twenty-five mile circle. Old associations, manners and superstitions linger in this outlying portion of the great Forest of Windsor, for the native population is practically undisturbed, despite the large number of public institutions that dot the countryside hereabouts. The huge blocks of buildings of the Brookwood Lunatic Asylum have been visible during much of the last five or six miles. At Addlestone, the next halt east of Ottershaw, are the Princess Mary Home for Girls ; the Surrey Workhouse ; and the College of St. George, a Roman Catholic seminary at Woburn Park. A famous old tree, called the Crouch Oak, stands, in a rather dilapidated condition, quite close to the village. Its reputed age is over eight hundred years, and one hears the stock legend of Queen Elizabeth having one of her state picnics beneath its branches. Wyclif is said to have used its shade for preaching, and as one might well conjecture the tree to have then been in its prime, the evangelist-reformer had an excellent pulpit.

After passing the gates of Woburn Park our road crosses the Bourne, and then accompanies the Wey Navigation to Weybridge, still a pleasant place although

a residential suburb. Here is the famous Oatlands
Park, once containing a Tudor palace, now the setting of
an hotel of high repute. Here are also a fine lake called
Broadwater, and much imposing timber. Weybridge
church, though otherwise of little interest, has a number
of sixteenth- and seventeenth-century brasses rescued
from the older building.

At Hersham, we rejoin our outward route from Esher,
and from the latter town traverse the suburban districts
of Thames Ditton and Surbiton and, by way of the
pleasant riverside gardens, soon arrive at Kingston
Bridge.

WAVERLEY ABBEY.

WINDSOR.

CHAPTER XII

THE THAMES TO WINDSOR

THE valley of the Thames between Kingston and
Maidenhead, and for many miles beyond, is
but semi-rural, and the banks of the historic stream,
wherever building is practicable, are lined with handsome villas and gardens ablaze with blossom during
seven months of the year, and not devoid of colour
through the remaining five. The hey-day of the river
may have passed and "innocuous banalities have
(perhaps) developed into raucous vulgarities," but the
happy voyager in skiff and punt may drift through
scenes still idyllic and peaceful enough to satisfy the
most exacting, even though the well-named water-
meadows themselves have been colonized by the builder
of bungalows, who is content to brave the perils of a
regular inundation by adopting a system invented
before ever Thames flowed over Runnymede.

It may be that to omit any description of such
glorious stretches of natural beauty as the wild glades
of Richmond Park, or to ignore the world-famed view
from the classic Hill itself, and the pleasant stretches
of greensward around old Ham and its quaint church

302

—historic localities that are rightly held in deep affection by all true Londoners—is to offend the susceptibilities of many readers, but our last journey must start from the busy market place of Kingston-upon-Thames—" the royal town where kings are hallowed," as its Saxon charter runs—where a block of stone, guarded by an imposing rail, is pointed to as the veritable coronation seat of seven Saxon monarchs. A few ancient houses still brave the bustle and busyness of modern Kingston, and several quaint corners invite the attention of pencil and camera, especially in those regions between Market Place and river.

At the Middlesex end of Kingston bridge is the quiet suburb of Hampton Wick. Here we may take a delightful stroll through the little-used Hampton Court Park. Of the thousands who visit the magnificent Palace Gardens, a mere dozen or so take the trouble to explore the region beyond the flower-beds. But they cannot be blamed. Few more delightful pleasaunces exist than the famous gardens, first laid out by the great Cardinal, extended and improved by Henry and each succeeding monarch, and in these latter days kept in order and beauty principally for the delight of King Demos. The picturesque courts of Wolsey's palace, and the stately quadrangles of Wren, re-echo the laughter of young folk from far-off Bow and Bethnal Green, though the decorous quietude of this vast retreat for pensioners of the Crown is usually respected, and the exuberance of holiday crowds finds its vent in the excitements of the Maze—a perennial joy—or under the chestnuts of Bushey Park across the way. The rather wearisome round of the " State " apartments, where are hung a number of fine and famous " old masters " among a perfect wilderness of mediocre paintings—furniture belonging to Dutch William—blue and white porcelain and some fine old iron fire-backs, is religiously performed. The tour has lately received the addition of the interesting kitchen below the Banqueting Hall, where we may study Tudor domestic arrangements and imagine the inferno of heat and smells when Great Harry dined in state above. The great Hall with its magnificent

roof and windows is perhaps the best thing in Hampton Court. Next come the Wolsey rooms, lined with oak panelling and commanding picturesque peeps from the windows, and the Haunted Gallery, with no fewer than three authentic ghosts, two of whom are Henry's wives.

THE MOAT BRIDGE, HAMPTON COURT.

Outside the Palace, to the west, the ugly bridge which leads to East Molesey strikes one incongruous note. Another consists of the vulgarities surrounding the one-time Tagg's Island, farther up the river, which has lately blossomed forth as " Palm Beach "—a place of revelry by night. Some day, when the bridge is declared unfit for modern traffic, we may have a structure more in keeping with the surroundings. And the " Karsino " may disappear, and Tagg's Island revert to a state of nature.

Hampton village, at the further end of the spacious green, has associations with the eighteenth-century stage, for both Thomas Rosoman, of Sadler's Wells, and John Beard, the operatic singer, are buried in the churchyard. David Garrick died at Hampton House in 1779 after a residence of twenty-five years. The front of the house was designed by Robert Adam and erected by the actor, who also caused the little Greek temple to be built as a shrine for Roubiliac's statue of Shakespeare, now in the British Museum. The churchyard is worth exploring for the interest of the names of personages upon the stones, most of whom were pensioners of the Crown at Hampton Court. The church itself preserves several monuments, notably that of Sibel Penn, nurse to Edward VI, and an extraordinary erection in memory of John Greg of Dominica. The building itself is of white brick and calls for no other remark.

Between Hampton and Sunbury, the river side is disfigured by the utilitarian buildings of the Metropolitan Water Board. Opposite Hampton itself is the white and green of Hurst Park racecourse. Farther on, down Sunbury Station Road, is another at Kempton Park, where there was once a Plantagenet palace. Our way is by the river bank, and presently the pleasant leafiness of Sunbury succeeds the monotonous banks of the reservoirs. The main street of the little town is on the margin of the river and the only open space is close to the ugly brick church. Some feeble efforts to improve the interior of this building have been entirely unsuccessful, and should stand to teach those who are out of sympathy with eighteenth-century architecture to leave such things alone, or destroy them altogether.

U

The fine red-brick mansion at the east end of the town is Sunbury Court, once the house of Percy Wyndham. Sunbury has been the residence of several well-known persons—Admiral Hawke, Lady Jane Coke and the Earl of Pomfret among others. A modern mansion called Charlton Court stands on the site of the ancient Cherdyntone Manor House, some two miles north-west—and not far from Littleton, a village lying away from main roads and, as yet, quite free of Suburbia. We may make the excursion for the sake of seeing an unspoilt remnant of rural Middlesex—a place of fat green meadows, of fine hedgerow trees, and old farm-houses and cottages. Apart from the dead flatness, and the " bogginess " of its lanes after rain, this district would compare favourably with the remainder of the county. Unfortunately, except for an occasional glimpse of the Surrey uplands, the only rising ground visible is the straight and monotonous ridge of the great reservoirs to the west.

Littleton church is a quaint little Perpendicular building of plastered brick containing several memorials of the Woods, Lords of the Manor, and twenty-four colours of the Grenadier Guards, of which regiment one of the family was, in 1855, Colonel and later, M.P. for Middlesex. Several other Woods were soldiers, and one, Charles, fought at Waterloo, besides being engaged in other battles of the Napoleonic wars. A window on the north side of the church was painted by Millais, who spent several holidays in the village. The window was presented to the church by Lady Millais in memory of those happy days.

To the south-east of Littleton, a lane brings us back to the Thames at Shepperton, a favourite resort of anglers and, although served by electric trains from

Waterloo, still retaining much of its old-time rural charm. This is a locality well advertised every year —during the season of Thames floods—by the illustrated dailies. Photographs depicting the housewives of the district shopping in boats, or watching their belongings floating across the Walton meadows, are regularly dished up to comfort those readers who cannot afford a bungalow up the river. Raised causeways, built many years before the word " bungalow " had come into the language, border the roadways hereabouts, and tell their own tale.

The late Perpendicular church here is more picturesque than interesting. All its details are poor, and the later tower of brick is undeniably ugly, but the position of the building is very pleasant.

Lower Halliford lies to the east of Shepperton, and is one of the most charming spots between London and Windsor. A pleasant green narrows down close to the river bank, where fortunate householders have their little detached gardens on the edge of the water. This is the best route by which to approach Walton, and though bungalow and villa are slowly eating up the parklands hereabouts, Walton Bridge still has rural surroundings and commands a wide stretch of the Thames, lazily flowing through lush meadows. Walton town is rapidly growing, however, and has a population of about twenty thousand, a busy market street and smart shops. Its old Perpendicular church, just off the main street, has, like so many others in Surrey, been badly mauled by the heavy hand of the tinkerer. The tower arch is fine and the Transitional arcade, a relic of the earlier building, has been left intact. The church possesses one or two interesting features, including a brass commemorating one John

Solwyn, keeper at Oatlands, who died in 1587. It is
said that while waiting upon Queen Elizabeth, who was
hunting in the park, Selwyn jumped upon the back of
a stag and cut its throat. This incident is depicted
upon the brass. Another memorial by Roubiliac to
Lord and Lady Shannon is rather overpowering in its
magnificence. A seventeenth-century " scold's bridle "
is preserved in the vestry, and the church possesses an
almonry for storing bread, kept for distribution among
the poor of Walton.

A pleasant river-path goes by Cowey Stakes, the
traditional spot where Cæsar is said to have forced

CHERTSEY BRIDGE.

the Thames passage, to
Dorney, where we cross
from Surrey to Middlesex
by the ferry. Here the
Wey joins the Thames, and
the waterways are made
intricate by a couple of
loops. Then, by Dockett's
Point, the path leads to-
wards Chertsey Bridge, with the bright green of
Chertsey Mead backed by the darker lines of the foliage in Woburn Park on the opposite shore. From
the bridge we get a delightful view down-stream,
with St. George's Hill and the spire at Weybridge
closing the vista quite effectually. It is to be expected
that this spot should be beautiful, for here, with their
usual aptitude for finding fine sites, the Benedictines
in 666 established the great Abbey of St. Peter, one of
the most famous of the English monasteries. Its
founder and first Abbot was Erkenwald, who afterwards
became Bishop of London. The Abbey was in ruins
for many years after a descent by the Danes, when

Abbot Broeca and his monks were murdered, but it arose in renewed splendour in the closing years of the tenth century.

The outline of the great church can be traced by the foundations excavated some eighty years ago, and may be seen by passing down a passage to the east of the churchyard. The chapter-house, a portion of the south aisle of the Abbey church, and a few fragments of the containing wall, are to be identified. A stream called the Abbey River winds across the meadows, and lends an added charm to the peaceful scene. A few tiles from the Abbey are preserved in Chertsey church, which has been so much rebuilt and altered that it has little to offer the antiquary. There is a small Flaxman memorial, and a tablet to Charles James Fox, who lived at St. Anne's Hill. A well-known story is connected with the bell here, rung as curfew, and dating from the fourteenth century. A maid, one Blanche Heriot, by clinging to the clapper and thus staying its ringing, is said to have saved the life of her lover, who had been condemned to perish at curfew.

Abraham Cowley died in the old half-timbered dwelling in Guildford Street called Porch House. The inscription reads, " Here the last Accents flow'd from Cowley's Tongue."

St. Anne's Hill, north-west of the town, is a pleasant walk and, although not over 250 feet in height, a fine view-point for the Thames Valley between Kingston and Windsor. Its slopes are clothed with trees and shrubberies which occasionally interfere with the prospect, but add greatly to the beauty of the hill. On the summit was once a healing spring called St. Anne's Well, and a few fragments of the saint's one-time chapel may be discovered by diligent search. Thorpe, nearly two miles from Chertsey, lies on the farther side of the hill. It is a most picturesque little place, quite unspoilt and rural. The restored church retains some of its ancient features, and of especial note are the two traceried squints on each side of the Norman chancel arch.

From near the site of Chertsey Abbey, a footpath crosses the meads to Laleham Ferry and the pretty village of that name. Here is Laleham House, once the home of Sir James Lowther—afterwards Earl of Lonsdale—and then of the Earls of Lucan. It was for a time the residence of Queen Maria of Portugal. Laleham church has Norman pillars and arches in the nave, and several interesting memorials upon its walls, but its chief interest is outside in the churchyard, where Matthew Arnold rests. It will be remembered that in William Watson's memorial lines, one stanza runs :—

> And nigh to where his bones abide
> The Thames with its unruffled tide
> Seems like his genius typified—
> Its strength, its grace
> Its lucid gleam, its sober pride,
> Its tranquil pace.

A group of cedars at the end of the village marks the site of Arnold's birthplace. In this house, Thomas Arnold lived for some years before he became head-master at Rugby.

From Laleham to Staines, past the curious loop called Penton Hook, the riverside is lined with smart bungalows and gay little garden plots. On the north bank is a church dedicated to St. Peter, built by Sir Edward and Lady Clarke. It will be a lasting memorial of the learned King's Counsel's connexion with Staines. The parish church is a monstrosity of the early nineteenth century, though the tower was perpetrated by Inigo Jones in 1631 and does the great architect no credit whatever. Its bald ugliness, however, holds a peal of bells of remarkable quality, and their music, heard from the water on a fine summer evening, is full of the peace of England's countryside.

The most important thing in Staines is the bridge which carries the great highway to the south-west over the Thames. It was at this spot that the Roman road crossed the stream on the way from Verulam to Silchester. The station was called Ad Pontes, and the later name was doubtless derived from the Saxon for "stone"—the Roman milestone, in fact. The bridge carries an enormous amount of traffic, not only for the Salisbury road, but also for the valley way to Windsor, Maidenhead and the west thereof. The main street of the town is in consequence a distracting and unquiet place for the pedestrian, who will quickly make his way back to the river bank.

Before dismissing Staines bridge, we may call to mind that in little more than a century no less than four different structures have stood here. A stone bridge finished in 1797 collapsed soon after it was opened, and was supplanted by a single iron span. This failed, and its successor, also of iron, was in turn declared unsafe in the course of a few years. The present graceful bridge was opened by William IV in 1832, and has been little altered since that decade of wonderful bridge-building in stone. Of the other dreadful iron structure carrying the railway, and utterly spoiling the down-stream vista, the less said— and seen—the better.

Staines has had few great days in history apart from that on which the Barons rode down its street to the bearding of John, but it may be mentioned that Sir Walter Raleigh was convicted of treason in the old Market Hall in 1603. The trial took place here in consequence of an outbreak of the Plague in London. There are several fine old houses left near the river bank. One is the Vicarage, and another called Duncroft House is said to occupy the site of the dwelling used by King John before the ceremony of signing the Great Charter.

London Stone, close to that arm of the Colne forming the boundary between Middlesex and Buckinghamshire, is a well-known object to frequenters of Staines Reach and the towpath. It was set up on the " Lamas " to mark the boundary of the City jurisdiction, and bore the pious motto, " God preserve the City of London." At one time the effect of the sea-tides was felt as far as this, and the authority of the City Fathers followed the swell. Now several locks and weirs intervene and render not only Staines, but Walton and Kingston also, definitely part of the Upper Thames. But still, up to this point, the bed of the river is controlled by the Conservancy and owned by the public. Beyond the Stone, it belongs to private freeholders.

Egham starts its rather mean and uninteresting length at the southern end of Staines bridge, in the long straight road running parallel to the ancient causeway raised by the monks of Chertsey above the narrow tongue-like extension of Runnymede. At the farther extremity of the town, two miles away, rise the ornate buildings of the Royal Holloway College, opened by Queen Victoria in 1886. Egham church is another dreadful example of Thames-side reconstruction. Its deplorably mean brickwork replaced a fourteenth-century building in 1822. Only two items are likely to interest the traveller—a tablet recording that the old chancel was built by Abbot Rutherwyke of Chertsey in 1327 ; and the memorial to Thomas Beighton, with its oft-quoted lines by David Garrick—

> Peculiar blessings did his life attend—
> He had no foe, and Camden was his Friend.

To the north of Staines, the flats of South Middlesex still hold a number of rural church-hamlets, soon to be swallowed in the tide of advancing London. We cannot hope that these future suburbs will have the pleasant spaciousness of those lately traversed, for the nature of the country is unlikely to attract the notice of the townsman with a few spare thousands to spend on " extensive and well-wooded grounds." This region already contains dreary Ashford and its rows of depressing villas. East Bedfont, however, still has much of its old-world charm despite the dangerous proximity of Feltham and the railway. The Bedfont yews are famous and elaborate examples of the art of clipping. By their date—1704—they have been in training for well over two centuries. The church takes secondary place in popular interest, but it has an unusual and picturesque tower, a Norman door and chancel arch, and two ancient wall pictures. Stanwell church, about two miles from Staines, is a fine building of various periods, with a chancel—below the level of the nave—containing eight arcaded seats said to have been used by the monks of Chertsey. A sumptuous monument, dated 1622, has kneeling effigies of Lord Knivet and his wife behind marble curtains drawn up to marble columns. The canopied tomb of Thomas,

Lord Windsor, who died in 1486, was used as an Easter Sepulchre by direction of the deceased.

From the pretty Green at Stanwell, a pleasant lane leads northwards to the Bath road, and just beyond this busy highway is another string of sequestered villages—Harmondsworth, called " Harmsworth," Sipson, Harlington, and Cranford. The first-named has the oldest church, much restored, however. It once belonged to the monastery of the Holy Trinity in Rouen, and afterwards the church and manor formed part of the endowment of William of Wykeham's new college, now Winchester School. The most interesting things here are the fine Norman doorway in the south wall and the large tithe-barn near by. Another celebrated doorway is at Harlington. This has even better detail than the former, and it is approached by a very beautiful oak porch. The village gave a title to Henry Bennet, one of the Cabal Ministers, but the clerk who made out the patent must have been a Caroline Cockney, and the new peer blossomed forth as Lord Arlington. The title is preserved in a well-known West-End street off Piccadilly. It can only be supposed that no system of checking the vagaries of the seventeenth-century scrivener was in vogue, for another and more famous nobleman became by mischance Duke of Devonshire, a region in which he had little or no interest, instead of Duke of Derbyshire, where he reigned as a petty monarch. And a dual error was committed, for Devonians are justly annoyed when the suffix is given to their county.

But we are wandering too far from the river and the tow-path on the south side thereof. This brings us, at about a mile from Staines, to Bell Lock Weir, near the western mouth of the Colne. The bright green of Runnymede stretches away to the left, flanked by the modest rise of Cooper's Hill. Somewhere in this pleasant water-meadow, probably because he had a wholesome fear of walls hung with arras, John sealed the Charter of Liberty. Local legend, probably of recent growth, persists in placing the historic site upon an island near the northern end of the great meadow, and here the innocent tourist is actually shown the stone used to support the document during the ceremony !

Cooper's Hill and the neighbouring Priest Hill vie with the Round Tower at Windsor in the excellence of their prospects. The views to the south-east from the former are, in a measure, impeded by the houses and trees of Englefield Green. But from the " Look-out," the sweep over Middlesex and Buckinghamshire, and far away beyond the towers of the Royal palace, is uninterrupted and entirely beautiful. It was probably at this spot that John Denham found inspiration for his lines commencing—

> Sure there are poets who did never dream
> Upon Parnassus . . .

The river between Rolls' Corner and the " Bells of Ousley " is delightful. Fine trees line the northern bank and mask the surroundings of ancient Ankerwyke, a Benedictine priory founded in the reign of Henry II. The present mansion was built in 1805. Just beyond the " Bells," crowded with river-parties in summer, is the ferry to Wraysbury or, to give the village its correct name, Wyrardisbury. The river may be crossed to visit the restored Early English church, if only to get the charming view Thamesward and to the hills beyond. The village itself, some distance farther, is most uninteresting.

Old Windsor has had little history since the Conqueror decided that the bold chalk bluff higher up the stream and commanding the valley was a more suitable site for the palace-fortress of soldier-sovereigns than the low mead and wooden home of the Saxon monarchs. This building was still used, however, until the time of Henry I, and some few years ago excavations resulted in the discovery of timber baulks which may have been part of the foundations.

The church is square in shape and, though partly restored, retains its Early English tower and chancel. The square windows with geometrical tracery are unusual and remarkable. Besides the church there is nothing calling for particular notice in Old Windsor, except that the churchyard holds the grave of " Perdita "—immortalized by the brushes of Reynolds, Romney and Gainsborough—and we may proceed without delay to the goal of our last journey—the " New " Royal Borough of the Winding Shore.

So overwhelming is the great mass of crenellated walls—sacred and secular—so long is the story—grave and gallant—that belongs to them, that Windsor town itself is overlooked by most of those who throng the short street between the railway stations and Henry Tudor's Gateway, or the Hundred Steps. And yet, though it has no interesting town church or medieval building of importance, it is a picturesque place with several first-class shops and hotels, and some fine old eighteenth-century houses. Modern developments have not yet succeeded in making Windsor a Cockney suburb, though motor-buses connect the town with the Underground at Hounslow, and an excellent train service transports the ladies of Windsor to Westbourne Grove in a little over half an hour.

One of the old houses—the one-time " King's Head " in Church Street—is now a museum containing several interesting articles referring to Shakespeare. Quaint fronts—interspersed with modern reconstructions—in Peascod Street make this the most picturesque thoroughfare, but the best houses are in and around Park Street. The Town Hall, usually ascribed to Wren, was partly his design, and there is an oft-told story of the pillars within the ground floor being placed there against the wish of the archi-tect, whose assur-ance that the upper floor would stand without their sup-port did not satisfy the nervous bur-gesses. So Wren gave them their pil-lars, but instructed the builder to leave an inch of space between abacus and ceiling.

THE ROUND TOWER.

Within are several portraits of the Hano-verian sovereigns, and statues of Queen Anne and her Consort adorn the exterior.

St. John's Church, though built in 1822, and with every outward appearance of that fact, is worthy of a visit. It contains some fine carving by Grinling Gibbons, and certain admired mosaics by Salviati, besides memorials of modern times. Holy Trinity Church is used by the garrison, and the volume of sound here on Sunday mornings is something to be remembered. Lovely are the voices of women and children, but how much grander, thrilling and inspiring is the deep roll of men's song in unison.

It would be useless to attempt, with the space at our command, any detailed description of Windsor Castle. In many ways it is the most interesting building of its kind in Europe, and contains within its precincts the most beautiful example of that truly insular form of Gothic architecture called Perpendicular. The Chapel of the Knights of the Garter, though apparently so regular and perfect in style, was commenced by Edward IV and finished by Henry VIII. It occupies the site of three earlier buildings. Of these the first was Norman, and the second a contemporary of the Curfew Tower—the oldest visible part of the Castle. The late restoration—an operation very different from some of those commented upon in these pages—has resulted in the rehabilitation of the " King's beasts " on the summit of the buttress pinnacles, from which the originals were removed by Wren as a precautionary measure.

Perhaps the most picturesque corner within the Castle is that occupied by the Horse Shoe Cloisters of Edward IV, opposite the west door of St. George's. Nevertheless, they are very obviously restored and have the polished and veneered appearance we have learnt to associate with Victorian refurbishings.

The interior of St. George's Chapel is magnificent in effect and in detail. The first impression, of great space and light, is the best. The over-ornamentation of the wall-space—little as that space is, for the church is nearly all windows—is unrestful though beautiful. The eye, taken by the straight lines of the columns to the roof, is again assailed by a mass of delicate detail in the rich tracery of the fan vaulting.

Modern taste does not see fit to eulogize the monument of the Princess Charlotte, placed in the north-west, or Urswick, chapel. For its date, it was a remarkably good achievement, and the charge of theatricality is due solely to the effect of the tinted glass window at the side. The Victorian Court sculptor—Boehm—is responsible for effigies of Leopold I and Queen Victoria's father. He also designed the cenotaph of the Prince Imperial in the Braye Chapel. More ancient memorials are in the choir—made colourful and splendid by the banners of the Garter Knights. But these have lost some of their once august companions — no Imperial double eagles now hang above the canopied stalls of Emperor-kings. It must be remembered that the association of Windsor with the Order, and with the Patron Saint of the realm, made it the central point to which the

St. George's Chapel.

chivalry of England turned in the reign of the third Edward and for centuries afterwards. Between the stalls, near the centre of the choir, is the movable stone slab leading to the tombs of Henry VIII, his Queen—Jane Seymour, and Charles I. Another vault, under the Albert Memorial Chapel, contains the coffins of four Kings—George III, his two sons and great-grandson. Edward IV rests in the north aisle, and near the south-eastern end of the choir is a slab of black marble covering the grave of the sixth Henry.

The most beautiful thing at this end of the chapel

is the magnificent iron screen below the Royal pew. This once formed part of the tomb of Edward IV and, though usually attributed to Quentin Matsys, is a fine example of native workmanship. Other tombs, too numerous to mention, which though eclipsed by those of Royal personages are of great interest to those who are well versed in the nation's story, are scattered around the great church. That knight of chivalrous fame who defended Raglan—the Marquis of Worcester —is buried here in a nameless grave. The ancestor of the Rutlands—Sir George Manners—has an altar-tomb, and the so-called King's Chapel is devoted to the family of Oliver King, Bishop of Bath and Wells. The painted panels in this little tomb-house are portraits of Edward IV, Edward V, Henry V, and Edward of Wales—the son of Henry IV. At the time of writing, preparations are being made for the last resting-place of Edward VII and Queen Alexandra, in accordance with the wishes expressed by the latter.

Beyond the east end of St. George's is the one-time Wolsey Chapel, re-named as the Albert Memorial Chapel. It was actually built by Henry VII for his own sepulture, but abandoned for the more imposing erection at Westminster. Henry VIII presented it to Wolsey. The black and white marble tomb, made to the order of the great Cardinal, but never used, now holds the remains of Nelson in the crypt of St. Paul's. The chapel contains the cenotaph of Prince Albert, of his son, Prince Leopold, and his grandson, Prince Victor. The building is of oppressive magnificence, the enrichment being the work of Sir G. G. Scott. Not a square foot of wall, ceiling or floor is without ornament or colour. The superficial decoration of Gothic has never been properly understood by moderns. It must be remembered that all medieval sacred buildings were rich with colour, and the reason that modern imitations of Early English—to take one example—are so lifeless and disappointing is due to the flat pallor of the interior walls. On the other hand, the Perpendicular style does not lend itself to vigorous colouring, so here we have another example of how not to do it—though it cannot be denied that the sumptuous and costly decoration of this chapel is, viewed in detail, of great beauty.

This pallor of newness pervades most of the Castle, with one or two exceptions, such as the Dean's Cloister, reached by the passage-way just traversed; part of the North Terrace; and the houses of the Military Knights. Successive sovereigns during the last hundred years or so have added to, and furbished up, the great range of buildings. The most drastic alterations and scrapping of old work took place under George IV, whose architect was the iconoclast Wyatville. However, a great improvement was then effected, for the Round Tower was heightened and the turret built, adding greatly to the dignity of the Keep, and also to the picturesque sky-line of the Castle.

The treasures of Windsor, shown to the public in the State Apartments, are surpassed in interest and value by those in the private part of the Castle, but these are, of course, only seen by the privileged few. Nevertheless, we may see magnificent pictures and tapestries, besides those many and various historic objects only to be met with in the home of a reigning sovereign. The finest room in the Castle—St. George's Hall—is two hundred feet long, and the Grand Dining Room, usually called the Waterloo Chamber, is another noble apartment. These, and the various state rooms, are all on the north side of the upper ward. The private apartments overlook the East Terrace with its beautiful sunk garden. Here, on Sunday afternoons, the band of that regiment of Guards which happens to be on duty plays pleasant music, not only to Royalty, but to His Majesty's lieges also.

Although the view from the Round Tower is of much greater extent—by its isolation one can see in every direction, and the legend says "into twelve counties"—the most pleasing is certainly that from the North Terrace. This takes in the picturesque roofs of Eton—framed in masses of foliage—the Thames meads and the parklands of Buckinghamshire, with even a hint of Stoke Poges church in the distance. The range of buildings on this terrace gives one a good idea of the general appearance of the Castle before its improvement. The Winchester Tower, built by Bishop Wykeham, has an inscription translated by the witty prelate as "this made Wykeham" when his King appeared to take exception to the assertion.

The so-called Hundred Steps take us back to the curve of the hill leading down to Windsor bridge—an unpicturesque one and unworthy of its surroundings. The bridge leads directly into Eton High Street, a narrow and crowded thoroughfare at most times. At the northern end are the various buildings of the famous school.

The College of Blessed Mary of Eton was founded by Henry VI in 1440. The beautiful Chapel was begun in 1441, and represents the gradual development—or decline—of Perpendicular during the next hundred years. The statue of Bishop Waynflete, first Provost, has been added to the west front. The greater part of the interior decoration is modern, and

includes Watts' "Sir Galahad" and a Burne-Jones
tapestry representing the Adoration of the Magi.
Of the original decorations, the most interesting are
the wall paintings behind the stalls, brought to light
a few years ago. The old choristers' vestry has been
turned into a War Memorial chapel, but the most
striking work commemorating the 1,157 Etonians who
fell is the bronze frieze in the colonnade below the
Upper School. This building dates from 1690. Its
panelled class-rooms are covered with the names of
scholars. Once cut by the boys
—doubtless the pioneers suffered
the usual penalty—the work is now
done by a practised hand with
official sanction. Lower School was
built by Sir Henry Wotton about
1630, and on the east of this is the
most beautiful front of all—a perfect specimen of early sixteenth-
century work, surmounted by a
clock tower.

ETON COLLEGE
CHAPEL.

The roll of scholars is, like that
of Harrow, a list of names high
in the annals of the nation, and include those of Fox
and Shelley, Walpole and Chatham, Peel and Gladstone, Howe and Wellington.

The oldest parts of the College are in the cloisters,
and on this side are the Playing-fields, a classic and
beautiful place of hallowed memories. The Poet's Walk
is named in honour of Gray, and the manuscript of his
Elegy is preserved in the New School library. The older
College library boasts the possession of a First Folio
Shakespeare and the manuscript of *Ralph Roister Doister*.
The author—Nicholas Udall—was a tutor at Eton.

In these fields football was first played, but the devotees of the sport would not recognize the original form, which still persists in the " wall game " between Collegers and Oppidans on the last week-day in November. The other wall game—" fives "—originated at Eton, and was played between the buttresses on the north side of the Chapel.

On the other side of the main street, Keate's Lane perpetuates the memory of Eton's most famous Head, who reigned in the early years of Queen Victoria. He was a muscular and exceedingly ugly man and, by modern standards, his disciplinary methods were brutal in the extreme. The slightest fault met with a severe flogging, and the years of his mastership soon became legendary. During his time, however, the school turned out a remarkable number of boys who were to become famous and successful men.

We must now briefly survey the country near Windsor and Eton. Slough, little more than a mile to the north, was our starting-place, so a short return eastwards will first be made to Datchet, best approached through the Playing-fields. This is a gay little town in summer, and the inhabitants appear to vie with one another in the display of colour in garden and window-box. Early Victorian Gothic is a marked feature of the domestic architecture, though there are a few old houses. The church was rebuilt in 1859, but retains some monuments from the old building, and also a notable brass to Richard Hanbury and his wife dated 1593. They are shown kneeling at an altar.

The great house of Datchet is Ditton Park, the residence of Lord Montague of Beaulieu. It is a large castellated building which replaced the old mansion, destroyed by fire in 1812. Ditton was once the property of Sir John de Molyns of Stoke Poges, and afterwards of Sir Ralph Winwood, Secretary of State to James I.

Clewer, on the road to Bray and Maidenhead, now forms the western suburb of Windsor, and is composed of large new houses and a number of small mean streets. The most conspicuous building is that of the Clewer Sisterhood, a community of ladies well known for their acts of charity and piety. Only a small portion of the original small Norman church remains, and the interior is not of great interest. This side of the river also is not particularly inviting, except for rearward views of Windsor Castle. From the opposite bank, in the direction of Boveney and Dorney, the prospect of the long fretted line of walls rising above the blue smoke of the huddled town is very English, and also very beautiful and moving in its suggestion of ordered peace and security.

Windsor Great Park is at first disappointing. The Long Walk, not quite three miles long, has lost much of its fine timber. The elms were planted at the Restoration, and for many years it has been dangerous to walk near them in a high wind. Herne's Oak, referred to by both Shakespeare and Harrison Ainsworth, was in the small Home Park. It was blown down in 1863 and the spot is now marked by a young tree. The conspicuous dome, blue-green in colour, on the east of the Long Walk is the Frogmore Mausoleum, containing the tombs of Queen Victoria and her husband.

At the end of this long avenue is a natural mound with artificial additions, bearing the heroic equestrian statue of George III, known to all the neighbouring

folk as the "Copper Horse." From this point onwards the Park becomes the region known as Virginia
Water and is very beautiful. Groves of magnificent
trees, especially in the neighbourhood of Cumberland
Lodge—the Ranger's house—alternate with masses of
undergrowth chiefly composed of rhododendron and
other flowering bushes that in June are worth a considerable journey to see. The lake was formed in
1746 by diverting several streams into a long marshy
hollow. The result, though not entirely natural, is a
successful piece of landscape gardening. Not so much
can be said for the exotic ruins scattered about the
eastern end of the Water. The ruins are real, having
been brought from Tripoli at the instance of George IV,
but they look ludicrously incongruous here.

Near the "Wheatsheaf" Hotel, we could join the
Bagshot road and proceed through beautiful pine
woods to Sunningdale and Sunninghill. The road to
the west goes by the Blacknest Gate to Ascot, a quiet
and pretty place for fifty weeks, and the glittering
scene, during the remainder of the year, of the Royal
Sport. From this point a return may be made to
Windsor by Queen Anne's Ride, with the massed
foliage of Windsor Forest and Cranbourne Chase on
the left and the sward, dappled with bracken and
heather, of the Great Park on the right. An occasional
herd of deer, lifting startled heads, and the white scuts
of rabbits disappearing in the fern, are the only living
things in the peaceful scene. Presently the lordly
towers of England's Castle rise blue on the sky in front
and the end of the journey has come.

AFTERWORD

THE itineraries in these pages have followed, with but few exceptions, practicable motoring-roads. To traverse, or even notice, the many field-paths between village and village, with a commentary on the intimate things of the countryside to be met with thereon, would be impossible within these covers. The allotted space, even under the present scheme, was found to be none too much before the sixth chapter had been finished and a drastic blue pencilling cancelled much descriptive matter from the first, or northern, half of the book—without, it is hoped, removing any information likely to prove of value in a conscientious exploration of the rural districts around the Metropolis. The Londoner is fortunate in the number of delightful footpaths through fields and woods to which he has access, and, as no adequate knowledge of the country can be claimed by those who never venture off the highway, the motorist is urged to leave his cushions to the care of some rustic host whenever he feels that a little pedestrian exercise is permissible and a likely track has been noted.

The appearance of a stile, half-smothered in tangles of honeysuckle and bryony, is a temptation to adventure the writer has seldom resisted. Often the shy path has led him to unsuspected folds of the landscape —lonely " dingles " and unsuspected watercourses.

Sometimes to skirt the inner demesne of an historic mansion ; over wide park-lands ; through dim and solemn woods. Sometimes the departure from the commonplace has resulted in discomfiture, and even disaster, but such chances are part of the essence of adventure. On one unforgettable ramble—with an important train at its end—one of these alluring, unknown short cuts appeared and was joyfully taken. After crossing several meadows and a couple of spinneys, the path suddenly dropped to a deep and mysterious green lane, lined with high and impenetrable hedges. Presently, however, the secrets of the leafy tunnel were revealed. Its solid way was at least a foot below the visible surface. A futile search for escape from this dreadful morass brought to light two long flat stakes, evidently used by someone whose business it was to negotiate the slough. By placing first one and then the other from tuft to tuft of rank grass—picking up the bridge just used and relaying it from the farther end of that one affording a precarious foothold—the quarter-mile *Via Dolorosa* was accomplished ; the unhappy wayfarer, daubed from head to foot in rich mud, accompanied from end to end by an interested and hilarious robin and several thousand flies. It is unnecessary to warn the reader of the exact locality ; both lane and footpath are long since lined with detached " Clovellys " and " Sandringhams."

Paths entered by swing-gates, though usually of less interest than the stile-track, are seldom traps laid by Pan to confound the townsman. They are mostly well-known and used rights of way, indicated as such upon the maps of the Ordnance Survey ; though it must not be taken for granted that all tracks marked thereon are thoroughfares. The explorer with un-

limited time may not object to retrace his steps through
a mile or more of cornfields and meadows after an
unpremeditated visit to a lonely and astonished farm-
stead, so the *other end* of the dotted line must be
carefully noted. It is needless to point out to the
reader of these pages that wandering from the path, or
ignoring boards marked " private," is no more *de
rigueur* than leaving the remains of the picnic meal
upon the wayside !

The sketch map which accompanies these pages is
merely a key to the position of the principal localities
described. The sheets numbered 85, 94–97, 105–108,
113–117, 124–126, of the popular Ordnance " one-
inch " map will be found almost indispensable in any
systematic exploration of the Home Counties, but it is
an expensive handful. The writer has for many years
used Bartholomew's " half-inch " maps in various parts
of England and Wales. The great virtue of the latter
consists in the contour colouring—invaluable in lonely
hill-country and not to be despised even in Buckinghamshire and Kent. The sheets required—from Oxford
and Cambridge to Canterbury—are 19, 24–26, 29–31.
The new Ministry of Transport maps are admirable
for motorists. Each road is coloured according to the
scheme of the Ministry for dividing the highways into
classes A and B, though there are many quite good
ways under neither category. The motorist carrying
these maps need never be at a loss. He has but to
drive to the next signpost and identify the numbers
thereon with those upon his chart. The Ministry's
maps—covering the same area—are numbered 24, 28,
29, 30, 33, 34 and 40. Both of these latter, and also
the official " one-inch " parent, are delightful things to
study in the arm-chair. They are full of intriguing

names and signs. Who can trace by lamplight the road from Chignall Smealey to Shellow Bowells without an overmastering desire to investigate further those entrancing places ?   Is Sutton Valence as lovely as its name ?   And surely the sun really does dance at Good Easter on that Sunday morning in spring.

The railway companies are generous in the facilities given to Londoners who have to depend upon the iron road for their outing. The Southern Railway is particularly obliging in issuing cheap tickets upon four days of the week, though it is difficult to understand why certain localities upon this system, entirely rural in character, are arbitrarily closed to the thrifty-minded explorer. Upon the Northern and Western lines certain days are set apart for the purpose of cheap trips, though " walkers' tickets " at slightly higher fares, available nearly every day and which enable the wayfarer to return from a different station, are a great convenience. They are obviously planned for the not too vigorous pedestrian, and it would be interesting to know who was responsible for choosing the itineraries. Did the General Manager himself pace the allotted number of miles, sinking at last upon one of his platforms, tired but happy, or was the duty deputed to a subordinate, who perchance shirked its actual performance and merely measured out the distance upon the Company's railway map—a chart innocent alike of contours and of houses of call ?

Lastly, there are the country bus services. What can we say for these convenient and popular means towards taking short, or even long, journeys ? They are not cheaper than the railroad, even when in active competition, and the fatigue consequent upon a trip by motor-bus from Central London to Dorking or

Farningham does much to spoil the pleasure of the holiday-maker. For short rural stages this method of transit is a great boon, and it would be ungracious and futile to gird at the impress of the town which flares through the green whenever a " General " goes by. The high roads around Dartmoor, the dales of Derbyshire, the solitudes of East Wales have long since been invaded by this entirely prosaic conveyance—for there is more romance in a dingy " local," puffing between Liverpool Street and Ponders End, than in a motor-bus labelled for Windsor itself.

It may be that while there still remains country between the Chilterns and the Downs, both motor-bus and railway train will belong to the history of an amusing past, and the only sane method of seeing the fair face of England's green and pleasant land will be the way of an eagle.

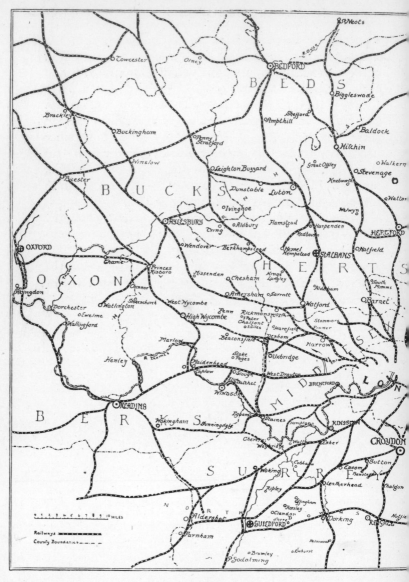

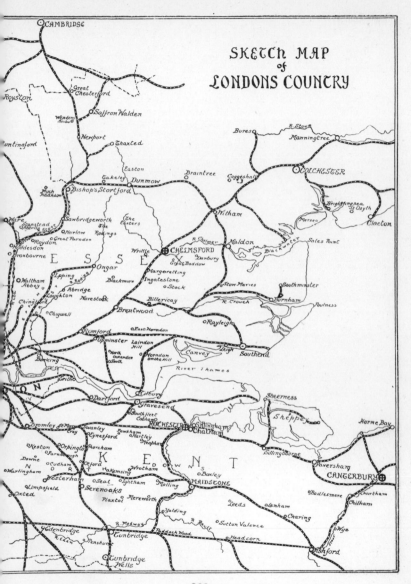

SKETCH MAP
of
LONDONS COUNTRY

CAMBRIDGE

Royston

Great Chesterford

Wendens Ambo

Saffron Walden

Huntingford

Newport

Thaxted

Easton

Bakeley

Dunmow

Braintree

Coggeshall

Bures

Manningtree

R. Stour

COLCHESTER

Brightlingsea
St Osyth

Mersea

Clacton

Much Hadham

Bishop's Stortford

Witham

Maldon

Sales Point

Blackwater

Ware

Stanstead Abbots

St. Margaret

Sawbridgeworth

The Easters

The Rodings

Harlow

Great Parndon

Roydon

Broxbourne

Hoddesdon

ESSEX

Ongar

Writtle

CHELMSFORD

Danbury

Great Baddow

R. Chelmer

Southminster

Waltham Abbey

Epping

Theydon Bois

Margaretting

Ingatestone

Stock

Stow Maries

R. Crouch

Burnham

Foulness

Abridge

Loughton

Blackmore

Navestock

Billericay

Chingford

Chigwell

Romford

Brentwood

East Horndon

Rayleigh

Barking

Ilford

Upminster

Laindon Hill

North Ockendon
South

Horndon on the Hill

Canvey

Leigh

Southend

River Thames

Erith

Dartford

Tilbury

Gravesend

Sheerness

Sheppey

Herne Bay

Bromley

St Mary Cray

Southfleet

Cobham

ROCHESTER

Gillingham

Chatham

Sittingbourne

Faversham

CANTERBURY

Keston

Orpington

Farnborough

Downe

Cudham

Warlingham

Westerham

Swanley

Eynsford

Shoreham

Otford

Fawkham

Hartley

Meopham

KENT

N   DOWNS

Kemsing

Wrotham

Ightham

Baxley

Malling

Badlesmere

Chartham

Chilham

Limpsfield

Oxted

Seal

MAIDSTONE

Leeds

Lenham

Charing

Wye

Edenbridge

Hever

Penshurst

Tonbridge

R. Medway

Paddock Wood

Plaxtol

Mereworth

Yalding

R. Beult

Sutton Valence

Headcorn

Ashford

Tunbridge Wells

Sevenoaks

333

TOPOGRAPHICAL INDEX

Printed in Great Britain for ROBERT SCOTT, Publisher, PATERNOSTER ROW, LONDON E.C.,
by BUTLER & TANNER LIMITED., FROME

THE ENGLISH COUNTRYSIDE SERIES

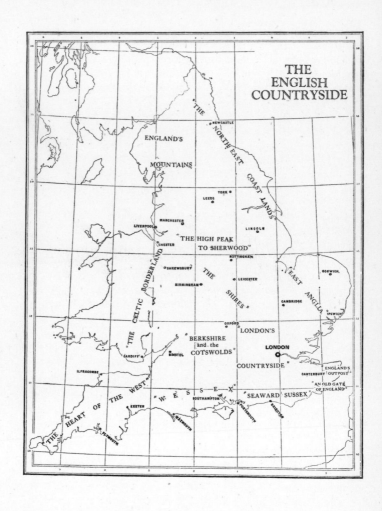

THE
ENGLISH
COUNTRYSIDE

"THE NORTH EAST COAST LANDS"

NEWCASTLE

ENGLAND'S

MOUNTAINS

YORK
LEEDS

MANCHESTER
LIVERPOOL
LINCOLN

CHESTER
"THE HIGH PEAK
TO SHERWOOD"

NOTTINGHAM

SHREWSBURY
THE

BIRMINGHAM
LEICESTER

"EAST ANGLIA"
NORWICH

"THE CELTIC BORDERLAND"
"SHIRES"
CAMBRIDGE
IPSWICH

OXFORD
LONDON'S

BERKSHIRE
and the
COTSWOLDS"
LONDON

CARDIFF
BRISTOL
"COUNTRYSIDE"

ILFRACOMBE
ENGLAND'S
CANTERBURY OUTPOST
"AN OLD GATE
OF ENGLAND"

"THE HEART OF THE WEST"
"WESSEX"
SEAWARD SUSSEX"
EXETER
SOUTHAMPTON
BRIGHTON
WEYMOUTH
PORTSMOUTH
PLYMOUTH

THE ENGLISH COUNTRYSIDE SERIES

This series is a departure from the cut and dried county handbook. Each volume deals with a well defined natural division of the homeland and ignores the arbitrary political boundaries of the shires. Sometimes the limits set by the editor follow the march-line of the ancient kingdoms of the first millenium—e.g. WESSEX, which became the cradle of the Empire. Again, in THE CELTIC BORDERLAND the district comprises a region second to none in its intense historic interest, for in the Marches of Wales—the Balkans of Britain in the early Middle Ages—was hammered out the stern stuff that has helped to keep our land inviolate. LONDON'S COUNTRYSIDE is a serious attempt at a concise record of the beauty and interest still remaining around the Great City and is written not only for the motorist and rambler, but for the consideration of those who are concerned in the future development of the Home Counties.

So with the remainder of the series—already published and in preparation. All have been carefully arranged to give a full, comprehensive—and yet concise and easily read—account of the English Countryside in each natural geographic division.

FROM PRESS NOTICES

" Forms a valuable addition to the shelf of the library devoted to home travel."—*Bookman*.

" Topography, Description, Anecdote and History, pleasantly blended and well illustrated."—*Westminster Gazette*.

" Tourists who use these books to help their eyes and their understanding will find their pleasures intensified and their perception made keen."—*Observer*.

" Delightful Itineraries."—*Truth*.

" Neither, History, Romance, or Guide Book, but all blended into one harmonious whole—books such as no traveller's hand-bag should be without."—*Morning Post*.

" The drawings and sketches add to the pleasure of reading these examples of the modern well-flavoured Travel Book."—*Times*.

ROBERT SCOTT, PUBLISHER, PATERNOSTER ROW, E.C.4.

SEAWARD SUSSEX

THE SOUTH DOWNS FROM
END TO END

By EDRIC HOLMES

With 100 Illustrations by M. M. VIGERS

CONTENTS

ENGLAND'S OUTPOST

THE COUNTRY OF THE KENTISH
CINQUE PORTS

By A. G. BRADLEY

Over 100 Illustrations by FRED ADCOCK

CONTENTS

7s. 6d. each.

ROBERT SCOTT, PUBLISHER, PATERNOSTER ROW, E.C.4.

EVERYMAN'S SUSSEX

THE COUNTRYSIDE
IN VARYING MOODS AND SEASONS

By RICHARD GILBERT

With 8 full-page Illustrations.

Foolscap 4to. Art boards. **3s. 6d.** net.

EVERYMAN'S YORK

A CITY OF HISTORIC MEMORIES
By CHARLES ROBERT SWIFT

Foreword by Sir JOSIAH STAMP, G.B.E. With 70 Illustrations by the Author and a coloured frontispiece.

Foolscap 4to. Art boards. **3s. 6d.** net.

ROBERT SCOTT, PUBLISHER, PATERNOSTER ROW, E.C.4.

THE HIGH PEAK TO SHERWOOD

THE HILLS AND DALES OF OLD MERCIA

By T. L. TUDOR

With 12 full-page Illustrations by FRED ADCOCK and 100 Sketches in the Text by the Author and from Original Photographs. With a Sketch Map of the District.

7s. 6d. net.

LONDON'S COUNTRYSIDE

—THE LATEST VOLUME TO BE PUBLISHED—

will be immediately followed by EAST ANGLIA, written by H. G. Stokes, and THE CELTIC BORDERLAND, by F. J. Snell. The whole of England up to the HIGH PEAK will then have been dealt with except the central area usually known as THE SHIRES. The latter will include the intensely interesting area of " Shakespeare's Country " and will be issued at an early date. The remaining districts —one comprised within the ancient borders of Northumbria, and the other that land of beauty and romance between the Pennines and the Irish Sea—will be duly dealt with by able writers and artists.

ROBERT SCOTT, PUBLISHER, PATERNOSTER ROW, E.C.4.

WESSEX

AN EXPLORATION OF THE SOUTHERN REALM FROM ITCHEN TO OTTER

By EDRIC HOLMES

With 12 full-page Illustrations by M. M. VIGERS and over 100 Sketches and Plans in the Text by the Author.

CONTENTS

THE HEART OF THE WEST

A BOOK OF THE WEST COUNTRY FROM BRISTOL TO LAND'S END

By ARTHUR L. SALMON

With 114 Illustrations by FRED ADCOCK

CONTENTS

7s. 6d. each.

ROBERT SCOTT, PUBLISHER, PATERNOSTER ROW, E.C.4.

AN OLD GATE OF ENGLAND

RYE, ROMNEY MARSH, AND THE WESTERN CINQUE PORTS

By A. G. BRADLEY

With 100 Illustrations by MARIAN E. G. BRADLEY

CONTENTS

BYWAYS IN BERKSHIRE AND THE COTSWOLDS

By P. H. DITCHFIELD, M.A., F.S.A.

With 12 Reproductions of old Plates and 30 Illustrations and Plans in the Text

CONTENTS

There are 25 divisions in all. The above is a summary only.

7s. 6d. each.

ROBERT SCOTT, PUBLISHER, PATERNOSTER ROW, E.C.4.